BALLERINA

SEX, SCANDAL,

AND SUFFERING

BEHIND

THE SYMBOL

OF PERFECTION

DEIRDRE KELLY

BALLERINA

GREYSTONE BOOKS

D&M PUBLISHERS INC.

Vancouver/Toronto/Berkeley

For my husband, Victor Barac:

A *pas de deux* we two shall make—
A dance without end,
Boundless and free—
Together a *tour de force.*

12 13 14 15 16   5 4 3 2 1

Greystone Books
An imprint of D&M Publishers Inc.
2323 Quebec Street, Suite 201
Vancouver BC Canada V5T 4S7
www.greystonebooks.com

Cataloguing data available from Library and Archives Canada
ISBN: 978-1-926812-66-3 (cloth)
ISBN: 978-1-926812-67-0 (ebook)

Editing by Nancy Flight
Copyediting by Anne Holloway
Jacket design by Jessica Sullivan and Setareh Ashrafologhalai
Text design by Setareh Ashrafologhalai
Jacket photograph by Iris Friedrich/fStop/Getty Images
Printed and bound in Canada by Friesens
Distributed in the U.S. by Publishers Group West

We gratefully acknowledge the financial support of the Canada
Council for the Arts, the British Columbia Arts Council, the Province
of British Columbia through the Book Publishing Tax Credit, and
the Government of Canada through the Canada Book Fund for our
publishing activities.

Greystone Books is committed to reducing the consumption of
old-growth forests in the books it publishes. This book is one step
towards that goal.

CONTENTS

PROLOGUE

PARIS, DECEMBER 18, 1961: Janine Charrat is backstage, preparing to rehearse the lead role in *Les Algues* for a performance on French television. The ballet is set in a lunatic asylum, and as Catherine, the woman who has lost her mind, Charrat is dressed in flowing white clothes and about to enter the scene holding a candelabra. Unbeknownst to her, someone has left the lighted prop next to the rosin box, and as Charrat rubs her ballet shoes into the sticky powder, her nylon skirt collides with the open flame and combusts.

The fire quickly engulfs her, the flames licking around her body, consuming her clothes and the pale, delicate flesh they were meant to protect. Like her character, Charrat becomes maddened, running wildly and screaming for help. Stagehands and fellow dancers gasp in horror at the sight of the dancer burning before their eyes. They rush to grab her, to throw her to the ground and stamp out the flames. But it is too late: nothing has been spared, with the exception of her pretty fox-like face.

The burning of the ballerina instantly makes headlines; all of Paris is riveted by the accident involving a beloved French celebrity, a dancer who first stole hearts when she was a twelve-year-old ballerina prodigy making her debut as one of the stars of Jean Benoît-Lévy's 1937 film, La Mort du cygne (Death of the Swan). Reporters swarm the Hôpital Cochin, a public assistance hospital on the rue du Faubourg Saint-Jacques, where the ballerina has been rushed by ambulance. They film for that evening's newscast crying fans, among them Charrat's fellow ballerinas—long-necked beauties with silk scarves tied tight around their heads—who are thickening the corridors. The cameras also capture Charrat wheeled in on a hospital bed, her eyes wide with shock. Her dark hair flows across the white pillow beneath her small head; an arm, badly burned, lies limply on the sheets. The camera closes in: the charred flesh is readily visible, peeled almost to the bone: a broken wing. A team of doctors and nurses pushes into the frame and rapidly wheels the bed down the brightly lit corridor toward an operating room. The blurred whiteness resembles a ghostly ballet.

"Janine Charrat became a living torch," declares a reporter, recapping the day's tragic event. "She sustained burns to between 60 and 70 percent of her body."[1]

It was a fateful episode in the life of the ballerina who had grown up in a Paris fire hall following her birth in Grenoble on July 24, 1924, during the dog days of summer. Charrat was destined to be a trailblazer—a gifted ballerina who defied the rules, an award-winning choreographer of experimental ballets created to reflect states of mind, among them Les Algues, considered her masterpiece. She also choreographed for film and television. The dark and dreamy dances she created for Benoît-Lévy's 1952 short, La Jeune fille aux allumettes (The Little Match Girl), showed Charrat experimenting with the atmospheric effects of fire to heighten the film's theme of disillusionment, a harbinger of things to come.

Charrat did not believe in movement for movement's sake. Ballet had to mean something. It had to have symbolic value as well as tell a story—a way of thinking that she learned through her collaborations with leading artists of the day, among them Jean Genet and Jean Cocteau. A Ballets Russes alumnus, Cocteau so admired Charrat's unique genius that he said she was a *"marcheuse solitaire…va au-delà des étoiles!"* (a solitary walker… who goes beyond the stars).[2]

In the television studio that day in 1961, Charrat seemed to be fulfilling Cocteau's prophecy. After the flames had been extinguished, she lay half-dead on the floor, still conscious, quietly moaning the same words over again: *"Comme Emma Livry!"* (Just like Emma Livry!).

In her delirium, Charrat invoked the name of an earlier French ballerina, another child prodigy, who had been burned alive in Paris just a century earlier, also while practicing her art: a sister in suffering. The similarity *was* eerily uncanny. Except that Charrat lived to tell the tale of how ballet, for all its transcendent beauty, is also fraught with hidden dangers.

Dancers beware.

1

THE FEMINIZATION OF BALLET
THE REIGN OF THE COURTESAN

SHE FLOATS ON AIR, a swan, sylph, or spirit haunting our imaginations from beyond the grave. Throughout her history (and it is a relatively brief one, considering that men dominated the art of ballet from its origins in the courts of the Renaissance until the Romantic era, when the cult of the ballerina took flight), the ballerina has been perceived as an otherworldly creature. Dancing in hard-tipped shoes that appear to lift her above the earth, she occupies a realm above the everyday. Historic lithographs of Romantic ballerinas show them with elongated necks, boneless arms, and flesh as pale and translucent as the wings pinned to their backs. The ballerina comes across as a feminine ideal, unblemished and ethereal, inspiration incarnate. The British novelist and poet Rayner Heppenstall describes the ballerina as "a woman on her points [who], because of the change in significant line and stress and action, ceases to be significantly a woman. She becomes an idealized and stylized creature of the Theatre... there is a kind of eternal virginity about her. She is inaccessible. She remains unravished."[1]

But the reality behind the curtain is another story. The history of the ballerina is tarnished by institutionalized suffering, starvation, poverty, and sexual exploitation. She has had to suffer enormous deprivation to maintain the ideal of the classical dancer as a symbol of perfection, enduring pain, frequent humiliation, and even starvation to create the illusion of weightlessness on stage.

From her beginnings as a dance professional in the seventeenth century until today, the ballerina's identity has been shaped by forces that go beyond those of mere art. More than an aesthetic symbol, the ballerina is also a social construct, a complex product of her time and place. If, as British sociologist Bryan S. Turner says, the body is the site of incorporated history, then the ballerina's body is the incorporated site of ballet history.[2] In the words of pioneering American ballet dancer and choreographer Agnes de Mille, "Theatre always reflects the culture that produces it": an observation that is true also of the ballerina.[3] Since the beginning, she has mirrored local conditions that contribute to the production of art and of historically specific ideas that govern her role and identity as a professional woman of the theater.[4]

But what were those conditions? What social practices and attitudes turned her into a type of idealized female in the first place? How is it that she appears to personify the dichotomy of spirit and flesh? What makes this wing-backed creature, a popular archetype, so fascinatingly inscrutable?

From the beginning, the image of the ballerina has been cast in contrasting ways. This is the source of her duality. From one perspective the ballerina is a subservient supplier of delights to male audiences and patrons, a concubine or prostitute. An opposing point of view sees her as an artist of the highest order, the embodiment of the loftiest cultural ideals and the image of femininity itself. A key contributing factor to these conflicting perspectives is that the ballet has been, since shortly after its inception, a meeting place of the social classes, a zone where aristocrats and commoners, rich and poor, commingle and negotiate their desires and identities. Ballet was an object of fascination for the daughters of domestic servants and of monarchs alike. For some girls, such as Anna Pavlova, the illegitimate child of a Russian laundress, ballet represented the road out of poverty. For others, such as Britain's young Queen Victoria, an avid ballet fan and collector of ballet dolls, it was a fantasy world where she could flee the cloistered loneliness of her overprotective upbringing.

That the rise of the ballerina coincided with an epoch of unprecedented radical social change is central to understanding her seemingly dual nature. As the age of agrarian feudalism and aristocratic privilege was being swept aside by the age of commerce, industry, and mass democracy in late-eighteenth-century Europe, the role of the ballerina was concomitantly being redefined. She went from being an amateur of noble birth to a professional of often humble origins, a creature of the marketplace subject to the whims and tastes of a paying audience. By the twentieth century, when ballet had become an established art form, the ballerina had become an object of both idealization and scorn in popular culture, particularly in the 1940 film *Waterloo Bridge*, where the ballerina, played by Vivien Leigh, becomes a prostitute whose death in the end symbolizes her fall from grace. Such conflicting messages about the ballerina have confused and confounded public perceptions of this iconic female artist while obscuring aspects of her real history. The fairy tale story lines of ballets in which maidens in tutus are rescued by handsome princes have long contributed to popular perceptions of ballet as an art form of the upper classes. This perspective, however, has tended to obscure the working-class origins of many ballerinas and the authoritarian nature of ballet culture, as well as the effort, dedication, and sacrifice increasingly demanded of the professional ballerina in doing her job. Pain in ballet is often denied, hidden behind a façade of skilful composure. This stifling of discomfort has produced a culture where deprivation and degradation co-exist alongside the pursuit of an ideal, often rendering the ballerina a victim of her own beauty and artistry. It's this Black Swan/White Swan duality that fascinates, intimating that there is much more to the ballerina than meets the eye.

THE PERSISTENT PERCEPTION of the ballerina as sublimely beautiful, breathtakingly delicate, and gracefully poised—perfection personified—stems from ballet's beginnings as a courtly art. From the very beginning of her history, the ballerina has been expected to embody aristocratic ideals of deportment, dignity, and decorum, values of etiquette developed in the courts of Europe but especially in the court of France. This is where ballet—the word is French, derived from the Latin *ballare*, meaning "to dance," and also from the Greek βαλλίζω (*ballizo*), meaning to jump about—was originally used to instruct boys and young men of the aristocracy in the proper positions for fencing and other military maneuvers. Ballets, when staged for court entertainment, were not the intimately enclosed presentations seen today on a stage; they were lavish and elaborate productions, often presented outdoors and for days on end, and employing whole battalions of soldiers, in addition to choreographed herds of stampeding horses, to create rigidly defined yet flowing patterns of movement representing the virtues of discipline and order. Women were not central to these displays of militaristic action. Men were the first ballet dancers, dancing female roles *en travesti* and wearing masks; at the beginning, ballet belonged to men, almost exclusively.

The star dancers were the kings themselves, and there was no challenging the status quo. Louis XIII (1601–1643) both danced and wrote ballets, among them *Le Ballet de la Merlaison*, which he created in 1635, casting himself in a comedic part. Louis XIV (1638–1715) was an even more committed balletomane, one of the art form's great practitioners; he made his debut in 1651, at age thirteen, in *Le Ballet de Cassandre*.[5] Louis XV (1710–1774) also danced and was a keen observer of the goings-on at the Paris Opéra. Louis XVI (1754–1793), however, appears to have abstained from dancing and even attending dance performances, which might help to explain his lack of popularity among the people. During his reign, ballet was not an integral part of court life; it flourished more on the professional stage, performed by men and women of low rank. Ballet's golden age belonged to the time of Louis XIV, when ballet was truly a noble pursuit. Throughout his reign, Louis regarded ballet as a most serious art. He was both observer and die-hard practitioner, said to have danced as many as eighty roles in forty major ballets until his early retirement from performing when still in his thirties.[6] His marriage to a pious queen who frowned upon ballet as unseemly for a king in middle age may have been why Louis stopped dancing: his body had given out. As a younger man, the king had excelled in fleet-footed sequences and airborne turns. At the same time as he lost his hair, he lost his stamina. To appear less than mighty when performing before his subjects would have been anathema to a king who had spread his reputation for invincibility on the wings of the ballet.

On one level, ballet represented an athletic pursuit for a pleasure-seeking king known to sequester himself inside a studio for up to six hours of daily practice. But ballet at the French court was also the means by which Louis maintained control over his courtiers. That need for control, which the discipline of ballet so forcefully represented, was a result of the violent upheavals of the Fronde, an attempted coup d'état by members of the nobility who wanted to challenge the existence of an absolutist French state. When Louis was just a boy, he was driven into temporary exile, together with First Minister Jules Mazarin, who reportedly had squandered "precious state resources on importing his beloved Italian dancers, singers, and designers to the French capital."[7] For Louis, this attempted rebellion was a traumatic occurrence he never forgot; it confirmed his belief that the nobility was a force whose energies needed to be carefully and calculatingly contained, much like the body when performing a ballet. Louis would craft himself as the choreographer, while his courtiers would serve as the performers of an intricately devised court dance in which the king would always play the central role.

Symbolizing the centrality of the king was a 1653 artistic and political tour-de-force, *Le Ballet de la Nuit*, which commenced at sunset and depicted a series of nocturnal scenes with mythological creatures representing chaos and destruction: the powers of darkness. At dawn, the fifteen-year-old Louis appeared as Apollo, Greek god of music, poetry, reason, and harmony. Befitting the god's identification with Helios, bearer of light, the young king's costume was aglitter with jewels. Louis was the sparkling center of a ballet symbolizing not only the ascendancy of his absolutist regime but also the role of the French king as a quasi-religious figure. Louis became known as the Sun King as a result of this role. At this time in history, ballet was the message. Being so favored, the art form grew in scope and authority throughout his reign.

More than just a divertissement, ballet was a way of life—at least at court. Ballet was both a mirror of society and a social ideal: reflecting the complex hierarchies within French society while at the same time providing concrete means of enhancing one's social status. Amateur performers of ballet included women, members of the nobility who danced for their own social class. These women were held to a high standard of behavior, "required to display elegance and skill above the common run of court ladies."[8] In allegorical ballets of the day, they personified Virtue but never Jealousy, Victory, Hatred, Fury, or Destiny.[9] They also symbolized ancient philosophical concepts of social order and cosmic harmony, as borrowed from the ancients. The expectation was that women be modest when dancing, even when performing dances that were inherently lively. Consequently, the first ballerinas specialized in dancing *terre-à-terre*, movements in which the feet barely leave the ground. Restrictions imposed on them by bell-shaped dresses upheld by imprisoning undergarments ensured that women's movements remained genteel and decorative, in comparison with those of their male counterparts: "With the fair sex, gentle movements and pretty gestures must be the fairest ornament," wrote the German dancing master Gottfried Taubert in 1717. "For here, with their legs covered under long dresses, high jumps and many capers will certainly not do, especially at a wedding, assembly, and so forth, and in common wear. Pretty steps and such variations can be chosen which well become a woman and likewise reveal her skill in dancing and thus take preference over the other steps."[10]

Matters of etiquette gradually became stamped into steps and positions of the body that emerged as the precursors of classical dance vocabulary. What today can be readily recognized as ballet's "first position"—standing with the legs together, heels touching, feet out-turned—originated as a relaxed stance enabling a gentleman to present himself frontally in the presence of the king. The gliding step in ballet known as the *chassé* originated from the curtsy of a lady shifting into an open or fourth position of the feet when she wanted to change direction without turning her back on her betters.[11]

Louis adopted ballet's intricate patterns of movement for ordering the social hierarchy at court; where one stood in relation to the king was a strong indicator of status. It was all strictly orchestrated, right down to the type of chair a lady was permitted to sit on, if permitted to sit at all. The level of detail was mind-boggling and was crafted to keep the courtiers in a constant state of social anxiety. There were rigid rules dictating how close one could stand to the king and on which side. Positioning was usually based on the prestige of one's ancestry, although character and talent—a talent for dance—could penetrate the ranks. This is true of Louis' own illegitimate sons, among the few allowed to challenge the king on the dance floor. As ballet historian Jennifer Homans cleverly observes, the king's courtiers and various hangers-on represented a veritable corps de ballet, leading even the formidable Madame de Maintenon, Louis's second wife, to quip that "the austerities of a convent are nothing compared to the austerities of etiquette to which the King's courtiers are subjected."[12]

Those at court had to keep up with, if not match, the physical prowess of the king if they were to enjoy a position of prestige, and this involved hours upon hours of study and practice. In this way, Louis, quite literally, kept the elite on their toes. Even the smallest misstep could prove fatal. Coordination was prized as much as exhibiting rhythm and poise and elegant posture—"straight spine, lifted chest, relaxed shoulders, long neck, erect head, hands and arms held without tension. It was the gesture of the aristocrat, as expressed on the dance floor. It was upper class demeanor converted into movement to music."[13] People who could not, or did not, dance well were ridiculed and made social pariahs. In Molière's comic play *Le Bourgeois gentilhomme* (1670), the principal character, Monsieur Jourdain, is scorned for failing to grasp the aristocratic ethos at the heart of his society, a blunder represented by his inability to master the minuet. "All the misfortunes of mankind, all the dreadful disasters that fill the history books, the blunders of politicians and the faults of omission of great commanders, all this comes from not knowing how to dance," the Dancing Master tells him. "Without the dance, a man can do nothing."[14]

Comporting one's self with elegance was also important for women, especially women of low birth who had nothing to lose but much to gain by using their wits, talent, and imitative powers to distinguish themselves through a mastery of their own bodies. Dancing manuals, which proliferated in those days, provided a road map for navigating the complex system of social hierarchies whose path led straight to the king. Jean-Philippe Rameau had been dancing master to the queen of Spain, and he penned two books on dance in which he stressed elegance in comportment as the means by which a woman could make her mark: "A lady, however graceful her deportment, will be judged," Rameau instructed. "For example, if she holds her head erect and her body upright, without affectation or boldness, it will be said: 'There goes a fine lady.'"[15]

This notion of the female dancer as necessarily daintier and more refined than her male counterpart has persisted and helps explain why ballerinas in our own time are presented as paragons of purity and virtue. The expectation is that a ballerina remains poised and dignified, no matter what the circumstances. In 1820, the Italian dancer, choreographer, and dance theoretician Carlo Blasis published his classic treatise on dancing, *The Code of Terpsichore* (1823), the first published analysis of ballet technique, and in it he stressed the importance of grand manners and courtly behavior among ballerinas: "Men must dance in a manner very different from women; the *temps de vigueur*, and bold majestic execution of the former, would have a disagreeable effect in the latter, who must shine and delight by lithesome [sic] and graceful motions, by neat and pretty *terre-à-terre* steps, and by a decent voluptuousness and abandon in all their attitudes."[16]

The convention would eventually change early in the eighteenth century, with the rise of professional ballerinas whose virtuosic feats were at first deemed shocking, precisely because performed by women. But Louis never appeared squeamish in the face of a lively, dancing woman. In fact, he was eager to encourage displays of virtuosity among women, often selecting females as partners in ballets he danced at a court. Among them was Mademoiselle Vertpré, who danced with him in *Le Ballet de la Nuit*.[17] This early ballerina, about whom little is known, also performed opposite the king in *Le Ballet de l'Impatience* in 1661, the same year Louis established the Académie Royale de Danse, the first institution dedicated to standardizing ballet. Later, more women continued to gain prominence in ballet when in 1669 the king established a theater with a school dedicated to training professionals of both genders for the stage.

One of the king's dancing masters, Jean-Baptiste Lully, managed that school. A native of Italy, Lully had also danced with the king in *Le Ballet de Nuit*, and was one of his favorites. Besides being an accomplished dancer, Lully was a gifted composer and musician, a member of the vaunted *Vingt-quatre Violons du Roi*, the king's personal violin ensemble. As well, he composed and staged ballets, mostly light fare suitable as court entertainments. A ruthlessly ambitious man, Lully aspired to create works on a larger scale. For this he needed his own venue. In 1672, through Machiavellian connivance, Lully commandeered his way to the directorship of the Académie Royale de Musique, later known as the Paris Opéra, purchasing from Pierre Perrin the letters patent originally granted him by the king in 1669 to run the public theater. Lully quickly cleaned house, replacing the old guard with men of impressive talent of his own choosing, among them choreographer Pierre Beauchamps, poet Philippe Quinault, costume designer Jean-Louis Berain, and playwrights Pierre Corneille and Molière, to create a new theatrical genre combining music, verse, dance, song and scenic design within an integrated whole.[18] Among the new productions were works created specifically for women, among the first of their kind. Typically, *opéra-ballet*, as these spectacles were called, replicated entertainments at court, making the Paris Opéra seem a mere extension of that royal realm, especially considering that until this time only members of the nobility were allowed to perform them.

But Lully generally found the nobility to be inferior as performers, particularly with regards to the ballet. Known for having defined a French style of music, Lully had quickened the pace of compositions created for dance, making it fly where previously it had decorously glided, only to discover that many of the aristocrats assigned to perform his ballets had difficulty keeping up. His solution was to look outside the nobility for people of talent to better dance his work. "He was obliged to choose novices, unspoiled by the traditions of their art, and laboriously train them to carry out his intentions," music historian Frederick H. Martens writes. "The dancers of his time… could see nothing but their own dance *per se*, all else, proportion, character, the relation of the dance to the expressive content of the music, was a matter of indifference to them."[19] Significantly, women were, for the first time, counted among the so-called novices whom Lully started to train for his own glorification. It is at this point in ballet history, and largely as a result of Lully's frustration with the prevailing system, that the first professional ballerinas begin to be noticed. Among them was Mademoiselle La Fontaine (1655–1738), the so-called "Queen of the Dance,"[20] who in 1681 appeared in a revival of Lully's opera-ballet *Le Triomphe de l'Amour* at the Académie Royale de Musique, the first recorded instance of professional ballerinas on the proscenium stage. La Fontaine performed alongside three other professional women dancers: mesdemoiselles Carré, Pesant, and Leclerc.[21] Other accounts of the ballet list mesdemoiselles Roland, Le Peintre, and Fernon,[22] suggesting there may have been other contemporaneous performances of *Le Triomphe de l'Amour* in 1681 but always with La Fontaine at the center.

Women like La Fontaine were happy to help Lully take on the role of ballet reformer. The theater offered them a chance to assert themselves in ways not typically allowed in society at large and on the basis of skill and looks. The latter was something they were born with. The former was something capable of being expanded upon through study and discipline. Many women dancers seized the opportunity to dance professionally, acquiring social prestige and, in some cases, vast stores of wealth even though their origins were humble. Their social mobility came courtesy of an art form that operated as both a political and personal tool for advancement, attracting and swaying power with its elegance and poise. The founding of a professional dancing school ensured that talent would eventually trump birthright as the means for social mobility for certain women in pre-Revolutionary France. Between the years 1700 and 1725, almost ninety professional female dancers were known to dance on the Paris Opéra stage.[23] The Opéra dance company, "which had so far been exclusively composed of men, was at long last opening up to professional dancers. Their growing presence became rapidly and increasingly felt and the first female celebrities of the prestigious troupe were soon to hold their own under the leadership of ballet master Guillaume-Louis Pécour."[24]

Lully had ensured that the nobility no longer danced as it once used to, but members of this privileged social class continued to form the majority of the ballet audience. In fact, the aristocracy never stopped exerting its privilege over the public theater, especially backstage, where the notion of "theater" constituted an entirely different moral universe than was depicted onstage.

Even so, the ballerina's rise to prominence came about almost by default. Having decamped for Versailles in 1682, Louis had hung up his dancing shoes for good and was no longer performing ballet; courtiers had to follow his lead, and soon ballet began to shed some of its importance as a court practice. Eventually this rarefied art of kings would open its doors to anyone with enough physical attributes, talent, and ambition to enable them to pursue it as a career, women included. The emphasis had shifted from ballets that showed group processions and geometric floor patterns to ballets that showcased the increasing virtuosity of the performers,[25] a development that grew out of the creation of the first proscenium arch stage in France, in 1641, at the Palais Cardinal—later known as the Palais-Royal—located next to the Louvre. Before this, ballets had been performed on the ballroom floor in large rectangular halls, with the audience seated on the periphery and the action facing squarely in one direction, toward the king.

When dances were raised to a platform at the end of the hall, a precursor to the proscenium stage, technical mastery of steps became more important than a mere presentation of harmony and order. Dancers were now facing toward an audience, their legs turned outwards from the hips for maximum frontal exposure.

This change marked a significant juncture in the history of the ballerina, as from this point onward she moved from decorative object to object of desire. In the geometrically patterned ballets at court, where ballerinas typically were arranged in procession, demonstrating allegorically suggestive floor patterns, the physical attributes of their bodies were de-emphasized.[26] But with the advent of the proscenium stage and an increased focus on individual technique in theatrical performance, ballerinas' bodies were more on display. What the dancing female body could do fired the audience's imagination as to what else it might do, behind closed doors. Ballerinas, as soon as they became professionals, no longer symbolized Platonic concepts of heavenly order and other philosophical ideas borrowed from antiquity. In the eighteenth century, bolstered by advances in stagecraft, they represented sex, the vital here and now of the flesh: erotic playthings exciting emotions, not just ideas, in the spectator.

Almost from the beginning, professional ballerinas were sexualized, and many came to lead double lives as courtesans. The ballerina-as-concubine was an open secret in French society, the status of the kept women being so widely accepted at the Opéra that a registry of female dancers' names was listed alongside that of their protectors.[27] The king's theater, for all its grandeur and gravitas, became known as "that house of ill-fame," as a disgusted French composer referred to it in the day.[28] The brothel of France.

These so-called protectors were male patrons of wealth and influence who paid for a dancer's keep and expenses and often shrewdly represented her interests within the theater. In exchange, she became her protector's mistress but not his property. There was a distinction. Thanks to their training in dancing and etiquette and well-honed skills of mimicry, ballerinas who knew how to act like aristocrats, although they themselves were not, attracted the attention of the upper classes, who sought them out for sexual liaisons. This is how many ballerina-courtesans rose to the top of their profession, as well as to the pinnacle of society, enriching themselves along the way. The talent ballerinas exhibited on stage often mirrored the dexterity they displayed behind the scenes in juggling several prominent lovers at once. Such women were not passive victims of patriarchy, as some might want to think, but active participants in the shaping of their own destinies, often with great pluck, aplomb, and humor. Ballerina-courtesans were among the first independent women; they did not live in brothels or bend themselves to conform to another's will. They danced to their own tune, so to speak, and so, for the most part, were not to be pitied but admired.

They sold themselves to men of influence, hoping to advance themselves both socially and professionally; yet to label such ballerinas prostitutes would distort the point of their existence. Ballerina-courtesans were, in a sense, a cut above. Certainly, in the eighteenth century, such dancers exuded a whiff of risqué glamor. They were celebrities, women prized for their beauty, charm, and physical talents, who became mistresses of kings or men of nobility or wealth. Their motivation, observes one dance scholar, wasn't love or affection; it was business: "Almost always, a courtesan is a beautiful poor woman who forms sexual alliances with wealthy men in order to improve her station in life, to increase her fortune, and to advance her social or professional career. Money, jewels, property, and other items of great value are always involved in the transaction. The courtesan is an amatory professional."[29]

Some ballerina-courtesans of the eighteenth century came from the corps de ballet, drawn from among the ranks of the poor, who bartered sex for the basics of life. But others were among the top-ranking ballerinas of their day, the world's first ballet superstars, for whom sex was as important a tool for social advancement as a well-honed technique radiating aristocratic manners.

Ballerina-courtesans were the unexpected consequence of the founding of a professional school intended to achieve perfection in the art of ballet, as directed by the king. When Lully, with the king's backing, started developing the professional dance and music academies within the Paris Opéra, he looked for people not of rank but of talent whom he could train to increase the prestige of French theater art. Thus Lully was able to give rise to the first professional ballerinas, who surpassed the limited capabilities of the aristocratic amateur by mastering ballets of increasing technical complexity and rigor. Discipline in the form of daily labor was required for these dancers to advance along with the art. To ensure that he had complete control over ballerinas at a time when women were still considered property, the chattels of their fathers or husbands, Lully freed them by law from all familial obligations. Dancers, as well as singers employed by the Paris Opéra (sometimes the roles were doubled), enjoyed an unprecedented degree of freedom afforded them by Lully's emphasis on creating artists devoted almost exclusively to their art forms. Ballerinas under his watch were servants of the king and were emancipated from parental and spousal control.[30] These cosseted *filles d'Opéra* were also protected from police harassment, deportation, and imprisonment. In matters of justice they were under royal protection.[31] This made them not only freer than most women in society at large but also able to seek and find patrons among the powerful and wealthy.

A private manuscript describing conditions backstage at the Opéra at the turn of the eighteenth century offers an idea of what obstacles professional women in the theater had to surmount: "Their fate depends on the one man who reigns as an absolute monarch over the Opéra [the Director], one who decides on whims their wages, whether low or high, and who stands above control or supervision. They are devoted to him like slaves in their constant fear of losing their position … They have no certification [*brevet*] and no contract and can be dismissed without compensation for the slightest reason."[32]

But the courtesan lifestyle was not without its risks: for instance, eighteenth-century Paris Opéra ballerina Mademoiselle d'Azincourt died in 1743 of venereal disease when she was just twenty-three.[33] And yet for the majority of these women, who came from nothing, there was so much more to gain: not only food, shelter, and clothing but also carriages, servants, jewels, furs, and augmented pensions on which to survive into advanced age. For such dancers, positioning themselves close to men of means was a maneuver to emulate in attaining success. Ballerinas had a number of incentives for moonlighting as courtesans: female dancers were generally paid less than their male counterparts, and yet they were responsible for living up to the high standards set by the Opéra's public image. An anonymous memoirist observed that "some women receive 400 livres, some 300 livres, and a very few at the top 1,000 livres, but what are these [sums] in comparison to what they must spend in decent cloths, linen, ribbons, accessories, shawls, trinkets, banquets, games, receptions, illnesses, medication, and rents in one of the most expensive districts of Paris."[34] But besides enabling them to afford the prestige associated with their onstage profession, ballerinas were also motivated to moonlight as courtesans as a result of the Opéra's murky recruitment practices. The Opéra Statutes approved by Louis XIV in 1713 specified that "actors, actresses, dancers and members of the Orchestra must have demonstrated their performing skill and received public approbation before being eligible for admission to the Opéra."[35] In real-life terms, such a policy often called for a lot of backroom negotiations in the form of favors and influence. For ballerinas, "it was tacitly understood that a distinguished sponsor should open the stage door for [them]."[36]

Some ballerinas abstained from the courtesan life, preferring to reside with their parents at home—for example, a Paris Opéra ballerina named Anne Haran.[37] But such dancers proved the exception to the rule. It was generally thought that no self-respecting ballerina went with fewer than three lovers at a time—one for prestige, one for money, one for love.[38] Some, like Émilie Dupré, a dancer from the French countryside, brazenly exceeded that figure. Mademoiselle Émilie, as the ballerina was known, had a great many protectors, all powerful men in French society who claimed her as their mistress—sometimes at the same time. They included the Duc Louis II de Melun, the regent Philippe d'Orléans, the Duc de Mazarin, and a Monsieur Fimarcon, a colonel who got into a dispute over the ballerina with the Comte de la Roche-Aymon, a musketeer, which ended in a duel.[39]

An even more colorful rags-to-riches story belongs to the ballerina Mademoiselle Delisle (1696–1756), the elder of two sisters employed by the company. She was mistress to Charles de Bourbon, Comte de Charolais. Through his generosity, she appeared on stage in 1723 dressed head to toe in a costume of solid silver to dance a solo in *Philomèle*, a lost opera by Marc-Antoine Charpentier. The sight was reportedly remarkable, especially given the woman's lowly origins. Jean-François Barbier wrote about her in his *Journal historique et anecdotique du regne de Louis xv*, saying that the costume cost 2,000 écus, roughly $60,000 in today's money: "This creature is pretty with a very beautiful figure," he continued waspishly. "Before being at the Opéra, she was a fifty-sous whore. She is very gratified now; the prince entertains her in his house and she lives in great style."[40]

Ballerinas of low birth entertained by royalty were not a uniquely French phenomenon. Sophie Hagman (1758–1826), a dancer at the Royal Swedish Ballet, entered the world poor as the daughter of a gamekeeper and rose to become the official royal mistress to Prince Frederick Adolf of Sweden. The Italian-born Barbara Campanini (1721–1799), another celebrated ballerina of humble origins, ended her days as a countess in Prussia. Frederick the Great was said to have adored her "boyish legs" and personally ensured that she attained prominence in his land.[41] The Venetian-born Giovanna Baccelli (1753–1801) was born into an itinerant Italian theatrical family but used her considerable sexual charms to rise to great heights in English society, eventually becoming the mistress of John Frederick Sackville, the third Duke of Dorset, who was ambassador to the court of Louis XVI (as well as ancestor to the writer Vita Sackville-West).[42]

Still, the most celebrated ballerina-courtesans came from Paris, where the backstage world of the Opéra was like "a foreign legion within the army of the Opéra—a legion recruited from the slums and composed, if you'd like, of more or less beautiful women but without any standard of conduct, incapable of dedication, study, and work,"[43] according to one of the theater's own directors describing the harem-like scene that existed behind the curtain. But within that seraglio were dancers of tremendous talent who skillfully navigated the demimonde of illicit sex—and on their own terms.

One such woman was Françoise Prévost (1680–1741), the first ballerina-courtesan to become famous as much as for her prowess on the stage as for her skills in bed. Prévost reigned at the Paris Opéra for almost thirty years as dancer, choreographer, and illustrious teacher. She was the first ballerina known to have shared her expertise with students, initiating a chain of apprenticeship—young dancers learning from senior female artists—that continues to this day. At least two of her students went on to command the highest accolades in the land, which says as much about her pedagogical skills as it does her ability to inspire others with her dancing talent. "Indeed, her personal way of investing steps with meaning would remain a reference point for female soloists throughout the 18th century."[44] She was a superlative dancer of low birth, being the daughter of a Spanish mother and a *piqueur*, the man who called the performers' roll at the Paris Opéra (he may also have been a dancing master), which could explain how she came early to be engaged there. She first appears on the rolls as a child performer under the name La Petite Prévost.[45] A charismatic performer, she danced in many of Lully's ballets, as well as those of Guillaume-Louis Pécour (1653–1729), the premiere choreographer of the French noble style. Prévost's roles encompassed everything from a shepherdess and a harlequin to a nymph, a faun, a bacchante, and a Greek—the latter likely due to her dark hair.

More significant were the roles she danced in works she created herself, solos and duets, the latter often danced with the celebrated male dancer Claude Ballon (1671–1744). Among them was her masterpiece, *Les Caractères de la danse*, a 1715 solo

depicting a series of amorous vignettes with Prévost playing
characters of both genders and a variety of ages. A fascinat-
ing chameleon of a work, it was composed of fragments of
social dances popular in their day—the *courante, menuet, bourée,
chaconne, sarabande, gavotte, louré,* and *musette*—set to an original
score by Jean-Féry Rebel, a member of the famous *Vingt-quatre
Violons du Roi.*[46] Prévost harnessed the shifting rhythms to suggest a mercurial variety of moods and characters, which she
danced with aplomb, playing an old man sighing for a young
beauty in one scene and in another a young woman so happy
in love she has nothing to complain about. The suite of four
individual yet thematically linked dances was Prévost's signature piece, showing off her versatility as a performer; it has
served to fix her star in the firmament of great ballerinas past.
The dance had both wit and humor. Prévost's contemporaries
all spoke of it highly, praising in particular the ballerina's skill
as a mime, not to mention her inherent grace, lightness, and
poise. Rameau was one of her biggest fans, describing the pro-
totypical ballerina as having "all the advantages of Proteus in
the Fable. She, at Pleasure, assumes all manner of shapes . . . to
enchant the Greedy Eyes of those that look on her, and to gain
the Applause of every Body which excites a noble Emulation
among the other Women Dancers."[47]

Prévost was celebrated as much for grace as for virtue. Such
was her public image, which she cultivated to the end of her
days. Before dying in 1741, at age sixty, she requested to be
buried in the Saint Theresa chapel belonging to Les Carmes
Déchaussés, which was next door to her house on rue Cas-
sette. She would be buried on hallowed ground.[48] But, in reality,
Prévost was a first-class courtesan who made a highly lucra-
tive living off her body, both on and off the stage. That she led
a double life was amply recorded in a 1726 legal document[49]

in which Prévost petitioned the courts to secure the life annuity of 6,000 livres[50] promised her by the French ambassador to Malta when she had been his mistress. Jean-Jacques de Mesmes was refusing to pay up, claiming that he was both emotionally and financially spent as a result of the dancer; he said under oath that she had stolen his heart.

Mesmes was the son of an important magistrate in France, who at one point had held the office of president of the Parliament. He owed his status within society to Louis XIV, who had personally appointed him ambassador to Malta in 1714 to keep the de Mesmes family on his side during a political dispute at court. The king at that time had wanted to appoint Louis-Auguste, his illegitimate son by his mistress Madame de Montespan as his successor over the rightful heir, Philippe d'Orléans, and needed this well-to-do family of the *ancien régime* to cast its vote in his favor.[51] If the king had not influenced his career, it is unlikely this scion of the house of de Mesmes would have succeeded on his own merits. A prominent contemporary described him as a man of "poor intellect and appearance, curiously dissolute… who in many ways was a disgrace to his position"[52]—which perhaps explains the rather foolish way he conducted himself when seeking to defend himself against the more canny (and cunning) Prévost.

The ambassador penned a tell-all journal of bartered desire, which was widely circulated in its day, damaging the reputations of both parties. Today, it offers a rare snapshot of what life was like for ballerina-courtesans of Prévost's spunk and caliber and so is worth reproducing here in large, juicy chunks. Mesmes starts by recalling his pre-ambassador days as a *chevalier* (knight) when he had first met Prévost, exposing not only his bungling impetuosity as a would-be lover but, more significantly, the secretive offstage existence of a ballerina known for playing virginal priestesses and other feminine ideals in ballets like Henri Desmarest's *Iphigénie en Tauride* (1704) and Lully's *Bellérophon* (1705) and *Thésée* (1707). Prévost was twenty-five at the time of the affair. While describing Prévost as "graceful and elegant," Mesmes observed that her origins were humble:

> She met the Chevalier [meaning himself] and fell for him, but she lived with her parents and their living conditions at first disheartened the aspiring lover. He found the family in a high and obscure chamber barely furnished with a *Bergame* hanging [a coarse type of hanging found in humble households] and four chairs upholstered in tapestry, the whole quite proper and clean nevertheless. The beloved object of the Chevalier's affection, who did not expect his visit, was caught in her domestic state: this was not a néréide from Neptune's court, laden with all the sea bounty, this was not Flora, Zephyr's lover, adorned with colorful spring flowers, this was *Fanchonette* [his nickname for her], dressed in striped *calmade* [thick material used as upholstery], coiffed with a dirty nightcap trimmed with a rose-colored ribbon, grubbier still. Her face was unmasked, her neck and chest were bare, revealing a sallow complexion and prominent muscles. Fanchonette stood thus, by a small fireplace, busy reviving ashes and a dying candle.[53]

Mesmes did not propose making her his concubine at this encounter but later arranged for a rendezvous in a back alley of the Palais-Royal, where the terms of their relationship were baldly laid out. Prévost's mother helped broker the deal, while the ballerina herself smoothed over the minor problem of her already having a lover:

> The bargain that was reached in the end was that he would take second place. He would be told when to visit and when to fill in when lover number one was absent, and he would also

pay the bills incurred at taverns and restaurants. This being settled, the lovers took immediate possession of each other that very night. Fanchonette got drunk as well as her mother and was in high spirits. The infatuated young man found her eyes tender, her teeth beautiful, and her skin soft to the touch. He spent the night basking in his great fortune, and that night was followed by others, all equally passionate.[54]

Mesmes kept Prévost in luxury for years, eventually purchasing for her, at her request, "a fully furnished apartment with cellar and kitchen, all manner of furniture, clothes for all seasons, not to mention a well-provided table," he writes. "No sooner than her desires were known they were met. Her dressers filled up with china, her wardrobe with gowns, and the ambassador delighted in hiding all kinds of jewelry in her drawers."[55] In return, she was faithful to him in her fashion: during their long-term relationship she gave birth to an illegitimate daughter. The father was not Mesmes but the Count of Middelbourg, Alexandre Maximilien Balthazar de Gand.[56] Prévost was caught several times by the ambassador in bed with other men, including a colleague from the Opéra, which is how the dancer had won the promise of the 6,000 livres annuity— her price for renouncing that lover, or so Mesmes claimed.

Prévost countered by saying the money was what he owed her, having borrowed from her ten times as much during the relationship for his embassy expenses. As to the allegations of whorish behavior, Prévost said nothing, determined to be known as her public knew her, as "Terpsichore the Muse, whom the ancients made to preside over Dancing."[57] Ultimately, the courts sided with her, granting her the 6,000 livres annuity. As soon as she got it, she put the bulk of the money into a trust fund to help her children and her grandchildren, setting them up comfortably for life. Prévost might have had loose morals, but she knew where her priorities lay. Promiscuity was the means to an end.

Prévost led by example; her own student, the illustrious Marie-Anne de Cupis de Camargo (1710–1770), who had studied with Prévost from the age of ten, also became a courtesan, eventually becoming a sexual rival to the more senior ballerina, who would continue to court men of influence well into old age. A fiery brunette celebrated for her bravura whirlwind performances, Camargo was a sexual powerhouse who rose into the upper echelons of French society assisted by several high-ranking lovers at once. In spite of their thirty-year age difference, Camargo and Prévost were said to share the same lovers—among them the handsome Paris Opéra dancer and ballet master Michel Blondy (1675–1739), who had partnered them both and bedded them both as well. The affair put a wedge between Prévost and Camargo. The French actress Adrienne Lecouvreur commented on their falling out in a gossipy letter to a friend: "Yesterday they played *Roland* by Quinault and Lulli [sic]. Although Mademoiselle Prévost surpassed herself, she obtained meager applause in comparison with a new dancer named Camargo whom the public idolizes and whose great merit is her youth and vigor. You may not have seen her. Mademoiselle Prévost at first protected her but Blondi [sic] has fallen in love with her and the lady is piqued. She seemed jealous and unhappy at the applause Camargo received from the public...The clapping gets so extreme that Prévost will be foolish if she does not decide to retire."[58]

In record time, Prévost ordered a tearful Camargo to the anonymous back row of the corps de ballet, refusing to create for her any more entrées, or choreographed entrances in the operas where ballet was a featured element.[59] Camargo might have lingered there, but one day when the male dancer David Dumoulin missed his cue, she brilliantly asserted herself back to center stage and improvised a solo as lightning quick as it was daring. The Italian author and sexual adventurer Giacomo Casanova saw Camargo perform in the sprightly *Les Fêtes véni-tiennes* and recorded his impressions: "I saw a danseuse who bounded like a fury, cutting *entrechats* to right and left, and in all directions, but scarcely rising from the ground, yet she was received with fervent applause."[60]

This time, Prévost couldn't ignore the tumult surrounding Camargo or stand in her way. Camargo had started to get hands-on instruction from leading male dancers, who admired her pluck and talent: Blondy, followed by Guillaume-Louis Pécour and Louis Dupré (1690–1774), known as Le Grand Dupré. Camargo benefited greatly from having these male teachers: they taught her attack and an air of nobility that enhanced her own lightness of touch and sensitivity to music.[61] More important, these men also showed her how to leap clear of obstacles cluttering her path to glory. With the same determination she reserved for her dancing, she continued to court them, as well as others, to advance herself into the upper echelons of French society.

Camargo had commenced her career at the Brussels opera house, and later in Rouen, where at age fifteen she had been appointed a solo dancer. But when she danced *Les Caractères de la danse* for her Paris Opéra debut on May 5, 1726, her fame exploded. In contrast to her chief rival Marie Sallé, she emphasized the escalating energy behind dances and not the moods of the characters, imbuing the solo with the bravura technique that immediately became her claim to fame: "Everyone beholds with amazement the daring steps, the noble, strong hardihood of Camargo," wrote the critic in *Le Mercure de France* following the performance. "Her *cabrioles* and *entrechats* were effortless, and although she has many perfections yet to acquire in order to come near to her inimitable teacher, the public regards her as one of the most brilliant women dancers to be seen, especially for the sensitivity of her ear, her lightness and her strength."[62]

Camargo's signature was vigorous movement performed to sprightly music. To move with even greater speed, she lobbed off the heels of her shoes to create the world's first dancing slippers, which allowed her greater contact with the floor in preparation for liftoff. To better show off her fabulous legwork, Camargo also shortened her skirts to around the midpoint of the calf, a modification in costume that precedes the adoption in the nineteenth century of the tutu, the ballerina's official uniform.[63] Camargo's costume reform was soon adopted by other ballerinas seeking freedom of movement.

By moving fast, Camargo was praised for dancing vigorously, like a man. Given the times, Camargo *did* dance like a man in that she was a virtuoso who gained attention not by dancing *terre-à-terre*, as had been the norm for women dancers of the day, but by rushing upwards into the air in performing *haute danse*, a masculine style of ballet where the feet barely touched the ground. In daring to defy the entrenched notion that women dancers should comport themselves with modesty when on the stage, Camargo set a new standard of heightened physicality for women in ballet. She was known for having a ninety-degree turnout, a radical doubling of the standard. Her specialty was *entrechats-quatre*, a rapid crisscrossing of the feet performed at the height of a jump, which she was said to have invented, though evidence exists of men having done it before her. At the very least, what can be said of this tricky step is that Camargo was the first female dancer known to have performed it.[64] Camargo was also adept at performing a step called the *gargouillade*, a sideways jump where the feet draw circles in the air, as well as *cabrioles*, leaps where one leg is stretched and the other beats against it. Audiences adored her athleticism and took to calling her by her nickname, La Gigotteuse—the woman who jigs.

Only once in her career did she dance the stereotypical female role of a Grace. With her tempestuous style of dancing and dark good looks, she was more often cast as a bacchante, a huntress, an Egyptian, or a bohemian.[65] These were earthy roles that lent her a heightened sexual allure, a reputation she took pains to encourage. The shortened hemlines also led to rampant speculation as to what else could be discovered beneath Camargo's skirts. Did she or did she not wear underwear? (She didn't.) If she jumped high enough, might a man sitting in the orchestra get to see the source of all her feminine power? (He might.) Such was the chit-chat of the day, and Camargo did little to stem the gossip. According to playwright and poet Louis Poinsinet de Sivry, writing in 1771, Camargo intentionally danced without the *caleçons de précaution* that soon would be de rigueur for ballerinas following her lead in lifting their legs above their knees, as prescribed by the Paris Opéra administration, "adopting the principle of executing all her steps under her, she always dispensed with that modesty garment worn by danseuses to avoid any offence against decency, notwithstanding the height of her *cabrioles, entrechats* and *jetés battus en l'air*."[66] Casanova, for one, delighted in the scandal, as observed in a letter he wrote to a friend around 1750: "That's the famed Camargo, *mon ami*, and you have arrived in Paris at the right time to see her...She was the first woman dancer who dared to jump: before her, women dancers did not jump, and the wonderful thing about it is that she doesn't wear drawers."[67]

Her sexual reputation had been established early, in 1728, when eighteen-year-old Marie was abducted, along with her thirteen-year-old sister, Sophie, by the Comte de Melun, the governor of Abbeville; he apparently was an overzealous admirer of Camargo's celebrated virtuosity,[68] following her from Rouen to Paris, ostensibly to watch her dance. The ballerina's father, Ferdinand-Joseph de Cupis Camargo, an itinerant violinist said to have been descended from the nobility, petitioned the French prime minister, saying his daughters were of high birth and should be treated as girls of good breeding, released back into his care or else married. His protests might have been part of an elaborate ruse to make Camargo respectable, if not socially well-placed.[69] No wedding took place. While Sophie was released back into the care of her anxious father, Camargo refused to leave her kidnapper's château, apparently having formed an attachment to her new and luxurious surroundings.

An illegitimate child was born of this dramatic escapade, whom Camargo never publicly acknowledged.[70] She later had other bastard offspring from her liaison with Louis, Comte de Clermont, the third and youngest son of Louis de Bourbon, Prince de Condé, whose mistress she became in 1736. He was an abbé of Saint-Germain-des-Près and a military officer who was also Grand Master of the Grand Lodge of France, the supreme Masonic authority in France. Other than bedding the king himself, Camargo could not have climbed the social ladder any higher than she did when she attached herself to this member of the illustrious Bourbon family. She stayed with Clermont for at least five years, from 1735 until 1740, during which time she retired from dancing, apparently at her lover's request, and bore him two children. They do not figure greatly in her story; it is doubtful they even survived her. Camargo made no mention of any children in her will.[71] She appears not to have been the mothering type. Innovations she introduced to ballet are what she wanted to be known for; these she carefully nurtured and jealously guarded. She was aware of her own talent and was determined to leave a legacy of ballerina boldness.

With Camargo, it was definitely a case of what-you-see-is-what-you-get. Although a trailblazer in her art, at heart she was just another *fille d'Opéra* with a string of lovers to keep her both sexually satisfied and wealthy. Camargo was quite openly a concubine, neither reserved nor subtle, and happy to drop her clothes when the occasion called. One such incident took place on June 15, 1731, at the Hôtel de l'Académie Royale on the rue Saint-Nicaise, headquarters of the Opéra's administration. Known as "the shop," it housed a rehearsal theater and studios, a library, and offices. It was also where many an after-party was said to be held, to the pleasure of the Opéra's high-ranking patrons.[72] This is where, at two in the afternoon, through windows opened wide to the street, Camargo was seen cavorting nude with other undressed ballerinas at a party organized by then director of the Paris Opéra, Maximilien-Claude Gruer, for some of his well-connected ballet patrons. Camargo was reportedly playing Venus, and to the letter, as captured by the French statesman and memoirist Comte de Maurepas, who wrote the following verse:

> Lorsque La Camargo, se montrant toute nue,
> Ah! Pour les spectateurs qu'elle agréable vue!
> Fit voir à qui voulut ce lieu plein de beauté
> Que l'on prive du jour sans qu'il l'eût mérité![73]

> Then that time when Camargo appeared completely naked,
> What a sight for those who saw!
> Anyone who wanted could see a kind of beauty
> That beforehand had been off limits!

Word of the party got back to Louis xv, who, at first, was amused. But public outcry led him soon after to relieve Gruer of his duties, not for acting the pimp, but for doing so without discretion. Ballet's prestige rested on it being perceived as an outward show of propriety and good manners; its reputation needed protecting.

Significantly, Marie Sallé (1707?–1756), appears to have been invited to participate in a similar, if not the same, orgy.[74] But she had refused, a moral stance misconstrued as insubordination, which in 1730 lead to an altercation with Claude-François Le Boeuf, another high-ranking Opéra administrator, ending in blows.[75] The prolific writer and ecclesiastic Antoine François Prévost d'Exiles (no relation to the dancer), who was Sallé's contemporary, alludes to an indecent proposal involving large sums of money, which Sallé declined, compelling her to seek patronage outside France. Assisting her flight from sexual harassment was the celebrated French philosopher Voltaire, who wrote for Sallé personal letters of introduction that she would use in London to secure patronage for her art. "If you ask me what they hoped to obtain from her by such a rich reward," Prévost writes, "I can best answer your question by avoiding an answer. The adventure … created an admirable impression in a country where virtue is ranked immediately below guineas."[76]

Ostracized from the Paris Opéra for refusing to yield her will (and body) to the whims of management, Sallé quit Paris for London, where she had family and well-connected English patrons, notably the Duke and Duchess of Devonshire, who bankrolled her productions. In London, Sallé enjoyed more artistic freedom, as well as higher wages, than was possible within the stifling atmosphere at the Paris Opéra. London is where she had first established an illustrious reputation, having made her mark there in 1716 at the age of nine as a child performer alongside her brother, Francis.[77]

When Sallé returned to Paris in early 1720, she became a favorite student of Prévost, who suggested that Sallé be her replacement in a 1721 production of *Les Fêtes vénitiennes*, the ballet providing Sallé with her Paris Opéra debut. Sallé was noticeably different from Prévost's other star student, and not just because she was fair where the other was dark. Sallé was known more for the nuanced expressiveness of her graceful gestures, in addition to her ability to inject a Prévostian sense of emotional verisimilitude into her dancing, rather than for the pyrotechnics displayed by her rival. She also differed from Camargo in that she choreographed her own works, often in collaboration with some of the greatest musical artists of her day, Rameau and George Frideric Handel (1685–1759) among them. The disparity in their approach to ballet set off a widespread debate in their day about who was better: Sallé, a cool blonde representing the Apollonian, or classical, strain in art, or Camargo, who was decidedly more Dionysian, or libertine. Not even as sage a man as Voltaire could decide: he apparently loved both ballerinas, praising them equally in his oft-quoted piece of poetry originally published in *Le Mercure de France* in January 1732:

> Ah! Camargo, que vous êtes brillante,
> Mais que Sallé, grands dieux, est ravissante!
> Que vos pas sont légers et que les siens sont doux!
> Elle est inimitable et vous êtes nouvelle:
> Les Nymphes sautent comme vous,
> Mais les Grâces dansent comme elle.[78]

> Ah! How brilliant you are, Camargo!
> But Sallé, great gods, how lovely!
> Your steps are so light, hers so smooth!

She is incomparable, yet you have something new.
You leap like the Nymphs, but she dances like the Graces."

The jury is still out. In fact, athletic prowess and dramatic
skill—aesthetic differences that these ballerinas personified—
remain the two principal criteria by which ballerinas are judged
today. More important, however, is how these two ballerinas of
extraordinary and diverse talents were able to shape the future
course of ballet by dint of their unique strengths and person-
alities. The differences in their approach to art mirrored the
differences in their approach to sex. Sallé reserved her seductive powers for the stage, where she was reported to dance in
a way that was subtly voluptuous; what she did behind the
scenes no one really knew. Sallé openly rejected the advances
of men and refused to have any part of the sexual orgies that
were a regular feature of Opéra life. Consequently, she became
known in the press as "the Vestal," one of the virginal attendants of the mythical goddess Diana, a virgin who also shunned
the company of men, preferring to surround herself with girls
and women who formed around her a type of Sapphic harem.
Having a reputation for being sexually reserved was so unusual
among ballerinas of the time that Sallé emerged as an enigma
and became more intriguing than Camargo in the public eye.
"Her aura of virtue, one of the 'wonders of the Opéra,' was a
constant source of amazement," writes one ballet scholar.[79]
Society painter Nicolas Lancret immortalized Sallé's identification with Diana by painting a portrait of her as the huntress, an
image inspiring verses by Voltaire and Louis de Boissy, praising
Sallé's modesty and virtue.[80] Sallé was an untouchable, and so
desire for her grew strong among her public, who put her up
on a pedestal, almost willing her to fall. And fall she did.

If she had any sexual affairs, they were covert; there is
no record of her ever having had a sexual relationship or any

indication of her having been anyone's mistress, making her unique for her time.[81] All of her most intimate relationships were with women. She traveled openly with a female companion whom she had met in 1724 in London, the French dancer Manon Grognet, who had performed alongside Sallé in a number of significant works.[82] At the end of her life, she lived in domestic contentment in Paris with an Englishwoman, Rebecca Wick, the *"aimable amie"* whom her biographer, Émile Dacier, thinks Sallé refers to in one of her letters.[83] To her, Sallé bequeathed her entire estate.

The suggestion that Sallé could be a lesbian did not endear her to the predominantly male ballet goers who had adulated her in poetry and in portraiture. Whether true or not, rumors that she was of the other persuasion came to a head when, on April 16, 1734, Sallé appeared at Covent Garden in drag for a ballet she had created for Handel's opera *Alcina*. In the ballet, Sallé played Cupid as a boy; given her need to inject sincerity of expression into her ballet work, Sallé defended her male costume as serving to heighten the veracity of the role she was playing. The audience didn't buy it; the costume was interpreted as a deliberate spurning of their desire. Affronted, the audience booed her off the stage, and Sallé was subsequently lampooned with coarse language in the press.[84] The Abbé Prévost wrote that wearing pants "suited her ill, and was apparently the cause of her disgrace."[85]

The incident upset Sallé greatly, compelling her never to set foot on an English stage again; it also spurred her on to retire early from the stage, which she did in 1740, at the youthful age of thirty-three. By comparison, her teacher, Prévost, danced until well into her fifties. Louis xv, a great admirer of the ballerina's talents, granted Sallé a sizeable pension and invited her to dance before select audiences at Versailles following her departure from the stage.[86] It was a testimony to how respected she had been as an artist, despite refusing to play by the sexual rules of her day.

When Sallé died on June 27, 1756, the result of an undisclosed ailment that took her life when she was just forty-nine, the passing of this remarkably gifted avant-garde eighteenth-century ballerina was barely noticed. There was no mention of her death in the French press.[87] Only the Duc de Luynes, a memoirist during the reign of Louis xv, commented on Sallé's "consistent and singular sagacity."[88] Presumably, Camargo knew of Sallé's passing, living at the time in the same quarter as her former rival, but she appears to have made no public statement. When Camargo died just over twenty years later in 1770, age sixty, she was still a household name. She was survived by a menagerie of animals that included six dogs, an equal number of parrots, three budgies, and twenty-two pairs of pigeons.[89] Having so many birds suggests that the ballerina never tired of flying.

Marie-Madeleine Guimard (1743–1816), however, did not just play by the rules; she bent them her way. The celebrated ballerina was not just a concubine but a pornographic priestess who orchestrated erotic performances for her high-class patrons to secure power and prestige within pre-Revolutionary French society. She openly abhorred the vogue established by Camargo earlier in the century for dizzying pirouettes, rapid rises to *demi-pointe*, and especially the raising of the foot as high as the hip.[90] Throughout her twenty-five-year career as a leading Paris Opéra dancer, Guimard advocated a return to the graceful, elegant dancing, the noble style, such as had originated at court. The push for a return to manners in ballet was ironic, given who was doing the pushing.

Guimard was of lowly birth, the illegitimate child of a woman who early on forced her young daughter into prostitution. But she was blessed with a natural intelligence and a buoyant wit that enabled her to manipulate the sexual market-place within her ballet world, making it work brilliantly for her. She was, in this regard, the first ballerina-courtesan as entre-preneur, her nose always on the money. In reading Guimard's story, it is clear she never allowed herself to play the victim. She was determined instead to own a stake in the flourishing back-stage sex trade, doing it the only way she knew how, by turning it into an act of the theater.

Her lifelong striving after material comforts may have been the result of a childhood tethered to want and misery, as outlined in her biography in 1893 by Edmond de Goncourt, member of the esteemed literary publishing family.[91] Her mother called herself the Widow Guimard,[92] although the man who had fathered her daughter, Fabien Guimard, an inspector of cloth factories from Voiron,[93] was very much alive, emerging, conveniently, when the ballerina was at the height of her powers at the Paris Opéra and in need of a good name. He signed the legal papers when she was twenty-one, granting her the legal right to use his name. She was popularly known as La Guimard, an artist no longer as footloose as her backstage reputation for slippery moral conduct suggested. That repu-tation was established when she was only fifteen, the year her mother consigned her "to a pair of dissolute men who made a practice of helping young girls in order to have them as avail-able as mistresses later on."[94]

These unscrupulous dancer-agents (said to be a Monsieur d'Harnancourt and the Président de Saint-Lubin[95]) placed Guimard in the corps de ballet of the Comédie-Française in 1758, when the young ballerina, presumably dashing all her mother's hopes for her, ran off with a penniless dancer by the name of Léger, with whom she had her first child. Throughout her life, Guimard would always have a soft spot for men of her own background. Among the other great loves of her life were the dancer and choreographer Jean Dauberval (1742–1806), creator of La Fille mal gardée (1789), the first full-length ballet about ordinary people, which is still performed by classical dance companies around the world, and the dancer-turned-satirist Jean-Étienne Despréaux (1748–1820), five years her junior, whom she eventually married during the outbreak of the French Revolution. Guimard is known to have also bedded a teacher at the Opéra's School of Dance.[96] Her dancer-lovers were impoverished. But she also had rich ones, whom she used to advance her social ambitions.

Guimard became acquainted with men of means after joining the Paris Opéra in May 1762, appearing there for the first time as Terpsichore, muse of the dance, in Les Fêtes grecques et romaines. She had been a last-minute replacement for her good friend and neighbor on the rue du Jour, the charming and coquettish Marie Allard (1742–1802), mother of the great nineteenth-century male dancer Auguste Vestris (1760–1842). The Paris Opéra star had injured her foot and was unable to perform. Guimard danced the role well enough that she was brought into the Opéra full-time as a danseuse seule, or soloist. The following year, having shown herself to be a gifted dancer with an abundance of talent and ambition, Guimard was promoted to première danseuse noble.[97]

Besides being a classical dancer in the noble style, Guimard early on demonstrated a flair for the dramatic; soon after joining the Paris Opéra, she was dancing demi-caractère roles in ballets by Rameau (Castor et Pollux) and André Campra (L'Europe galante), as well as more than one hundred other roles.[98] Her best role was Nicette, the simple farm girl in Maximilien Gardel's 1778 comic ballet La Chercheuse d'esprit, a part that delighted her audience for being in stark contrast to Guimard's worldly offstage image.[99] At the beginning of her career, Guimard also danced Prévost's *Les Caractères de la danse*, a piece from the old repertory, performing it as Sallé might have done, with an emphasis on natural grace and simplicity of gesture. Her contemporary, the artist Élisabeth-Louise Vigée-LeBrun, wrote that Guimard conveyed "a sort of suggestion, using tiny steps," and "the audience loved her more than all the other dancers."[100]

Guimard's rapid rise through the ranks of the Paris Opéra and the ease with which she was able to harness public opinion for her benefit paralleled the speed with which she plowed through a series of high-ranking men as a born-to-it courtesan. She had a discerning eye for protectors and established lasting alliances only with those who could most help her become a powerful figure within the Opéra and in society at large. Thanks to extensive and detailed police reports documenting the comings-and-goings of Opéra employees and their influential patrons, a practice of state spying that had been established by Louis XIV and that continued unabated for more than a century, much is known about Guimard and her remarkably well-placed connections.[101] She was not known to have been a beauty. She was unfashionably thin and was parodied in the press as "*la squelette des graces*" (the skeleton of the Graces).[102] And yet powerful men found her irresistible, perhaps drawn by her legendary reputation as a genius of erotic foreplay.

Her aristocratic lovers included Jean-Benjamin de Laborde, first gentleman-in-waiting to the king, governor of the Louvre, and amateur composer. She became his mistress when she was twenty and stayed with him for ten years. The relationship produced an illegitimate daughter in April 1763, whom Guimard forced Laborde to acknowledge publicly to spare the child the ignominy of her own upbringing.[103] While involved with Laborde, in 1768 she also became mistress to Charles de Rohan, Prince de Soubise, who made her an allowance of 6,000 livres a month, in addition to gifts of jewels and gold.[104] The two protectors were publicly acknowledged as *l'amant utile* (the lover with his uses) and *l'amant honoraire* (the lover bestowing prestige). They not only tolerated each other but made way for another of Guimard's lovers, Jean Dauberval, known as her *gerluchon*, the name given to the man who was loved and favored by a woman with a known protector.[105]

As if her bed weren't already crowded enough, around 1772 Guimard also commenced a sexual affair with the powerful Louis-Sextius de Jarente de La Bruyère, Bishop of Orléans, one of the Catholic hierarchy's most highly placed officials. At a time when members of the theater were denied the last rights and forbidden to be buried on church ground (a fate suffered by the great Molière, for one), Guimard's intimate partnership with a member of the ecclesiastical elite was nothing short of a tour-de-force. It perhaps explains why, one time when she was ill, a sermon was delivered from the pulpit of Notre Dame on her behalf, in which the faithful were urged to pray for the ballerina's speedy recovery, their Hail Marys incongruously spent on bolstering the spirits of the larger-than-life Mary Magdalene in their midst.

But the people probably would have prayed for her without being asked. She was known for her generosity with the poor, going door to door to give food to the destitute during the harsh winter of 1768, a good deed commemorated in an etching that survives of the dancer as a gorgeously frocked Saint Madeleine, entitled *Terpsichore charitable, ou Mademoiselle Guimard visitant les pauvres*.[106] Such a self-serving portrait might have been an eighteenth-century version of spin; the dancer's notorious backstage life was popular gossip, and perhaps the same people who had advised her to legalize her name had also suggested she develop a persona of Virtue to counter the image of Vice that fired the imaginations of all who knew her name. She was also respected by many of her peers, having on several occasions raised the issue of dancers' rights with management, including parity in salary for female dancers. She enjoyed the protection of those associated with the court and did as she pleased, knowing she was immune from persecution.

Guimard organized a dancers' revolt against the Opéra administration, targeting Jean-Georges Noverre (1727–1810), a ballet reformer and former Sallé pupil who then was the company's director. Guimard had danced in Noverre's work and the choreographer had openly praised her: "Mlle Guimard... never courted difficulties, a noble simplicity dominated her dancing," he said. "She danced tastefully and put expression and feeling into all her movements."[107] But together with her peers, namely Gardel and Dauberval, she disliked Noverre's pompous way of delegating and was responsible for getting him ousted. Those who feared her called her *La belle damnée.*"[108] Those who admired her did so cautiously: "Everyone acknowledges her talents," Denis-Pierre-Jean Papillon de La Ferté, the superintendent in charge of ceremonies within the king's household and at court, said in 1783. "She still looks very young on the stage; if her technique is not outstanding, her gracefulness makes up for it; she is very good in action ballets and pantomime, is enthusiastic and works hard, but she is an enormous expense to the Opéra, where her wishes are obeyed with as much respect as if she were the director."[109]

Guimard's power extended beyond the Opéra and into the heart of the French, where she held sway as the beguiling hostess of one of the most daring salons in pre-Revolutionary Paris. The men of rank who served, simultaneously, as her

various lovers were united with her in an enterprising business arrangement, with their mistress emerging as creative
director, if not CEO. The enterprise consisted of a series of pornographic theaters built expressly for Guimard by members of
the power elite. The first of these so-called Temples of Terpsichore (named for Guimard's first star turn on the Paris Opéra
stage) appeared in 1768, a classically designed edifice built into
one of Soubise's mansions at Pantin, with generous financial
support by Laborde.

Demi-elliptical in shape, the 240-seat theater boasted
blue-marble Ionic columns, rose-and-cream-colored wall pan-
els, and elaborate vases full of flowers.[110] The stage was about
twenty-one feet wide, with a lush blue curtain that was barely
fifteen feet high and an orchestra pit that lay almost two feet
below. Surrounding the stage were grilled loges and curtained
vestibules; spectators could watch the pornographic presentations, which frequently appeared along with dancers, singers,
and actors recruited from the Comédie-Française and the Paris
Opéra, in private and with impunity. These sequestered boxes
were also large enough for patrons to indulge their own erotic
fantasies, should they desire; the shows were intended to be
interactive. According to the anonymous *Mémoires secrets*, an
erotic diary of the day, when the audience became excited by
what they saw on stage, the "orgies which often celebrate this
nymph, 'La Guimard,'" passed into legend.[111]

But five years into the enterprise, Soubise wanted out;
he felt the theater was distracting him from developing the
careers of other protégées within the Paris Opéra and so with-
drew his support. Guimard next turned to her other lover, the
Bishop of Orléans, convincing him to bankroll a second and
much more elaborate five-hundred-seat pornographic theater inside a custom-built mansion, this one on the rue de la

Chaussée-d'Antin, nearer the center of Paris. Built in 1772 in the rococo style, it was designed by Louis xv's own architect, Claude Nicolas Ledoux, and decorated on the interior by a series of famous artists, among them Jean-Honoré Fragonard and François Boucher, both of whom contributed original paintings and sculptures. The structure had a marble colonnade, as at Pantin, but the interior was even more elaborate: "a sculpted fresco of Apollo crowning Terpsichore, 'galant but not indecent' tapestries, silver ropes, a salon opening onto a small winter garden, a dining hall with terrace, a bathing apartment, and grilled loges that were 'delicious boudoirs.'"[112]

Guimard's new residence epitomized the luxury and frivolity of the age: "The entire salon is painted with murals," observed the author Friedrich Melchior, Baron von Grimm, in a letter written in 1773, "and Mademoiselle Guimard appears in them as Terpsichore with all the qualities that can show her off in the most seductive way in the world."[113] The porno shows were an extension of the salon; Guimard made herself continually desirable by ensuring that everyone who was anyone would want to sit at her table. She accomplished this by hosting three suppers a week, with entertainment, at her sumptuous new residence. One supper was for highly placed members of court and government; a second supper was for artists, writers, and scholars; the third was, to quote the Mémoires secrets, "a veritable orgy, where one found the most seductive and lascivious women and where luxury and debauchery attain their zenith."[114]

But nothing good lasts forever, not even good sex; by 1785, Guimard was facing financial difficulties and was forced to sell the Temple of Terpsichore to make ends meet. Ever resourceful, she came up with the idea of auctioning off the property through a lottery. She sold 2,500 tickets at 120 livres a piece, two examples of which are conserved in the Bibliothèque Nationale in Paris.[115] She raised nearly 300,000 livres from the lottery, but the Comtesse de Lau, who was the winner, immediately sold the Temple Terpsichore for double the money to the French banker Jean-Frédéric Perrégaux, also Guimard's friend. There were no hard feelings; Guimard and Perrégaux maintained a warm relationship, especially after 1787, when her money woes seemed well behind her.[116] Louis XVI had that year granted her a 6,000 livres annual pension in recognition of her contributions to Parisian society (and doubtless in more ways than one). His wife, Marie Antoinette (1755–1793), was a fan of the dancer, calling on her for fashion and beauty advice, Guimard being a well-known clotheshorse with a taste for simple gowns of pastel shades made from expensive materials. In a single year, 1779, her stage wardrobe alone had cost 30,000 livres.[117] But when the French Revolution struck the following year, the pension disappeared and so did the extravagant wardrobe.

Although a well-loved artist, Guimard also represented all the corruption, debauchery, and blasé privilege of the *ancien régime*. She had no more protectors: Soubise and Laborde both lost their heads to the rabble. Guimard had to go into hiding. She retreated with Despréaux to an out-of-the-way attic apartment in Montmartre, where soldiers were said to be too lazy to climb the hill to get her.[118] There, she lived a little like Marie Antoinette playing milkmaid at Versailles; she became a gardener and grew her own vegetables. Yet the lure of the theater remained strong. Her health was weak; she had survived smallpox, which reportedly marred the face on which she had so studiously practiced the art of maquillage.[119] With Despréaux's assistance, she devised a third pornographic theater, featuring marionettes, whose doors she opened to only a very small circle of her former habitués.[120] She appears not to have danced again.

When Guimard died, on May 4, 1816, the public had already forgotten her. She was buried without notice. A brief obituary made no mention of her accomplishments.[121] It was up to her husband, who had called her his best friend, to correct the record. Seven months following his wife's death, he wrote a letter to a friend extolling her virtues: "Among women dancers Mme. Guimard-Despréaux was superior to all the others because nature had endowed her with intrinsic, and one might say, spiritual grace."[122] It was easy for him to say; the Temples of Terpsichore, those theaters of the erotic which Guimard had so expertly managed, disappeared along with the *ancien régime*. Time would be the ultimate judge of her accomplishments, and indeed time has been kind to the dancer who once made herself look youthful by making up her face each morning in imitation of the painterly images of her as the Muse of the Dance that once decorated her more opulent surroundings. Today, her likeness is preserved in a bust that sits inside the Palais Garnier, casting an eye over the generations of ballerinas who have followed in her wake. Guimard remains a reminder of ballet's traditions as well as its darkest secrets.

That Guimard's memory is immortalized within the gilt-edged halls of the Paris Opéra, shrine to the art of ballet, shows that in her time the ballerina-courtesan was not a social pariah; nor was she a victim. Ballerinas like Guimard, together with Camargo and Prévost before her, were singular sensations whose remarkable dancing talents encouraged a sensualizing of the female body, which previously had been denied by the Platonic ideals demonstrated by processional ballets at court. When seen frontally on a stage, the first professional ballerinas excited emotions within their spectators. They were adulated, adored, and desired; for ballerinas like Guimard, Camargo, and Prévost, such attention was ultimately empowering. Sallé found it intrusive and shunned the advances of her male patrons, choosing to relish her sexuality on her own terms. For the most part, she was allowed to do so, living out her days with a female companion as she had wanted.

Eighteenth-century ballerinas enjoyed freedoms denied other women by dint of performing at a time when ballet was a major concern of the state. Some benefited greatly from being able to live as they chose, free from persecution by the law and the constraints of an absolutist society. This is not to deny that sexual exploitation of the ballerina existed at this time. Rather, ballerinas gave as much as they got: they were wily creatures who knew how to manipulate their public image for private gain. A dancer like Guimard was subverting convention at a most dangerous time, the eve of the French Revolution, and could very well have lost her head for dallying in decadence. But she survived, saving herself with typical aplomb and a wicked sense of humor: hats off to her. While the kings of France exploited their people, enslaving them to poverty and hardship, Louis XIV gave women dancers, especially those of low birth, a way out of their misery. It wasn't a perfect world; prostitution did, and does, have a dark side. But to deny these women their due because they chose to barter their bodies for social advancement would be a disservice to their legacy as pioneering ballerinas. The ballet might have operated as a seraglio, but for the dancers who made the system work for them, it was a source of salvation. These ballerina-courtesans gained independence and fame, dancing their desires.

But not everyone was as fortunate.

2

PIMPS, POVERTY, AND PRISON
THE CORPS DE BALLET IN
NINETEENTH-CENTURY FRANCE

BY THE END of the eighteenth century, the ground in ballet had shifted. The *ancien régime* had been replaced by a new class of ballet patron eager to emulate the privileges and entitlements that had been the birthright of their social predecessors. The rise of the bourgeoisie in the nineteenth century produced an audience composed of a new mercantile class of industrialists, financiers, and lawyers, the parvenus of Parisian society. They created a new wave of theatrical entertainment at the Paris Opéra, which increasingly was being bankrolled by private money and not by the state, as had been the case in Lully's time. Ballets of this era were expected to be emotionally uplifting and cleansing; ballet moved away from the noble dancing style of Guimard, Sallé, and Prévost and toward a new virtuosity that was more ideally feminine than that embodied by Camargo.

Women during this era were to be protected and adored; they were set up high on pedestals, embodying such virtues as chastity, piety, and fidelity with respect to marriage, a highly valued institution among the new middle class. Art mirrored these bourgeois concerns, in particular the Romantic ballet,

which flourished in France during the first half of the nineteenth century and showcased works where the ballerina was
cast in the new role as the ideal woman. This idealization operated as a subterfuge to what was really going on behind the
scenes, where ballerinas, for the most part, were poor, hungry,
and desperate for social advancement. But they put on a good
show, skillfully hiding the sins of their profession. They were
the whores who helped the wives look worthy of enshrining.

Works of this period were intended to be morally instruc-
tive and included the seminal *La Sylphide*, an 1832 ballet that
depicted a young man who, after choosing sensual adventure
over the promise of conjugal bliss, is punished by losing not
only his object of desire (the otherworldly Sylph in the title)
but also his status within society, which turns its back on him,
leaving him alone and isolated, a Byronic figure of Romantic
suffering. The Swedish-born ballerina Marie Taglioni (1804–
1884) danced the first performance of *La Sylphide*, which had
been choreographed by her ballet-master father, the Italian-
born Filippo Taglioni (1777–1871). He had created the principal
female role with her in mind, using it as a vehicle for his daughter's unique strengths as a ballerina able to rise to the tips of
her toes while dancing, a relatively new phenomenon. He also
gave her wings, creating choreography that highlighted her
innate buoyancy. Marie Taglioni had perfected a technique of
seeming to hold onto the air while jumping, a feat of extreme
breath control, creating the illusion of flight. It was a remarkable achievement, and it turned Taglioni into the poster girl for
the era. *Terre-à-terre* dancing was no longer the goal for women
dancers. The demand was for aerial flights of fancy, the idea
being that women were unconnected to the mundane matters
of the earth; they had become sublime creatures of the air.

Robert le Diable, originally produced in 1831, was the work
that gave birth to ballet's new wave; at the center of the five-act

grand opera was *La Valse infernale*, a crazed dance for a troupe of ghostly nuns led by Taglioni, again dancing choreography created by her father. Emerging from their tombs, their bodies and limbs spiraling and undulating to the swooning melodies of Giacomo Meyerbeer's haunting score, these white-clad ballerinas gave birth to the *ballet blanc*, a new genre of ballet in which female dancers became spectral images of themselves: vapors more than real women. Ballet became so ethereal an art that male dancers in the new century began to look out of place. Their virile capering, which had so dominated in the eighteenth century, was suddenly out of fashion; in a world constructed from tulle and satin ribbons, male dancers were perceived at best as effeminate and at worst, disgusting.[1] A host of male dance critics helped fuel the increased feminization of ballet in the nineteenth century, among them Jules Janin (1804–1874) and Théophile Gautier (1811–1872). Their highly subjective prose-poem critiques rated a dancer's sex appeal along with her technique. Their writings appeared frequently in the popular press and were widely read, fanning emotions, including amorous desire, among a growing audience for ballet.[2]

Women were now the leading exponents of a ballet whose feminine values of lightness, buoyancy, and delicacy started pushing it into new and unchartered artistic territory: the exodus of men from ballet was met by legions of young women lining up at the theater door, ready to take their place. Most came from the ranks of the poor, who looked on ballet as an attainable job and a relief from the drudgery of their everyday lives.

There were so many girls applying to enter the ballet that they began taking over parts formerly reserved for men, performing *en travesti* as men had once done early on in ballet history when there had been a shortage of women. The roles were most certainly reversed: "Once this fragile woman had access to center stage, the image of robust heroism was disarmed, and the mythic areas ballet could tap were enlarged: now the real world, whether courtly or rustic, interpenetrated with an ideal world, each word with its own hierarchy of positive and negative forces."[3]

This was the era not only of the great Marie Taglioni but also of Carlotta Grisi (1819–1899), the first Giselle, and Lucile Grahn (1819–1907), the first star ballerina of Copenhagen. Following immediately in their footsteps were the equally brilliant ballerinas of the Second Empire: Fanny Cerrito (1817–1909), Carolina Rosati (1826–1905), Léontine Beaugrand (1842–1925), and finally, Marie Taglioni's student Emma Livry (1842–1862), said to be the last of the Romantic ballerinas. Each was a celebrity in her day, well loved and well paid. But the popularity and success of this new generation of winged dancers belied an even coarser backstairs reality than may have existed in the eighteenth century, when the ballerina was still under the protection of the king.

In the nineteenth century, ballerinas increasingly became the pawns of wealthy entrepreneurs, many of them members of the Jockey Club de Paris, a gathering of the elite of nineteenth-century France, who, just as they did with horses, traded dancers for sport, swapping them among each other as sexual partners, as illustrated by an amusing anecdote that survives today: a young member of the corps de ballet is seen to be pregnant and when a member of the Paris Opéra administration asks her who was responsible for putting her in the family way, the girl innocently replied, "Some men you don't know."[4] Gentlemen of the Jockey Club kept boxes at the Paris Opéra, using them as salons and places for sexual encounters. They were a powerful social group who saw to it that no opera featured a ballet in the first act, so as to enable them to linger over their dinners and chat up the ballerinas in the wings before their entrances. They ensured that the practice of ballerina-courtesans continued to flourish; but where eighteenth-century ballerinas like Guimard could wrest control of their situation, in the nineteenth century it seems that many more could not. The Opéra's murky backstage world had become more officially a place of institutionalized prostitution. French author Ludovic Halévy documented the phenomenon in a trilogy of fictionalized stories based on his observations of the desperados he routinely met backstage at the Opéra. Published in 1883 as one volume under the title *Les Cardinals*, the plot followed the exploits of Madame Cardinal, a fictional woman of the concierge class, who sells her two young daughters, Virginie and Pauline, both members of the corps de ballet of the Opéra, to a pair of wealthy Jockey Club admirers, with her husband's consent. The parents are the main focus of the tale; the daughters are more a sideshow existing on the margins, just as real prostitute-dancers of the corps de ballet might have been perceived at that time. Their feelings, thoughts, desires didn't matter; they did as they were told.

Young ballerinas were expected to be seductive; it was built into their daily instruction. "My good friends, be charming, sensual," instructed Auguste Vestris, the brilliant ballet-dancer-turned-ballet-master, to the young dancers in his charge. "Indicate through movement the greatest transports of passion. It is imperative that during and after your variations you inspire love and the box and orchestra and seat holders should want to carry you off to bed."[5]

The identification of the ballerina with prostitution was so pronounced at this time that when Danish dancer and choreographer August Bournonville went to Paris in the 1840s seeking to advance his career, he wrote letters home in which he referred frequently to the moral depravity encountered backstage at the Opéra, lamenting its detrimental influence on the art of ballet. Observing that poverty bred desperation, on his return to Copenhagen to direct the Royal Danish Ballet he resolved to pay his dancers, male and female, a fair and equitable wage to keep them from having to prostitute themselves, thereby elevating the moral worth of ballet (at least in Denmark). In this way, Bournonville, a churchgoing Lutheran and devoted family man, created a school and style of ballet in stark contrast to that found in Paris, one based, unusually, on non-sexist and egalitarian values. Meanwhile, in France, at least where the ballet was concerned, it was business as usual.

After the old Opéra on the rue Le Peletier had burned to the ground in 1873, Charles Garnier had designed a new building to replace it. Opening its doors, the new Palais Garnier was custom-built for both theatrical spectacles and sexual sport. There, under the gilded rooftop decorated with statues dedicated to Apollo, Harmony, and Poetry, fortunes were squandered, reputations sullied, and affairs brazenly carried out in the exalted name of the ballet. Napoléon III, head of the Second Empire, was such a backstage regular at the Opéra that he kept a private room there.[6] Baron Georges-Eugène Haussmann, the city planner who had redeveloped Paris with a view to keeping filth from clogging the sewers, kept as his mistress the Paris Opéra dancer Francine Cellier, housing her in a series of increasingly expensive apartments on the boulevard Malesherbes. His indiscretion was well known and served as gossip for the tabloids until 1877, when the ballerina mysteriously vanished from history.[7]

Haussmann might have fared better had he conducted his affair as other men of his social class did—within the confines of an ornately decorated room especially made for close encounters of the amorous kind as practiced by French ballerinas and their top-hatted patrons.

The *foyer de la danse*, as this room was called, of the Palais Garnier was ostensibly an open studio where dancers came to take class and rehearse. But that was just the outside view. In writing about the new building, Garnier himself explained that "above all, the Foyer is intended as a setting for the charming swarms of ballerinas, in their picturesque and coquettish costumes."[8] Lined with gilt-edged mirrors and hung with chandeliers, the room was where wealthy male patrons or subscribers known as *les abonnés* came to watch and mingle with the dancers on display, eyeing them as if they were show ponies. These predatory men, "Adonises-over-forty," as the French social-realist writer Honoré de Balzac once called them,"[9] were an elite group, exclusively male, who paid dearly for the benefit of wandering at will through the backstage corridors of the Opéra. The cheapest *abonnements* were a little under 1,000 francs a year for a single seat one night a week; a more coveted loge in the *avant-scène* cost almost 30,000 francs a year. A 1991 study done of the nearly five hundred names listed for the 1892 and 1893 season reveals that "around a quarter of the subscriptions were held by major financiers and two out of every five belonged to members of the nobility, while other groups included industrialist and commercial magnates (9 percent), the liberal professions (21 percent), and public officials (10 percent)."[10] These prominent Opéra spectators used the *foyer de la danse* for social display, business deals, and private liaisons. The last they accomplished by flirting with the dancers in the *coulisses*, or wings, watching them closely in rehearsals and besieging them in their dressing rooms both before and after performances; nothing and no one interfered with their pleasure. Their money is what enabled the theater, operating since 1830 as a financial enterprise beyond state control, to enrich its coffers.[11] The Opéra was a private club for those privileged by fortune.[12]

Omnipresent and omnipotent in the backstage world of the Paris ballet, these men were almost impossible to ignore. In spite of their fatigue, young dancers before, during, and following a performance were encouraged to smile and flirt to win themselves an *abonné*, often by their own mothers. "I heard a singular lecture made by the mother of an artist to her daughter," writes Dr. Louis Véron, a medical professional appointed director of the Opéra in 1831, in his memoirs. "She reproached her for acting too coldly toward those who admired her. 'Be kinder, more tender more eager! If not for the sake of your child or mother, at least for the sake of your carriage!'"[13]

Acquiescing to the advances of an *abonné* was often the difference between a life of penury and one of privilege for dancers at the Paris Opéra, from the highest ranking to the lowest. Some dancers who participated in the sexual intrigues that were part and parcel of ballet at that time came from the upper reaches of the Paris Opéra company's dancing hierarchy; among them, Taglioni's archrival, the Austrian-born Fanny Elssler (1810–1884), a sensual dancer (Gautier, who adored her, called her a "pagan"), became the mistress of Leopold, Prince of Salerno, son of King Ferdinand of the Two Sicilies, with whom she bore an illegitimate son. The great Taglioni (whom Gautier said was a "Christian dancer") tended to keep a low profile with regards to matters of the heart, but there were hints that she, too, indulged in illicit affairs behind the screen of her pure-as-snow public persona. But few were fooled. The popular press openly discussed her carriages and teams of fine horses, her treasure chests bursting with jewels, and the opulent surroundings of her palatial home on the shores of Lake Como in Italy—all code for the spoils of the courtesan life. Taglioni also had a child out of wedlock, whom she bore in seclusion after begging time off from the Opéra, allegedly for a bad knee. She used the nonexistent injury to cover her pregnancy and, when found out, reportedly laughed about it.[14]

But illegitimacy and other consequences of pursuing social advancement while lying on their backs was no laughing matter for ballet's rank and file, paraded into the *foyer de la danse* for the voyeuristic pleasure of this behind-the-scenes audience. They occupied the company's lowest rung and were among the anonymous members of the corps de ballet; there were hundreds of them, supporting the illusion of splendor that danced before the footlights.

These were the "gutter sylphs," as Dr. Véron called them,[15] and they were culled from among the city's most wretched poor, street urchins for whom the ballet represented an opportunity for advancement. But scores of these bedraggled, malnourished, sexually exploited girls in the corps de ballet had almost no real chance of dancing out of the misery they were born into. They were popularly known as *les petits rats*, for how they seemed to gnaw at everything in sight, desperately hungry for life and its material goods.

Gautier is credited with being the first to use the metaphor of a rodent to describe the young dancers scurrying about the Paris Opéra in his essay, "Le Rat," a piece of piquant writing devoted to these poor children of the theater. He applies an affectionate tone when describing these "eminently feminine" creatures in the wings, mockingly explaining how they came to get their name: "*Nous pensons que le rat a été appelé ainsi, d'abord à cause de sa petitesse, ensuite à cause de ses instincts rongeurs et destructifs*" (We think the rat got her name first off because of her smallness and second, because of her gnawing and destructive tendencies), wrote Gautier in the paper published in his 1865 collection of Paris-inspired essays, *Quand on voyage*.[16] "*Comme son homonyme, il aime à pratiquer des trous dans les toiles, à élargir les déchirures des décorations, sous prétexte de regarder la scène ou la salle, mais au fond pour le plaisir de faire du dégât*" (Like its namesake, the rat likes to practice making holes in the curtains, expanding on the rips already there in the decor, under the pretext of watching the stage or the audience, but really just doing so for the pleasure of doing damage).

But elsewhere in the essay, Gautier suggests that the Paris Opéra rats are more the victims of other people's destructive pursuits of pleasure, calling them "poor girls" and "frail creatures" offered up as sacrifices to the Minotaur that is Paris, city of insatiable desire, "*qui dévore chaque année les vierges par centaines sans que jamais aucun Thésée vienne à leur secours!*" (which each year devours its virgins by the hundreds with no hope of a Theseus coming to save them!).[17] Behind Gautier's flowery language lurks a grim truth about the reality faced by these young dancers.

Typically, *les petits rats* came from poor backgrounds and single-parent families. Enrollment records of the Paris Opéra reveal that around 1850, "more than half the certificates of engagement at the school of dance indicate that the children had no known father and that their mothers were concierges, [or] laundresses."[18] Other young dance students "were daughters of the common people, of hired hands from the workshop, the shop or the office, retired or humble performers, concierges."[19]

Many came on foot to the Opéra from as far away as Montmartre, Batignolles, or the Hôtel-de-Ville neighborhoods for their dance lessons, rehearsals, and performances. They returned past midnight to these far-off areas in rain or snow, driven by need. "I paid many compliments to one mother on her young daughter, whose beauty was growing every day," writes Dr. Véron. "'We are very unfortunate, nonetheless,' she told me, 'and I have to give her to whoever wants her, just to have enough to eat.'"[20]

Although many girls applied, not all were chosen. The Paris Opéra had standards; potential dancers had to have the right body type to get in. Throughout their time in the school, they also had to give evidence that they were developing their muscles in a way conducive to performing the rigorous steps and balances of French ballet. Dancers were routinely scrutinized from a medical point of view to ensure that they had the right physique: "I often had to put a stop to lessons for those sickly, feeble children, already looking like little old men, for whom such exercise was debilitating rather than fortifying," Dr. Véron continues. "The mothers and their allies the ballet masters respectfully fought my opinion, but a sense of justice made me obdurate."[21]

Girls who passed the initial examination could advance themselves on the basis of talent, and that was the hope that made them endure an often grueling regimen meant to take them out of the gutter and onto the world's stage. The exercises used to mold scraggly rats into alluring symbols of airborne femininity were said to be especially punishing in the late 1800s. An anonymously penned memoir by *"un vieil abonné"* (an old subscriber), now known to be the novelist Paul Mahalin,[22] records some of the barbaric practices used to break in young bodies. He itemizes "boxes, rings, straps and bars... an entire torture apparatus," before elaborating on how a dancer/student "imprisons her feet in one of those grooved boxes. There, her heels back-to-back and her knees turned out, she accustoms her poor martyred feet to remaining, by themselves, in a straight line."[23]

Young dancers were also obliged to attend class regularly or else face stiff fines or dismissal. Protocol, as established between 1870 and 1900, was strict. Students as young as five trained at the dance conservatory until they passed the examinations that allowed them a spot in the corps, usually between the ages of twelve and fourteen. Depending on training, dedication, and capacity for attracting influential patrons, dancers could progress steadily through the five ranks defining the dancing hierarchy within the Paris Opéra: *premier* or *deuxième quadrille* (classifications assigned dancers in the corps), followed by *coryphée* (minor soloist), and next by *sujet* (equivalent to second soloist) and *premier sujet*. The ultimate designation was *première danseuse* or *étoile*, the highest level for a female dancer at Paris Opéra. (The same hierarchy applies to the Opéra ballet company today.) Rigorous annual and biannual examinations determined advancement, with appropriate adjustments made to dancers' pay as they rose through the ranks.[24]

If and when a young dancer graduated from the school and into the parent company, her financial situation didn't improve much: junior members of the corps de ballet were never well paid. Their monthly salaries were between seventy-five and eighty francs. Persistent poverty forced many members of the corps de ballet to become prostitutes just to make ends meet, if not to afford the fifteen-franc tarlatan skirts and six-franc satin pointe shoes required for taking daily class at the Opéra. This often meant finding a generous protector "who would ensure them a decent existence."[25]

In exchange, the little rat yielded unquestioningly to her patron; she was putty in the hands of the wealthy and more powerful, allowing herself to be shaped according to another's will: "I have a passion for novices, 'little rats' still in poverty," declared Richard O'Monroy, the Paris-born novelist and apparent connoisseur of the ballet, in 1893. "I like to be the patron who discovers newborn talents, who, in spite of pronounced collarbones and red hands, prerogatives of their awkward age, reveal future curves that facilitate the first steps in the career from the beginning in a *quadrille* set all the way up to the principal ballerina."[26]

The road to the top was hard, paved with pain and deprivation; dancers took class every day, six days a week, often arriving hungry. The concierges who manned the rear entrance sometimes fed them soup to keep them from fainting. Daily class was usually followed by a full day of rehearsal, plus performances at night. The hard work and long hours, often on an empty stomach, made the dancers appear "exhausted, almost dead, puffing like a steam engine," according to one eyewitness, Opéra enthusiast Charles de Boigne, who observed the dancers in class.[27] This image of the ballerina as physically spent and machine-like contrasted sharply with her popular image as a delicate fairy, winging toward eternity. Other ballet observers were able to see the disconnect between the public's idealized perception of the ballerina and the brute realities of her everyday existence: "We cannot imagine the courage, patience and incessant work required to become a talented dancer," wrote the French composer and music writer Albert Vizentini in 1868. "The true dancer is obsessed with her art and sacrifices everything to it. At sixteen as at thirty, she must undergo the same painful exercises; stretching at the *barre*, lifting oneself at the knees, *pliés*, *écartés*, leaning back until the limbs creak in unison, exhausting oneself, making oneself continuously hoarse, accepting neither fatigue or sluggishness, these are the daily routines of the dancer who, after attending classes from nine

until one, and rehearsal from one until four, appears in the evening with a smile on her lips to perform as a sylph as if nothing
had happened."[28]

Working conditions endangered dancers' health. A document from the time, a letter of complaint to a public health
official in London, where life for young ballet dancers was no
different than for those in Paris, drew the inspector's attention
to venues whose cramped, dirty gaslit rooms were overrun by
rats and other insalubrious features. In each of these rooms,
the letter writer observed, up to a dozen girls at a time, "all per-
spiring from strenuous dancing have to spend the evening to
earn a living. These conditions are liable I should say to lead to
consumption and other illnesses."[29]

Corps de ballet members tended to suffer in silence, rarely
protesting against a system that fed off their youth and labor.
What made the life tolerable was the sense of belonging to a
community of other dancers, each driven by a shared loved
of dance and the hope for a better life. The company felt like
family, all the girls rooting for each other—a situation not
uncommon among members of today's corps de ballets. There
was solidarity in numbers, producing what social scientists
refer to as "collective effervescence," a feeling shared by members of a like-minded group of individuals who manage to
transcend obstacles by being united in a common cause. "Luxury and poverty hold hands," says Dr. Véron. "The one came in
a carriage, the other in sandals; but a spirit of camaraderie per-
vades their little world. She who is penniless does not grovel;
she who is possessed of luxury is not arrogant."[30]

The director paints a rosy picture. But there was a dark side
to this world of economic extremes. Careers could be made or
broken at whim and lives ruined. "Some girls," Dr. Véron drily
observes, "were abandoned as soon as they became mothers."[31]
There were other threats besides. When the Franco-Prussian

war cut off food supplies to Paris, forcing the temporary clo-
sure of the Opéra, the Italian-born ballerina Guiseppina
Bozzacchi died of starvation on November 23, 1870, her seventeenth birthday. Her family was in dire straits and could not
save her. Bozzacchi had been a rising star in Paris, and her loss
was tragic.

The life of the ballet girl was indeed harsh, and the choices
she had to make just to survive sometimes backfired on her
and her family members, who had rested all their hopes for success on her malnourished shoulders. An 1859 article published
in London Society entitled "The Ballet Girls of Paris" played up
the flip side of the pleasure-seeking fantasy for those ballerinas who gambled with their bodies and lost, saying that they
were to be found "in hospitals, in streets begging, or worse, in
asylums, in gaols, at the solemn little Morgue by the banks of
the Seine—very rarely that we do not hear of them in places of
misery, in the somber realms of wretchedness. Their lives are
frail and brittle, and break often under their burdens."[32]

Marie van Goethem was one of those girls.

She is better known as The Little Dancer, Aged Fourteen, the
insolent-looking ballerina sculpted by Edgar Degas (1834–
1917) for a two-thirds life-size creation whose debut took place
in Paris at the Sixth Impressionist Exhibition of 1881. She
was, at the time of the statuette's unveiling, a member of the
corps de ballet, one of 140 dancers employed by the Opéra. She
had just been promoted the year before after two years in the
dance conservatory, which she had joined in 1878, at the age
of twelve.[33] She was not yet a full-fledged ballerina; she was,
like many members of the corps, a girl whose future would be
determined by her past.

Research bordering on detective work executed in the
1990s by Martine Kahane, an authority on the history of
the Paris Opéra, reveals that Marie was born into precarious

circumstances that appear to have scarred her for life.[34] Born June 7, 1865, Marie was the middle daughter of three girls of Belgium-born parents who had relocated to Paris between 1861 and 1862, perhaps in search of a better life.[35] The oldest girl was Antoinette, born 1861 in Brussels, and the youngest was Louise Joséphine (also called Charlotte), who was born in Paris in 1870 and who died there in 1945. Kahane says that "the three sisters' childhood [took] place in a geographic and social environment that exert[ed] a heavy toll. The young girls, probably streetwise, spent more time in the street than in the dark and joyless hovels that make up the district's poor dwellings. The Bréda district, Marie's birthplace, was one of the poorest, most squalid locations for Paris prostitution."[36]

The sisters' father was said to be a tailor, and their mother a laundress, who was also a known prostitute; once in Paris, the family moved through a rapid series of apartments, all located in the 9th arrondissement: "The frequent changes in residence are an indication of poverty, of the inability to pay rent on time but could also be considered an indication of vagrancy bordering on prostitution."[37] The family's financial situation no doubt worsened after Antoine van Goethem died, around 1870, leaving his wife to raise the three girls on her own, seemingly without a profession; 1870 also marked the start of the Franco-Prussian War, which introduced tremendous privations to Paris, including starvation. It was a desperate time in the history of the city, and the semi-criminal van Goethem family was obviously doing all it could to survive.

They lived close to Pigalle and the red-light district but also within walking distance of artists' studios such as that belonging to Degas, who kept lodgings on the lower slopes of Montmartre. The artist knew the van Goethems, and as early as 1873, when the family lived on the boulevard de Clichy, Degas appears already to have started sketching the children, each of whom were students at the École de Danse, the Paris Opéra dance school. A notebook dating from around 1874 makes a reference to "Antoinette Vangutten—aged 12," suggesting the older sister might have sat for some of his earlier dance paintings.[38] But it was Marie who appears to have posed more frequently for the artist, both clothed and nude, affording Degas an opportunity to study her anatomy from every angle and at close hand. Degas was a committed studio artist, often working from live models paid between six and ten francs for a four-hour sitting at a time when a pound of meat cost a franc.

Degas was classically trained at the École Nationale Supérieure des Beaux-Arts in Paris, as well as in Naples, Florence, and Rome, where his banker father, a prominent member of Second Empire society who later in life lost all his money, had supported his son in furthering his art studies. But Degas was a pioneering modernist. In his paintings, he slyly alluded to the backstage violence of the ballet through images of dancers yawning, drooping, or staring catatonically into space. The other threat, that of the ever-present *abonné*, the man who, single-handedly, could determine a dancer's destiny, Degas rendered almost satirically, using the presence of small-figure dark-suited men hovering in a picture's background: storm clouds who at any minute might thunder down on the petal-like tulle of his dancers' tutus. When Degas came to make the statue of Marie, modeling it by hand from wax during a two-year period—the only sculpture he exhibited in his lifetime—he took pains to capture the young dancer's psychological makeup, presenting her idiosyncratically in ballet's relaxed fourth position, with most of the weight falling onto the back leg. Her bony legs are widely turned out, and her thin arms are pulled back with hands tightly clasped. Her pointy chin is thrust high, and her eyes are semi-closed, as if lost in a dream, if not interminable boredom. She wears a real tarlatan tutu such as she might have worn to the studio for practice, and there is a ribbon in her plaited hair. She looks defiant if not impudent; she is not at all one of those fantastical creatures of the ballet stage but a girl who looks half-starved and brutalized by life and her profession.

This lack of conformity to classical precepts of beauty shocked many who first laid eyes on the meter-high, partly colored and clothed sculpture of a young ballet student to which Degas had added real hair; the general consensus was that she was a grotesque: "I don't ask that art should always be elegant, but I don't believe that its role is to champion ugliness," declared an outraged Elie de Mont in La Civilisation.[39] "This opera rat has something about her of the monkey, the shrimp, the runt. Any smaller and one would be tempted to enclose her in a jar of alcohol."[40]

Perhaps worse than ugly, the young dancer was seen as immoral, embodying all the vice of both her class and profession. The critic Paul Mantz, writing in Le Temps, stated that in choosing this less-than-desirable-girl as his model, Degas had "picked a flower of precocious depravity from the espaliers of the theater."[41] For the art historian and collector Charles Ephrussi, who owned some of Degas's ballet paintings, the figure represented "the Opéra rat in her modern form, learning her craft with all her disposition and stock of bad instincts and licentious inclinations."[42] The French literary critic Henri Trianon likened her to a "young monster" that belonged in a museum of zoology or anthropology."[43]

Yet, this strange little statuette also had its supporters; many saw it marking a turning point in the history of modern sculpture. Joris-Karl Huysmans, writing in L'Art moderne, praised it as "the only truly modern attempt I know of in sculpture."[44] The critic Paul de Charry called it "extraordinarily real," adding that the "model is perfect."[45] French writer and muse of the Impressionists Nina de Villard declared it to be "the leading expression of the new art." Even Ephrussi understood this, despite expressing moral revulsion over the choice of subject matter; he called *The Little Dancer* "a new endeavour, an attempt at realism in sculpture."[46]

The subject depicted by the sculpture of *The Little Dancer* was a member of the corps de ballet, a thin, tired, deliberately unsexy specimen of the rats who populated the Paris Opéra, a crystallization of ideas that Degas had been experimenting with for decades in his ballerina paintings. Degas was forty-seven at the time of the unveiling, but he had already been exhibiting his evocative images of ballerinas for almost a decade, starting in 1871. Degas haunted the backstage world of the Opéra, depending on the generosity of wealthier friends with subscriptions to get him backstage and into the *foyer de la danse*. His interest in the dancers went beyond the erotic, the glamorous, and the conventional. While his brother kept a ballerina as a mistress, there is no documentation to support that Degas himself ever had sexual relations with any of the ballerinas he portrayed and befriended. He was more interested in the cold, hard stamp of hard work and fatigue he saw imprinted on their bodies. He depicted them not as objects of desire but as spent and sweaty athletes, caught up in the banal act of their training. In sonnets, Degas extolled the truths and the illusions he encountered at the ballet: "One knows that in your world/Queens are made of distance and greasepaint," he wrote around 1889. "The dance instils in you something that sets you apart/Something heroic and remote."[47]

The Little Dancer, Aged Fourteen was by far his most controversial work. The statuette didn't sell, and Degas never exhibited her in public again, preferring to live with her in private for the rest of his life, jokingly referring to her as his daughter. After Degas died in 1917, at age eighty-three, the sculpture was cast in bronze in Paris. Several of these bronzes are now in major international museums, including the National Gallery in Washington, which has the most. The original wax statuette appears not to have survived.

She is loved and admired today. One of the few bronzes in public hands sold at auction in London in 2009 for just over $19 million, a record price for a Degas statue. But in the day, *The Little Dancer, Aged Fourteen* was a figure of great controversy. The storm of mixed reactions that swirled around the sculpture's debut—people hating it or loving it as if it were a real person—was linked to the ongoing popularity of ballet in nineteenth-century Paris. Dancers, even unknowns like Marie van Goethem, triggered a visceral response in a citizenry for whom ballerinas were like pop stars, aggressively celebrated and intrusively scrutinized as touchstones of collective erotic desire. Outside the Opéra, photographs of ballerinas were widely circulated in the tens of thousands and their stage performances analyzed; a subgenre of newspaper reporting called *"coulisses"* journalism and salacious memoirs fed the public taste for ballerina gossip and rags-to-riches stories within the confines of the Palais Garnier.[48] Female dancers, once marginalized, now preoccupied the popular imagination. "Far from being an esoteric activity followed by the few, ballet at the Opéra filled the gossip columns and reviews, featured in cheap illustrations and widely read novels, and supported a cult of personality that has few rivals even today," observes contemporary Degas scholar Richard Kendall. "Analogies have been proposed with cinema in the golden age of Hollywood or television in our own time, but both cases fall short of the mark, missing the extraordinary fusion of the highest artistic standards with the most blatant and officially sanctioned vice, and the concentration of both in a single edifice, the Palais Garnier."[49]

Marie wasn't one of the ballet girls often gossiped about, existing beyond the range of the Opéra's celebrity radar, and so it is not known if she took a patron when recruited into the Paris Opéra at the bottom of the pay scale after passing her exams in 1880. She and her sister Charlotte had both become company members; they earned bonuses for their participation in some shows, in addition to yearly salaries. Marie had an annual contract of 900 francs, or a monthly salary of 75 francs plus bonuses, while Charlotte had an annual contract of 852 francs, in addition to the bonuses she earned while dancing. In May 1880, with salaries and bonuses combined, Marie earned a monthly wage of 109 francs and Charlotte 82 francs.[50] Their older sister, Antoinette, never had a contract and worked as an extra doing mostly walk-on roles, paid by performance. She had early on become a prostitute to supplement her meager earnings. By 1882, she was serving a three-month sentence in the notorious Saint Lazare prison for having been caught stealing 700 francs from a john—a date with an *abonné* gone terribly wrong.

It seems that Marie and her sister were, initially, more disciplined. They never ran afoul of the Opéra administration but appear to have been dutiful employees. In 1880, both sisters appear in the premiere performance of Louis Mérante's *La Korrigane*, starring Rosita Mauri (1849–1923), the leading ballerina of her day; in the ballet, Marie plays a peasant and Charlotte a sprite.[51] In 1881, the year of the debut of *The Little Dancer, Aged Fourteen*, they are together again, dancing in *Le Tribut de Zamora*; this time, Marie is a slave and Charlotte a street performer.

The sculpture shows what Marie looked like at this time— her body long, lean, lithe, and well suited to dancing the roles in the Opéra's ever-expanding classical repertoire. It seems that although she came from the criminal fringes of Paris, she had the physique that would enable her to move rapidly through the ranks of one of the world's most demanding ballet academies.[52] The statuette confirms that she had a pronounced turnout of the legs and feet, originating from the pelvis, a quality she either was born with or acquired in the ballet studio.[53] She also had flexible ankles, permitting her to create with her body a fluid, classical line. Degas gives a sense of her progress in presenting Marie as an older, more prominent ballerina in a pastel entitled *Dancer with Long Hair Bowing*, produced in the mid-1880s. In this portrait, she appears to be fulfilling her promise as a ballerina: she is no longer a rat but a *sujet*, or soloist, and is surrounded by her own little-girl attendants.

Soon after, Marie disappears from sight. There is confusion as to what happened to her. Lillian Browse, whose 1949 book, *Degas Dancers*, includes first-hand interviews with some of the artist's surviving models, says that Marie enjoyed an association with the Opéra until 1914.[54] But other accounts suggest that she was fired from the ballet in 1882, which appears closer to the truth. Never having been a celebrity like the courtesans within the Opéra, Marie didn't figure much in the gossip columns detailing the comings and goings of the leading ballerinas of the day. She merits only one mention, when still fifteen and just starting her dancing career, which appeared in the local newspaper, *L'Événement*, on February 10, 1882. The anonymously penned column refers to a "Mademoiselle Van Goeuthen," identified as a "model... for painters, who is frequently seen at the Brasserie des Martyrs, the Nouvelle Athènes café and the bar of the Rat Mort." These were not the kind of places young ladies wanting a future in ballet were meant to be seen. The Rat Mort, at 7 rue Pigalle, was an all-night establishment popular with artists (Degas was a regular) and others eager to meet easy women. Marie, that skinny dancer with a prickly attitude, was hardly the type. But her mother, you could say, had insisted, having prostituted her, along with her older sister, to the world of the demimonde, presumably because she needed to put food on the table. It would be Marie's undoing.

"I could tell you things to make you blush or make you weep," the anonymous newspaper writer continues in his column about Marie. And then he says nothing more.[55]

By June of that year, Marie's name was stricken from the company's roster for having missed eleven ballet classes during the month of April. She was unemployed and likely in desperate straits. Last seen at the Chat Noir nightclub in 1882, she was accompanying her now much more popular younger sister, Charlotte, described insinuatingly in the press "as a pretty *petit rat* who could very well become a first ballerina in a few years" (provided she behaved).[56] After that, Marie is never heard of again.

Charlotte did behave, and the prophecy about her career at the Opéra did come true. The youngest van Goethem sister enjoyed a long and fruitful association with the Paris Opéra, entering the dance school in 1880, at age ten, and retiring in 1933, at age sixty-four.[57] She rose steadily through the ranks. She started her dancing career as a member of a *quadrille* group in 1883, becoming its leader in 1887; in 1889, she became a soloist. She danced until 1907, at which time she retired from the stage and became a teacher within the school. For a brief time, in 1927, she instructed Yvette Chauviré, a grand *étoile* of the Paris Opéra, described as France's greatest ballerina. At the end of her days, Charlotte claimed that she also once posed for the great Degas. It is now supposed that she is the ballerina depicted in the portrait called *Dancer* (circa 1895) in the Bibliothèque Nationale in Paris. The ballerina's bracelet and brooch are identical to jewelry worn by Charlotte in a photograph of her in costume, taken before 1898.[58] If she is the same dancer, not only was she a Degas model who made good but a *petit rat* who clawed her way to the top of her profession on her own merits—that is, her dancing skills.

Marie, on the other hand, ends our story much as she started: the subject of much speculation. Like the statuette that bears her likeness, she remains an enigma. In 2003, the Paris Opéra attempted to make sense of her life through the creation of a new work inspired by her image as originally captured by Degas. *La Petite Danseuse de Degas* featured original choreography by chief ballet master Patrice Bart and a new score by contemporary French composer Denis Levaillant. Based, in part, on the given facts of her life, the plot follows Marie as a young student, taking class and dreaming of rivaling the top *danseuse* and working after hours as an artist's model. What happens next in the ballet is semi-fictional: pushed by her mother into prostitution, Marie attaches herself to an *abonné*, is caught stealing from him, and goes to Saint-Lazare prison, after which she is expelled from the Opéra and becomes a laundress, as her mother professed to be. At the ballet's conclusion, Marie climbs inside a glass box and assumes the pose in the Degas statue that has made her world famous and forever frozen in time. It was an original creation. But like the sculpture in its day, the ballet received mixed reviews, including this one by a critic who observed the premiere performance: "The program notes almost read like a sociology text, while the dance impulse gets lost along the way."[59]

The poor girl never could win.

3

BONFIRE BALLERINA
DEADLY DANGERS OF THE
ROMANTIC BALLET

There are perils dire
Which oft beset the Ballet Girl,
And worst of all is Fire!
Most deadly of the deadly foes that threaten player folk,
An enemy who never sleeps, whose power is ne'er broke,
While of the groups Theatrical, the greatest risk who run
Are lightly costumed ballerinas—Escape for them is none.
A spark upon the muslin dry, then instantly it lights into a flame,
Like lightning's flash, at sea, on summer nights,
A blazing mass of agony, all maddened, quick they fly,
Yet fly not from the enemy who dooms them thus to die
That shrivels up the glowing limbs, and face and form, alas!
Leaving of female loveliness a charred and calcined mass.
Ah, happy if they die at once, and from Life's stage retire,
Than linger on in torment from the all-remorseless fire.

ANONYMOUS VICTORIAN POEM

CÉLESTINE EMAROT WAS another *petit rat* of the Paris Opéra. When the theater's director, Louis Véron, spoke of young corps de ballet dancers who were abandoned by their *abonné* lovers once they became pregnant, he may well have been thinking about her. Born in 1824 as Marguerite-Adélaïde Emarot, she had changed her name to Célestine as early as 1837—the first time her name appears on a list of the École de Danse students.[1] She enjoyed a fourteen-year career with the parent company, dancing minor parts in works by Jean Coralli (1779–1854), Jules Perrot (1810–1892), Joseph Mazilier (1801–1868), and Arthur Saint-Léon (1821–1870).[2] She had been a pretty adolescent but not a particularly good dancer. Her reviews were mixed, if not scathing. She was considered a mediocre talent at best: Charles de Boigne described her as "rococo," or old-fashioned, in his book, *Petits mémoires de l'Opéra*.[3] Others were less kind in describing her shortcomings: "She filled secondary roles adequately enough but failed miserably when called upon to take an important part, such as the Abbess in *Robert le Diable*," writes dance historian Ivor Guest, an authority on ballet of the Second Empire. "Many gentlemen whose memories of Taglioni were still vivid could not bear to watch her in the role and retired to the Foyer, while laughter was heard from the pit."[4]

She doubtless owed her career more to the first in a series of her protectors, Baron Charles de Chassiron (1818–1871), a French diplomat and prominent member of the Jockey Club de Paris. Like his titled peers, Chassiron was an habitué of the notorious *foyer de la danse*, where sexual assignations between dancers and certain privileged members of the audience were openly arranged. There, the comely Célestine had caught his eye. She was fifteen, he twenty-two when they started their affair. The liaison was encouraged by Célestine's mother, Jeanne-Léontine Emarot, an unmarried linen worker from

Dijon who had come to Paris in 1834 in search of a better life for herself and her illegitimate child. Getting her daughter into the Paris Opéra and pimping her to male ballet patrons of means was how Jeanne-Léontine had hoped to save them both from poverty. But all her hopes appeared dashed after Chassiron abandoned his teenaged lover when, nine months after their first encounter, she gave birth to a baby girl on September 23, 1842 (some accounts say 1841). Chassiron refused to claim paternity for the child, who (pity for her) grew up to be his spitting image—receding chin and all.[5] He later shuffled off to marry in 1850 Princess Caroline Laetitia Murat, the daughter of Prince Napoléon Lucien Charles Murat, himself the grandson of Caroline Bonaparte.[6] Chassiron also abandoned his wife when, as an attaché of the French Embassy, he embarked on a long journey through Asia, about which he wrote a book, *Notes sur le Japon, la Chine et l'Inde: 1858-1859-1860*—a carefree adventurer until the end of his days.[7]

Célestine eventually moved on, netting a new lover, also a member of the Jockey Club, who would keep her, if not in luxury, at least spared from having to prostitute herself—and, more importantly, her own daughter—to survive. Becoming mistress to Vicomte Ferdinand de Montguyon (1808–1876), a fervent balletomane, was, in fact, largely motivated by a need to protect her daughter, an only child whom she had baptized Jeanne-Emma Marie Emarot at the church of Notre-Dame-de-Lorette in Paris on December 14, 1843. Célestine might have been spotty as a dancer, but as a mother she was a veritable diva of domestic control. Regardless of her middling dancer's salary of between 3,000 to 6,000 francs a year, she personally saw to it that her daughter got an exemplary education at the Institution des demoiselles Cathonnet, a convent run by nuns on the rue du Faubourg Poissonnière, tapping Chassiron for the funds. For the rest of her life, Célestine would do all that she could to safeguard her child from following in her mother's footsteps.

As it turned out, her daughter fulfilled her mother's wishes—but with a twist. She became a dancer but avoided the corps de ballet entirely, on the basis of her extraordinary talent. Fate had blessed the ballerina who would become known the world over as Emma Livry, a name chosen to distance herself from her mother's risible reputation, with an abundance of innate talent as well as a wiry and plastic body. Unfashionably thin for her time and extraordinarily plain, Emma was nonetheless possessed of a pliancy and buoyancy that would quickly distinguish her from her peers. There was much expectation that Emma, a French-born dancer, would restore to Paris the prestige it had fast been losing in favor of a new generation of pyrotechnical ballerinas from Italy who were giving the dancers of the Second Empire a run for their money.

Montguyon was Célestine's lover, but he also took on the role of father-figure to young Emma, helping to raise her but ultimately micro-managing her career as a ballerina in whose interests he had invested heavily. He had the reputation as a gambling man, and in Emma he saw his winning hand, a chance at making his mark. He wagered that she would be the greatest ballerina of all time, and to make good his bet he scrupulously stage-managed her public image and her career at the Paris Opéra. He used his status as a member of the Jockey Club to influence management to give his protégée special attention, leveraging his relationship with Napoléon III to tighten the screws. He also made sure the royal couple were aware of Emma, apprising them of her progress through written correspondence and inviting them to see her take class.

Montguyon's masterminding of Emma's career was unfolding almost a decade following the bloody events of 1848, a year marked by revolutions across Europe but particularly in Paris, where the citizens had overthrown the "bourgeois monarchy" of Louis-Philippe I (1773–1850), replacing it with the Second Republic, under the leadership of an elected president. Montguyon was closely associated with this new and increasingly conservative political organization, his best friend being its leader's half-brother. In 1851, Louis-Napoléon Bonaparte (nephew of the first emperor, Napoléon I) disbanded the Second Republic to establish the Second Empire, crowning himself Emperor Napoléon III. Montguyon was there, close to the source of power, and knew how to exploit the reigning sentiments of the day. As Friedrich Engels has written on this period of French history, "The Second Empire was the appeal to French chauvinism...a French empire within the frontiers of the old monarchy."[8]

Anything that stoked the fires of French pride at that time was sure to get the public's attention, if not support. By publicly bruiting the fact that Emma was Paris-born. Montguyon launched a public relations campaign, promoting her at the expense of Italians then headlining the art, namely Guiseppina Bozzacchi (1853–1870), Amalia Ferraris (1830–1904), Carolina Rosati (1826–1905), and Fanny Cerrito (1817–1909), dancers known for their virtuosity and bravura displays of technique. The French school, as had been epitomized by Taglioni, was more vaporous and more poetic. Emma, while as technically proficient as the Italians, would be cast as Taglioni reborn, dancing in ways that were deliberately understated, to stress the point that she was innately a French ballerina, an artist as opposed to an acrobat. The public would eat it up.

The upshot of all this backstage maneuvering was that Montguyon ultimately convinced the French author and dramatist Alphonse Royer, then director of the Opéra, to take her into the company not as a member of the corps de ballet, as was usual for newcomers recruited from the school, but to promote her straight to the top, to the vaunted position of principal dancer. The girl had talent, and so there was little fear that she would sully the company's reputation as a result of incompetence. She was a child prodigy, hand-picked for greatness by her first teacher, Caroline-Dominique Venetozza (born Caroline Lassiat), Célestine's former colleague within the corps de ballets, and later one of the most sought-after dance instructors in all of Europe. She had also coached Adèle Grantzow (1845–1877), Léontine Beaugrand (1842–1925), and, later, Guiseppina Bozzacchi (1853–1870), other notable ballerinas of the Second Empire who also rose to the top as a result of her guidance. But Emma, whom she first started training when the dancer was eleven, was Mme Dominique's most brilliant student, surpassing all expectations in her mastery of classical dance. She had quickly endorsed Montguyon's suggestion that Emma bypass ballet's lower ranks in making her debut as a principal dancer.

Montguyon then went a step further, inciting some ballet observers of the day to accuse him of hubris when he insisted that for her premiere Emma dance the lead role in La Sylphide, the work intrinsically linked with ballet's still reigning queen, at least in memory, La Taglioni, who by then was living in retirement at her estate in Lake Como. Montguyon negotiated the inclusion of the ballet into Emma's initial contract with the Opéra: "Engagement as première danseuse for one year, starting from 1st July, 1858. Debut to be in La Sylphide. Only to dance in pas de deux, or in pas seule and pas de deux, with corps de ballet. No other person whatever to be allowed to dance her role. These conditions accepted, the Director of the Opéra shall himself fix her emolument after the third performance of La Sylphide."[9]

Adept at promotion, Montguyon then got word to Taglioni herself, idling in Italy, that there was a new dancer in Paris, said to be as great as she had been in her halcyon days as a ballerina superstar. Taglioni had a well-known jealous streak; she was notorious for having carefully guarded her ballet roles, possessing them fiercely against all rivals for her crown as the world's pre-eminent Romantic ballerina. She had been known also to sideline male dancers who she worried had a talent equal to hers and who might get more applause. It is how she, early on, had managed her celebrity status within society. The idea of an upstart, a mere wisp of a girl, threatening now to overtake her legend was perhaps too much for her. Up she got from Como to head straight to Paris, probably planning to cause a scene. But one peek at Emma in class preparing for rehearsals for *La Sylphide* was enough to stop the great Taglioni dead in her tracks. She knew instantly that she had met the next great ballerina of France. Believing she had seen herself reincarnated in Emma, she wrote in her diary, "*Il est vrai que je ne me suis jamais vue danser, mais je devais danser comme elle le fait*" (It is true that I never saw myself dance, but I must have danced as she does).[10]

La Sylphide, as performed by the precocious Emma, took place at the Paris Opéra's Salle Le Peletier on October 20, 1858, and the reviews were unanimously ecstatic. For critics who had grown accustomed to the flashy, bravura style of the Italians, Emma's gentle grace and airiness—which hearkened back to ballet's origins as a French court art, redolent of dignity, decorum, and, above all, restraint—struck them as something new and fresh, a complete surprise. Critic Paul de Saint-Victor wrote in *La Presse*.

> *Mlle Emma Livry est de l'École française, de l'école aérienne. Elle s'enlève une plume qu'on souffle; en retombant, la plume devient flèche et se pique dans le parquet sur les pointes d'acier. Ses entrechats sont nets, ses parcours arpentent la scène avec une rapidité fantastique. Elle a, dans*

*les temps penchés, cet aplomb de marbre qui fait songer à ce que serait
l'inclinaison d'une statue. Elle a surtout cette chaste et correcte élégance
qui est la distinction de la danse française.*[11]

(Mlle Emma Livry is of the French School, of the light and
airy school. She rises, wafted up like a feather. In its descent,
the feather becomes an arrow and pierces the floor with its
tips of steel. Her *entrechats* are neat, her progress across the
stage strides with fantastic rapidity. Her *penchés* have a marble-
like composure that makes one imagine a bending statue. She
has especially that pure and correct elegance that is the distinct attribute of French dance.)

Poet Théophile Gautier also praised Emma's debut, writing
that she captured the transparency of her French-made ethereal art:

*Elle appartenait à cette chaste école de Taglioni qui fait de la danse un
art presque immatériel à force de grâce pudique, de réserve décente et
de virginale diaphanéité. À l'entrevoir à travers la transparence de ses
voiles dont son pied ne faisait que soulever le bord, on eût dit une ombre
heureuse, une appearance élyséenne jouant dans un rayon bleuâtre; elle
en avait la légèreté impondérable, et son vol silencieux traversait l'espace
sans qu'on entendît le frisson de l'air.*[12]

(She belonged to the pure school of Taglioni who made
dance an art that is almost ethereal thanks to its chaste gracefulness, its proper reserve and its unsullied translucence. On
glimpsing her through the transparency of her veils of which
her foot lifted only the edge, one would have said she was no
more than a lucky shadow, an Elysian presence playing in a
beam of bluish light. She had the imponderable weightlessness of a shadow, and her noiseless flight traversed the space
without the audience hearing even the tremor of the air.)

Taglioni allowed herself to be carried along by the Emma-mania then sweeping the nation. She asked to return to the Paris Opéra and in 1860 was appointed *inspectrice des classes*, a position she held until 1870. She also made preparations to choreograph her first and only ballet, *Le Papillon*, which she was creating as a vehicle for Emma, whose training she had taken over; it was said that Taglioni shared with Emma all her air-borne secrets during private classes, just the two of them, held at the Opéra behind locked doors. She loved her like a daughter and wanted the best for her. She was willing to step aside to let the younger dancer shine. Taglioni gave Emma a gift that elegantly summed up her feelings, a portrait of herself on which she had written, "*Faites-moi oublier. Ne m'oubliez pas*" (Make me forgotten, but don't forget me).[13] It was the ultimate compliment, coming as it did from the greatest ballerina in the world.

With an eye fixed on her protégée's future, Taglioni determined that Emma should have her own signature ballet, just as she had had, and with composer Jacques Offenbach creating his first and only score for ballet, she set out to make a full-length, three-act work that, like *La Sylphide*, would feature a winged creature of the imagination as the central motif. Just as she had been identified with the sylph, she wanted Emma to be associated with the butterfly. Taglioni believed this role would enhance Emma's ephemeral allure and get audiences once again talking about the ballet which, in the second half of the nineteenth century, had started losing ground to French grand opera, then in the ascendant. She wrote the libretto in collaboration with Jules-Henri Vernoy de Saint-Georges, one of the creators of *Giselle* and of *Le Corsaire*.

The story concerned Farfalla (Italian for "butterfly"), a girl turned into a butterfly by a wicked sorceress whose spell can only be broken by a lover's kiss. At one point in the convoluted story, Farfalla's wings are singed when she draws close to a burning torch, which almost kills her. Emma played the part only too well. No one knew it at the time, but the scene was prophetic and would be responsible for making *Le Papillon*, an otherwise forgettable ballet, known in history as the work that unintentionally predicted the tragic end to Emma's life. The rave reviews that accompanied the November 26, 1860, premiere gave no hint of the tragedy to come: "[*La danseuse*] *acquit la seule chose qui lui eût un peu manqué jusque-là: une grâce parfaite*," wrote Paul d'Ambert in *Le Nain jaune*. (The dancer acquired the only thing she had slightly lacked up to then: perfect gracefulness.) Emma alone made *Le Papillon* an instant success. Napoléon III himself came twice to see it; the sculptor Jean-Auguste Barre, who had made a practice of immortalizing select French ballerinas of the Romantic era in statue form, created a figurine of Emma as the Butterfly (a delicately painted, hard-paste porcelain version of is in the Theatre Museum in London).[14] Inspired by the success of *Le Papillon*, Taglioni was said to be embarking on a new ballet that would again star Emma, this one tentatively entitled *Zara*.[15] The world lay at her feet.

But there never would be a sequel. Within a few short years of the ballet's premiere, Emma would be dead, after colliding with an open flame on the stage of the Paris Opéra, later succumbing to her wounds after eight long months of agonizing suffering.

The accident took place on November 15, 1862. The occasion was a revival performance of Daniel Auber's rabble-rousing opera *La Muette de Portici*, scheduled to be performed at the Paris Opéra with an all-star cast. The night in question was a dress rehearsal but a hot ticket, nevertheless. The seats in the theater's auditorium were filled with spectators, including Célestine, sitting next to Montguyon in his private box. Taglioni was also in the audience, awaiting the debut of her protégée in the role of Fenella, the mute in the opera's title, a mimed part always played by a dancer. Taglioni had herself previously performed it (the role was created for her in 1828), and she thought it would suit Emma; Taglioni had personally coached her, believing again that the role would further enhance Emma's reputation as a neo-Romantic ballerina. Besides Emma, the attraction was the tenor, Giovanni Matteo Mario, one of the most celebrated singers of his time. Everyone in the house that night was brimming with excitement, including Emma who, in advance of her entrance in Act II, came down earlier than usual from her dressing room, fully dressed in her bouffant tarlatan skirt costume with corset, to sit on a bench she had especially requested be placed for her in the wings. Backstage, she sat quietly as she listened to Mario raise his voice to the rafters:

"*Amis, la nuit est belle*" (Friends, the night is beautiful).

"*Sur le rivage, assemblez-vous*" (Assemble yourselves on the shore).

Mario joined his voice with the singer playing Pietro to sing the famous duet "*Amour sacré de la patrie*" (Sacred Love of the Homeland).

As soon as the song ended, Emma prepared to take her place backstage on a rock from which she would appear in the next scene, gazing out at what was supposed to be the Bay of Naples. She never made it.

When she stood up from the bench, she shook out her skirts to make them look full and round for her entrance. The act of fluffing her costume fanned the flames of a nearby gaslight. The skirt ignited like dry straw, instantly engulfing Emma in flames.

Crazed with fear, she ran out from the wings, looking, according to one terrified eyewitness, like a human torch. Her running served to fuel the fire, which licked upwards around her body, burning her legs, her back, and her upraised arms. She let out three blood-curdling screams, described by a doctor who was in the house that night as a "sound the ear would not soon forget."[16] She kept running in circles around the scenery as horrified cast members watched helplessly.

A backstage fireman rushed to grab Emma. But fear had made her strong, and she pushed him away, sprinting away like a madwoman. One of her fellow dancers, Edouard Pluque, later to become a ballet master at the Paris Opéra, tried in vain to save her himself, burning his hands in the effort. The other cast members were by this time frightened of losing their own lives and had rushed out onto the street in their costumes.

Another fireman (nineteenth-century theatres illuminated by candles and gaslights commonly employed firemen) ran from behind the wings and tackled Emma to the ground. He rolled her in a moistened blanket, succeeding finally in snuffing out the flames. His name was Jacques Muller, and the emperor would decorate him for bravery, rewarding him with a cash gift of 300 francs. For his efforts, Pluque got 200 francs.[17]

Amazingly, Emma was still alive, despite sustaining burns on up to 40 percent of her body. As soon as the blanket was off her she stumbled to her knees to say a prayer, saying later, "Quand j'ai vu ces flammes, je me suis sentie perdue" (When I saw the flames, I thought myself lost).[18]

Two doctors of the Paris Opéra, Laborie and Rossignol, carried the dancer to her dressing room to immediately offer first aid. Painstakingly, they removed what remained of her costume. She had been wearing a leotard, eleven fine-cloth skirts, and a corset.[19] All that remained was a fragment of her belt and some strips of fabric, the remnants of which can today be seen in the Paris Opéra Museum, where what is left of Emma's costume has been preserved in a tiny coffin-like box. The stays of her corset had become encrusted into her flesh. These the doctors painfully removed, one by one. Célestine reportedly took one look at her daughter stretched out in her dressing room, writhing in agony, and fainted.

Wrote Laborie in his medical notes, "*Le feu avait déterminé des brûlures d'une très grande étendue, envahissant les deux cuisses, les reins, le dos, les épaules et les deux bras… Son état paraissait très grave, non par le fait de la profondeur des brûlures, mais par le fait de leur étendue*" (The fire had caused burns which extended over both thighs, the loins, the back, the shoulders and both arms. Her condition appeared very grave not so much from the depth of the burns as from their extent).[20]

Taglioni, desperate to help in some way, grabbed a jar of makeup grease and began applying it to Emma's charred flesh. The doctors also applied cotton wool over Emma's body, which appeared to them as an open wound.[21] She lay cocooned for thirty-six hours, before being carried home on a stretcher to her modest apartment. There, she was placed on her stomach, arms stretched out at both sides of her charred torso, and there she lay for 131 days, watched over by two nuns and attended to by three physicians, who ordered her be fed with juices from meat provided by a local butcher.[22] Her mother also paid the city to cover the street below with straw to soften the sounds of horses and carriages passing by.

As freakish as such an accident might seem today, death by fire was a common occurrence for ballerinas throughout the nineteenth century. It was just one of many backstage dangers that routinely threatened dancers' lives. Taglioni once narrowly escaped being maimed or killed when an overhead piece of scenery came crashing down during a performance of *Robert le Diable*; she saw it coming and was able to jump away in the nick of time.[23] Dancers in Romantic ballets were often hoisted aloft on wires, which sometimes became entangled in sets and scaffolding, leaving the poor creatures dangling precariously in midair before a horrified audience. The risks associated with the Romantic ballet were so great that the Paris Opéra offered danger pay to those dancers brave or desperate enough to be yanked by pulleys some thirty feet above the ground without a safety net. Opéra director Louis Véron says in his memoirs that the airy illusions of the Romantic ballet used to cause him anxiety, worried as he was for dancers' safety: "I had personally inspected all the safety locks, the chain links, and the stays by dint of which the sylphs were attached to a number of metal wires, and though I attended all the trial runs, made with weights much heavier than those of our young dancers, I trembled lest some accident expose our twelve or fifteen flying corps girls to peril," he writes. "As they each were accorded a salary of ten francs, practically the entire corps de ballet—courageous women and children—begged for the favor of being suspended."[24]

But fire was a more elusive foe. Gaslighting, also known as limelight, was a relatively new piece of stagecraft, introduced at the beginning of the nineteenth century. The subtle and mysterious effects of gaslighting played no small role in the development of the Romantic ballet. Gaslighting allowed for house lights to be dimmed for the first time in theater history, giving rise to a heightened sense of onstage illusion. Choreographers of the day took advantage of the innovation, creating supernatural spectacles whose phantasmagorical imagery was augmented by the softly glowing light. But while gaslighting brought radiant drama and otherworldly atmosphere to Romantic ballet, it also ushered in a new set of risks for ballerinas, dozens of whom caught fire when their flimsy tutus brushed too close to an open flame. Scores perished as a result. Among them was the English dancer Clara Webster, who died after catching fire backstage at London's Drury Lane Theatre during a performance of *The Revolt of the Harem* on December 14,

1844. Two half-sisters of the famous playwright Oscar Wilde, both dancers, also died this way; one reportedly tried to help the other when her costume caught alight but was burnt to death herself.[25] There were gaslighting victims also in North America, on September 14, 1861, at the Continental Theater in Philadelphia, where seven young ballerinas at once caught on fire, all subsequently dying.[26] Emma had herself witnessed a fiery backstage accident involving a fellow ballerina, which had taken place during a dress rehearsal for *Le Papillon*, about a year before her own catastrophe. The skirt of Maria Baratte, a *petit sujet*, had ignited on an open flame, setting her instantly on fire. Luckily, she was saved from death by a quick-thinking stage-hand but not before her hand was badly burned.[27]

The situation was so dire that the medical establishment rallied to draw public attention to what it called "this holocaust of ballet girls." An article that appeared in 1868 in the British medical journal *The Lancet* entitled "The Ballet-Girl's Hardship: A Needless Fate" sounded the call to arms:

> Have our readers ever reflected on the courage required by the ballet-dancer's profession? The risks she runs are hardly less frequent and far more formidable than those which the soldiers of the line or the man o' war's man gets so much credit for facing. It is but one thing to take your chance of being sabered or hit by a bullet; but it is another (and to our mind) a much more terrible ordeal to pirouette in combustible gauze before the foot-lights, or, worse still, to be pinioned to an iron niche in some precarious perch, amid a blaze of light and within leap of the flame from a thousand burners. Yet this is the experience which myriads of poor girls have to encounter night after night that juveniles may be entertained and bawdy crowds amused.[28]

And yet precautions had been put in place in many theaters, including the Paris Opéra, which, not coincidentally, had also caught fire, burning twice to the ground before the end of the nineteenth century. Stage curtains were laced with steel to help contain fires if and when they broke out on stage. In 1859, the French state issued a decree demanding all people employed by theaters use a newly invented chemical bath retardant in which props and costumes were dipped to make them more fire resistant. The process, known as carteronising after its inventor, Jean-Adolphe Carteron, was effective. But it had a major drawback, at least where the dancers were concerned: the chemical yellowed their muslin skirts, making them look dark and dingy. The chemical also stiffened them, compromising the illusion of lightness and buoyancy ballerinas of this era worked so hard to achieve. Many dancers consequently refused to follow the government order:

"*Bah!*" wrote the corps de ballets dancer Mlle Schlosser in a letter to Opéra management that survives in the theatre's archives, "*On ne brûle qu'une fois, mais on porterait tous les soirs de vilains jupons*" (Bah! We'll burn but once, but have to suffer those ugly skirts every night).[29]

Emma was among those who protested against the forced use of le *carteronage*. In a handwritten letter to management on Friday, November 23, 1860, asking to be exempt from having to dip her costumes in the fire retardant, Emma argued for the triumph of aesthetics over safety:

> *Je tiens absolument, Monsieur, à danser les premières représentations du ballet avec mes jupons de danse ordinaires et je prends sur moi la responsabilité de tout ce qui pourrait m'en arriver. Pour le dernier tableau, je ne le danserai avec un jupon carteronisé. Je ne peux pas m'exposer à des jupons qui seraient laids ou qui n'iraient pas bien. Comme je trouve que*

*l'administration a raison dans le changement qu'elle veut opérer, au bout
de quelques représentations je demanderai moi-même à opérer, la substitution pourvu qu'elle ne nuise pas à l'effet des costumes, ce que je crains.*

Mille compliments empressés, Emma Livry[30]

(I insist, sir, on dancing all first performances of the ballet in
my ordinary ballet skirt, and I take it upon myself all responsibility for anything that may occur. In the last scene, I am
willing to dance in a treated skirt, but I cannot wear skirts
that would be ugly, or that would not become me. However,
as I feel that the management is quite right to bring into force
the proposed alterations, I will ask myself after a few performances, for a substitution to be made, provided that it will not
spoil the effect of the costume, which is what I fear.

With best wishes, Emma Livry)

She had effectively authored her death sentence.

When the end drew near, Emma seemed increasingly
prescient of her impending doom. When French writer Ernest-
Aimé Feydeau (father of comic playwright Georges Feydeau)
came to the home she shared with her mother on rue Lafitte to
interview her as part of his research for his 1865 novel, *Le Mari
de la danseuse*, Emma told him she didn't fear death by fire.[31]
This macabre confession was sparked when Feydeau explained
to her how in his book the dancer-heroine burns to death.
Emma allegedly then turned to her mother, always hovering
in the background, and said, "*Mourir brûlée... cela doit bien faire
souffrir*" (To be burnt to death, that must be very painful). She
paused before adding, perhaps with a note of delicious melan-
choly as befitting a dancer molded in the Romantic tradition,

"*C'est égal, c'est une belle mort pour une danseuse*" (All the same, it is a fine death for a dancer).[32]

It was a case of being careful of what you wish for.

Indeed, Emma seems to have resigned herself to her fate. Throughout her long recovery, during which she lay face down for months on a makeshift stretcher, her arms spread out by her sides, she endured without question the agonizing treatment of fresh lemon juice squeezed into her wounds to keep them bacteria-free;[33] she never screamed, as instructed by her doctors who had warned her that any movement she might make could rupture the tender tissues newly forming across her back and lower limbs. "*Je veux vivre! Dieu! donnez-moi du courage*" (I want to live! God! Give me courage), she whispered to a family friend who had come to visit her during her convalescence.[34]

Her main concern, it seems, was for her courtesan-mother, whom Emma had recently convinced to take her first communion, at age thirty. One can only imagine the depths of despair in which Célestine had been plunged, watching helplessly as her only child, her pride and joy, the daughter she had tried desperately to keep from being consumed by the predatory men at the ballet, was devoured by flames. She remained by Emma's side, and when it was all over, she ended up as she had started—poor. Montguyon did what he could for her, but after the accident their relationship was never the same. He was said to be devastated by Emma's tragedy. During her recovery, he stood watch over her and was quick to make sure that reports about her demise were seen as premature. He is probably responsible for a string of incredible news reports that followed soon after the accident, claiming that Emma was on the mend and would soon be dancing again. It was even suggested that the Paris Opéra was preparing for her imminent return to the stage. It was wishful thinking, a final act of airy illusion. Montguyon always was a gambling man. But the die had been cast.

Emma took her final journey in the spring of 1863, supported by a brace of doctors hired to help her sit up, dressed head-to-toe in white, and waving feebly from her coach at the crowd of curious onlookers who had lined the road to watch her. She was on her way to Compiègne, where the emperor and empress had put their country house at her disposal, but she made it no further than Neuilly-sur-Seine, where her mother had rented an apartment. When the coach stopped, she was assisted into her mother's home. There, she suffered another in a series of convulsions that had beset her for months. Emma knew she couldn't go on.

She ate a light supper on the night of July 26, 1863, and toward eleven o'clock that night, a slight smile on her lips, tears rolling down her cheeks, she died.[35] The cause of death was said to be blood poisoning, brought on by the weakened state caused by her wounds.

The funeral service took place three days later, at Notre-Dame-de Lorette. Emma, again dressed in white, was laid in a coffin cloaked in white cloth, a virgin's farewell. The cortege that lead the way to Montmartre Cemetery was accompanied by a dozen young girls from the corps de ballet of the Paris Opéra, also dressed in white, holding the cords of the procession. Behind them walked the two nuns who had attended Emma while she lay ill, crossing themselves as they said their prayers. The whiteness of the funeral procession, symbolizing both Emma's purity and the pristine values she fought to preserve in ballet, contrasted dramatically with the black of the many mourners who had come to bid Emma farewell.[36]

Gautier covered the sad event for his newspaper, *Le Moniteur*, and wrote that he saw two white butterflies fluttering teasingly over Emma's coffin, as if inviting her back to dance. He concluded by saying that the dancer who danced like a butterfly had become one—"*a brûlé ses ailes à la flamme*" (burning her wings in the flame).[37]

It was flowery language, but in a strange way it was true: Emma had died as she had danced—in the heat of her chosen profession. The inscription on her tombstone was equally poetic: "*O terre, sois-moi légère; j'ai si peu pesé sur toi*" (Earth, tread lightly on me who so lightly weighed on you).

As an epitaph, it summed up Emma's dancing—light, ethereal, buoyant. Yet it also served to obscure the fact that far from being removed from terrestrial matters and concerns, Emma was very much of this earth: an artist strategically molded in the image of another, an emblem of French national pride, a victim of her own human frailty, if not her popular image as a diaphanous dancer.

There was a starker reality: Célestine had to pawn her jewels to pay for Emma's medical bills, totaling almost 27,000 francs. Montguyon pleaded his mistress's case to the emperor, who, on humanitarian grounds, granted Célestine a 40,000-franc gratuity plus a 6,000-franc annual pension. When the Second Empire fell in 1871, making way for the Third Republic, the new government refused to honor her pension, and Célestine was forced to move to a smaller apartment at 19 avenue de la Grand-Armée. There, the former dancer lived alone, dying of cancer in 1892, aged sixty-eight.[38] She had outlived her daughter by thirty years.

Where ballet was concerned, Paris had changed for the worse. Emma's death was the turning point. After she died, Paris would never again be the world capital of ballet. Even Taglioni moved away after Emma's death, settling in England, where she became an instructor of dance and manners to members of the British elite, before returning to France via Marseilles, where she passed away in 1884. Emma remains a throwback to another time, her "imponderable lightness," as Gautier put it, now almost forgotten except as a footnote to *Le Papillon*, a ballet rarely performed today. All ballerinas sacrifice something of themselves for their chosen profession. But Emma gave her entire life, dying needlessly as a result of wanting to preserve an immaculate ideal of ballet as a transcendent art form. At her funeral, Paris Opéra ballet master Lucien Petipa delivered the eulogy; he spoke of Emma's brilliant career, emphasizing its brevity: "*Quand tout te souriait, la jeunesse et le talent; quand la sagesse et la vertu étaient tes guides; quand, à seize ans, tu avais conquis la première place; quand les succès te tendaient la main à chaque pas, quand la presse et le public t'entouraient des plus vives sympathies, un accident affreux a suffi en un instant pour tout anéantir*" (When everything—youth and talent—was smiling at you, when wisdom and virtue were your guides, when at sixteen years old, you had conquered first place, when successes greeted you with every step, when the press and the public enveloped you in warmest affection, a terrible accident was sufficient to obliterate everything in an instant).[39]

Emma was gone and so, it could be said, was the French Romantic ballet. After Livry, the Paris Opéra grew increasingly stagnant, hobbled by an unwillingness to let go of tradition. By this time, many of the top French practitioners had already started to move to Russia in search of greater opportunity, and there were more of them on their way. They included Marius Petipa (brother of Lucien), the French-born ballet master and choreographer who would soon transform the Russian ballet, making it the best in the world. Ballerinas performing his works would rise to the occasion of his dynamic ballets, becoming dazzling virtuosos in their own right. Among them was

Pierina Legnani (1863–1930), born the same year that Livry died. Out of the ashes of one ballerina comes another to take her place. An Italian virtuoso, Legnani would help take ballet in a new direction as a prima ballerina in Russia, where she originated the dual role of Odette/Odile in *Swan Lake* (1895), today the world's best-loved ballet, and the female lead in *Raymonda* (1898). These important works foreshadowed the rise of the Classical era in ballet, initiated by *La Bayadère* (1877) and epitomized by *The Sleeping Beauty* (1890). Petipa choreographed all of these ballets and more, crafting them as showcases for the singular talents of the epoch's other leading ballerinas: the Russian-born Ekaterina Vazem (1848–1937), the first Nikiya, and the Italian-born Carlotta Brianza (1867–1930), the first Aurora, among them.

France had ruled the art of ballet for two hundred years. And yet the established French practices of ballet would not soon be forgotten, not least of all the practice of concubinage, which would flourish in the land of the tsar before being replaced by a more novel—or modern—type of sexual control over the ballerina.

ABOVE French ballerina and experimental choreographer Janine Charrat was scheduled to dance the role of the madwoman in her own ballet, *Les Algues*, when her diaphanous costume caught fire on a lit candelabra inside a Paris television studio, engulfing her in flames. LIPNITZKI/ROGER-VIOLLET/GETTY IMAGES

Habit d'Indienne du balet du Triomphe de l'amour

ABOVE The first recorded instance of professional ballerinas on the public stage was *Le Triomphe de l'Amour*, staged in 1681 in Paris by Jean-Baptiste Lully, the man responsible for giving women dancers a leg up in what was then a male-dominated art form. GIANNI DAGLI ORTI /THE ART ARCHIVE AT ART RESOURCE, NY

FACING PAGE Eighteenth-century ballerina Françoise Prévost was the leading female dancer of her day, ruling the Paris Opéra for almost fifty years. She was also a well-known courtesan, whose dual reputation is captured by this historic portrait of her as a dancing bacchante. RÉUNION DES MUSÉES NATIONAUX/ART RESOURCE, NY

FACING PAGE, TOP Courtesanship flourished at the Paris Opéra throughout
the eighteenth century, earning the theater the nickname the Brothel of France.
V&A IMAGES, LONDON/ART RESOURCE, NY

FACING PAGE, BOTTOM Young ballerinas were frequently pimped by their
own mothers, who viewed ballet as a means to social advancement. VISUAL ARTS
LIBRARY/ART RESOURCE, NY

ABOVE Marie-Anne de Cupis de Camargo was a pioneering dancer who, by
trimming her hemlines, revolutionized technique for the ballerina while
adding an erotic dimension to ballet. THE ART ARCHIVE AT ART RESOURCE, NY

ABOVE The Paris Opéra ballerina Madeleine Guimard was a wily ballet
survivor, outwitting not only the French Revolution, which wanted her head,
but also the sexual exploitation rampant in ballet of her day by spearheading
a series of pornographic theaters for the French elite. GIANNI DAGLI ORTI/THE ART
ARCHIVE AT ART RESOURCE, NY

FACING PAGE Ballet's reputation for sin was hidden in the Romantic era
behind the popular image of the ballerina as a frail creature of the air. Marie
Taglioni epitomized the new ethereal ideal, even while, behind the scenes, she
indulged in such earthly pleasures as extramarital affairs and hoarded treasure.
EILEEN TWEEDY/THE ART ARCHIVE AT ART RESOURCE, NY

FACING PAGE, TOP The ballerina's notoriety as a creature of vice is captured by this nineteenth-century caricature in which reproving ecclesiastics inspect dancers for signs of moral depravity. EILEEN TWEEDY/THE ART ARCHIVE AT ART RESOURCE, NY

FACING PAGE, BOTTOM At the Paris Opéra, the administration permitted paying subscribers to cruise the notorious *foyer de la danse* in search of sexual adventure with willing dancers. GIANNI DAGLI ORTI/THE ART ARCHIVE AT ART RESOURCE, NY

ABOVE This image of ballerinas in Vienna shows that the ballerina-courtesan trend was not confined to Paris. The backstage show was in many ways as entertaining—if not, for some, more so—as what was presented on stage. ALFREDO DAGLI ORTI/THE ART ARCHIVE AT ART RESOURCE, NY

FACING PAGE Marie van Goethem was the real-life model for Degas' multi-media statuette known around the world as *The Little Dancer, Aged Fourteen*. Her emaciated body marks her as one of the *petits rats* who comprised the corps de ballet in nineteenth-century Paris. GIANNI DAGLI ORTI/THE ART ARCHIVE AT ART RESOURCE, NY

ABOVE The two-pronged reality of the ballet girl's existence is captured in this poignant drawing: by day, she toils anonymously in her own poverty; by night, in tutu and makeup, she carries on her bony shoulders the illusion of ballet as an escapist art form, even as she prostitutes herself to the highest bidder. RÉUNION DES MUSÉES NATIONAUX/ART RESOURCE, NY

THÉATRE DE L'OPÉRA. — Accident arrivé à Mlle Emma Livry pendant la repétition de *la Muette de Portici*.

FACING PAGE Emma Livry was the last of the great French Romantic ballerinas. Her signature role was the butterfly, which she first performed in
Le Papillon, a ballet whose plot about a winged creature dying after it collides
with an open flame eerily prophesied her own demise. ADOC-PHOTOS/ART
RESOURCE, NY

ABOVE Gaslighting claimed the lives of many ballerinas in the nineteenth
century, among them Emma Livry, whose tarlatan skirt caught fire during a
dress rehearsal for Auber's La Muette de Portici in 1862. She died eight agonizing
months later. MUSÉE CARNAVALET/ROGER-VIOLLET/THE IMAGE WORKS

FACING PAGE Early in the twentieth century, Russian ballerina Anna Pavlova brought ballet to the masses through a series of international tours that she produced and headlined. Devoted to ballet to the exclusion of much else, she danced herself to an early grave. CULVER PICTURES/THE ART ARCHIVE AT ART RESOURCE, NY

ABOVE Mathilde Kschessinska attained the rare rank of *prima ballerina assoluta* in her native Russia on account of her pirouetting powers and her well-known sexual affairs with high-ranking members of the ruling Romanov family, among them the last tsar, whose mistress she was. HIP/ART RESOURCE, NY

ABOVE Ida Rubinstein was a member of Diaghilev's famous Les Ballets Russes in the early twentieth century. She expertly manipulated the press to her advantage, feeding it details of her many steamy love affairs to ensure she remained in the public eye. GIANNI DAGLI ORTI/THE ART ARCHIVE AT ART RESOURCE, NY

FACING PAGE Girls! Girls! Girls! George Balanchine attained almost cult-like status among his ballerinas when he was chief ballet master of New York City Ballet. He coined the phrase "Ballet Is Woman," but he was the one in control. BERNARD GOTFRYD/PREMIUM ARCHIVE/GETTY IMAGES

FACING PAGE Balanchine's preference for long-legged ballerinas with narrow hips, long arms, and small heads established a new feminine ideal in ballet so difficult to attain it sparked a global epidemic of eating disorders that persists, to a large degree, today. MARCO SECCHI/GETTY IMAGES ENTERTAINMENT

ABOVE, TOP Complications from an eating disorder cost a young Boston Ballet ballerina her life. Her grieving mother unsuccessfully sued the company for urging her daughter to diet. JOHN STOREY/TIME & LIFE IMAGES/GETTY IMAGES

ABOVE, BOTTOM Not all dancers are victims. These ballerinas from the American Ballet Theatre led the New York City Labor Day Parade to draw attention to their fight with company management. EARL DOTTER;
WWW.EARLDOTTER.COM

FACING PAGE National Ballet of Canada principal dancer Kimberly Glasco is the swan who roared. After her artistic director abruptly fired her, the ballerina sued, scoring a series of legal victories. PETER TYM; WWW.PETERTYMPHOTOGRAPHY.COM

ABOVE, TOP After overcoming anorexia, Jenifer Ringer of New York City Ballet made headlines when, following a performance of *The Nutcracker*, a critic accused her of eating one too many sugar plums. PAUL KOLNIK

ABOVE, BOTTOM Misty Copeland of American Ballet Theatre is a black and buxom ballerina breaking down barriers. She performs here with Prince on one of his world concert tours. KEVIN MAZUR/WIREIMAGE/GETTY IMAGES

ABOVE, TOP The former prima ballerina of the Royal Winnipeg Ballet Evelyn Hart equates the end of her dancing career to a loss of identity.
ALEX WATERHOUSE-HAYWARD

ABOVE, BOTTOM After surviving ballet's dark side, Gelsey Kirkland teaches the next generation of ballerinas about the enduring beauty of classical dance.
ANDREA MOHIN/THE NEW YORK TIMES/REDUX

4

STRIVING AND STARVING FOR ATTENTION
THE CHANGING ROLE OF THE BALLERINA
IN THE TWENTIETH CENTURY

NOBODY BETTER cultivated the image of the modern ballerina as a waifish workhorse than the Russian-born choreographer George Balanchine. Born in St. Petersburg in the early part of the twentieth century, he arrived on the scene at a time when ballerinas were athletic superstars who outshone the choreographers laboring behind the scenes. But Balanchine would change that, shifting the audience's attention away from the ballerina and toward ballet itself. Until he stole their crown, ballerinas had ruled in Russia for close to two hundred years.

The Russian ballet flourished with the help of French dancers, ballet masters, and choreographers, who had been coming to Russia since the early eighteenth century. Russia offered higher salaries to foreigners representing the latest European artistic movements and fashions; Russian rulers personally invited ballet practitioners from Paris as part of a larger cultural shift that saw French introduced as the lingua franca at court. Russia in the eighteenth century consisted largely of landowners and serfs; the ruling elites wanted to bring the country out of the rural past and toward a sparkling cosmopolitan future: imitating Paris, and all that the city had to offer by way of culture and manners, was seen as a viable way forward. Ballet was one of the ways Russia would push itself into a new era of European-influenced sophistication. As ballet historian Jennifer Homans observes, ballet first came to Russia as etiquette, not art: "This mattered: ballet was not initially a theatrical 'show' but a standard of physical comportment to be emulated and internalized—an idealized way of behaving."[1]

Among the first French ballet masters to come to Russia was Jean-Baptiste Landé, invited from Paris to teach etiquette and poise to young cadets at the military academy. After presenting a ballet performance in 1735, Landé became a favorite of Empress Anna (1693–1740), helping her to establish Russia's first ballet academy in St. Petersburg in 1738. The Imperial Ballet School, later known as the Mariinsky, would help Russia establish a reputation as a world leader in ballet. Although Landé taught ballet to members of the ruling class—one of his students was Catherine the Great, whom he tutored soon after she arrived in Russia in 1744—dancers within the academy generally came from the lowest segments of society. They were serfs or the children of serfs, a carryover from the popular practice of serf theater that flourished within the extravagant settings of Russia's private country estates. In 1778, a second ballet academy was established in an orphanage in Moscow, where ballet evolved as a combination of imported European high culture with Russian folk art. From the outset, Russian ballet was rooted in the culture of the disenfranchised—people who had nothing to lose but much to gain by striving for excellence through dance.

These early dancers were regarded as private property or as wards of the state and could be arbitrarily imprisoned, abused,

sexually exploited, and sold off.[2] And yet, within the confines
of the ballet, a certain freedom could be found for those dancers with talent and other salable charms. As among the poor of
Paris during the reign of Louis xiv, many were able to rise to
prominence within society via dance. Among them was one
of Russia's earliest ballerinas, Avdotia Istomina (1799–1848),
an orphan who became one of the greatest ballerinas of her
country as well as among the best paid; within fifteen years
of launching her dancing career, she was drawing a salary of
15,000 rubles, a small ransom. Istomina was celebrated for her
speed and for the number of pirouettes she could execute in
succession. She was taught by her countrywoman, Evgenia
Kolosova (1780–1869), known for her nuanced interpretations
of peasant dances, and by the French ballet master Charles-
Louis Didelot (1767–1837), who had been invited by the tsar to
become director of the Imperial Ballet. The first Russian ballerina to dance on pointe, Istomina made her debut in 1815 and
caused such a sensation that several men died in duels fighting for the privilege of being her lover; she was reputed to have
been a grand courtesan. The Russian poet Alexander Pushkin
(1799–1837), enamored of her dancing genius, immortalized
the ballerina in his verse-novel, *Eugene Onegin*: "Istomina stands:
she,/while touching with one foot the floor,/gyrates the other
slowly,/and suddenly a leap, and suddenly she flies,/she flies
like fluff from Eol's lips/now twines and untwines her waist/
and beats one swift small foot against the other."[3]

Istomina's command of Russian society was tragically brief:
in 1848 she died of cholera. She had been the first of the Russian ballerinas to embody the Romantic tradition of ballet
then sweeping Europe, and in her wake came a series of high-
ranking ballerinas from Paris who kept the passion for ethereal
dancing alive in the East. Among them was Marie Taglioni,

who came to St. Petersburg in 1837 to perform her signature ballet, *La Sylphide*, a work that would leave a lasting impression on the development of Russian ballet. Taglioni's rival, Fanny Elssler, came to St. Petersburg in 1848 on the personal invitation of Tsar Nicholas, a fervent admirer of the ballerina's talents. Elssler ended up spending three seasons in Russia, dancing in Moscow and St. Petersburg in French-flavored ballets like *Giselle*, *La Esmeralda*, and *La Fille mal gardée*, among others.

Several Parisian-bred male dancers also left their mark on the Russian ballet, including Jules Perrot (1810–1892) and Arthur Saint-Léon (1815-1870), both of whom served as ballet masters and choreographers when in Russia—to mixed reviews, leading Saint-Léon once to challenge a critic to a duel. By far the most successful French choreographer on Russian soil was Marius Petipa (1818–1910), who at once signaled the end of the Romantic ballet and the advent of the classical ballet with feature-length works that combined dance, mime, and symphonic music. Petipa's intricately crafted dance ensembles presented a kaleidoscopic display of shifting shapes, patterns, and rhythms that raised ballet to the level of opulent spectacle. Dominating the St. Petersburg stage from the 1860s through the 1890s, Petipa's grand-scale choreography was based on a strict adherence to the classical tenets of dance as developed in the court of the French kings. During his long career in Russia, Petipa staged approximately seventy-five ballets for the Imperial theaters, including two of his most famous: *The Sleeping Beauty* and *Swan Lake*, the latter created in collaboration with the Russian-born choreographer Lev Ivanov (1834–1901), both set to commissioned scores by frequent Petipa collaborator Pyotr Tchaikovsky (1840–1893). The influence of *The Sleeping Beauty* on Russian ballet cannot be overestimated; it inspired the next generation of Russian ballet greats, among them Sergei Diaghilev whose Ballets Russes in 1921 restaged Petipa's

1890 version of the ballet, renaming it *The Sleeping Princess*, a homage to the French influence on Russian ballet.

Petipa's genius was evident too in his working relationships with ballerinas; in his ballets, he placed the ballerina front and center, using her pointe work as a focal point (a practice that would flourish into the twentieth century when adopted by the world's next pre-eminent choreographer, an Imperial Ballet alumnus steeped in the Petipa tradition, who would bend the classical ballerina-centric ballet his way—but more on that later). Petipa celebrated virtuosity and created dance passages where ballerinas could dazzle with their technique. But eventually, his style was seen as formulaic; by the dawning of the twentieth century, when academic classicism began to be pushed aside by a growing desire for expressiveness and naturalism in ballet, Petipa fell out of favor. His defenders, not surprisingly, were those ballerinas whom he had made into stars: Pierina Legnani but also Virginia Zucchi (1849–1930), another Italian-born powerhouse for whom Petipa had created an entire solo on pointe. Zucchi was eventually banned by the tsar from the Imperial stage, allegedly as a result of an affair with an aristocrat gone wrong. The world of the concubine was one Petipa knew about but did not indulge in. His first wife (he was married twice) was a Russian ballerina to whom he devoted his talents, as he wrote in his memoirs: "I had aided greatly in the success of my first wife. I had done everything that I could to help her attain the highest position on the ballet stage, but in our domestic life we were unable to live long in peace and harmony."[4] A family man, Petipa's interest in his leading ballerinas was mainly professional. He left it to his royal patrons to ignite the offstage fireworks for which some of his ballerinas became celebrated, chief among them being Mathilde Kschessinska (1872–1971), the last of the ballerina-courtesans linked to the tsar.

Kschessinska was a poor but gifted student of Russia's Imperial Ballet School, the daughter of popular Polish character dancer Felix Kschessinsky, who early on groomed her, as well as a son, for a dancing career. Being a theater man himself, he was well aware that young dancers under the protection of the tsar would want for nothing. The state-sponsored school provided them with clothing, food, and shelter, in addition to superlative instruction in dance, etiquette, and academics. Students had their own servants who tended to their every need. Driven to the Imperial Theater in horse-drawn carriages manned by attendants in immaculate uniforms, they frequently were presented to members of the royal family for whom they would do a performance and later be rewarded with a gift given personally by the tsar, the tsarina, their children, or other members of their entourage. It is how, when still a young student, Kschessinska first caught the eye of the tsar. How could he not notice her? Kschessinska was a pirouetting virtuoso, with a vivacious and ebullient stage presence, who believed in communicating meaning through dance. Audiences adored her. "I was not one of those who dance themselves silly and think of nothing but details of execution, of turning out their knees, who are hypnotized by technique at the expense of acting," she said in her published memoirs, *Dancing in St. Petersburg*. "Where there is no mime, technique must obviously be followed; but in scenes of powerful drama, where everything rests on the emotion, one can safely forget one's knees!"[5]

But the ballerina nicknamed the Mighty Mathilda also gained fame of another sort—as mistress of the Russian nation. She was what might be called a looker: blessed with a pretty face, flashing eyes, and an ample bosom. As a child during a year-end recital at the Imperial Ballet School, she attracted the attention of the tsar, who later actively encouraged a backstage meeting with his son, Russia's next monarch. While barely out of her teens, Kschessinska became the mistress of Nicholas II, the last tsar. She simultaneously conducted an affair with his cousin, Grand Duke André, whom she ultimately succeeded in marrying after the tsar, and other members of his immediate family, were executed by Bolshevik revolutionaries in July 1918.

Kschessinska often performed on stage wearing the jewels her aristocratic lovers showered upon her for being their shared courtesan: dog collars of diamonds, tiaras encrusted with cabochon sapphires, and ropes of pearls mixed with chains studded with precious stones that hung down to her knees—the state's treasures.[6] Up-and-coming Russian choreographer Mikhail Fokine (1880–1942) had tried to curtail this ostentatious habit, ordering her to dance unadorned in the new, stripped-down modernist ballets he was creating when he became the new ballet master of the Mariinsky following Petipa's forced retirement in 1903. She apparently never forgave him, even though later in life she conceded the jewels sometimes got in the way of the show: "My diamonds and other precious jewels were so valuable that they raised delicate problems," she wrote, describing the behind-the-scenes drama that had accompanied her 1911 performance in London of a *pas de deux* from *The Sleeping Beauty*. "On the advice of Agathon Fabergé, the famous jeweler's son, who was also one of my great friends, I had entrusted the dispatch of my jewels to his firm, the London branch looking after them until my arrival. Two catalogues were made and each piece of jewelry was numbered: I had only to know the numbers of the jewels I needed every evening, without giving further details. At the appointed hour an official of the firm, who was also a detective, brought them to me in my dressing-room and prevented any unauthorized person from entering; when the performance was over, he took the jewels away again."[7]

Kschessinska received as payment for her sexual services not only gemstones and jewelry but also a sumptuously decorated palace in the most fashionable neighborhood of St. Petersburg, a gift from the tsar. One of her lovers also gave her a son said to be of noble blood, though his father remains unknown; in her memoirs, Kschessinska proudly refers to her illegitimate child as *tsarevich*, or son of a tsar.

But admiration, and also tolerance, for Kschessinska waned as the new century, with its novel ways of presenting ballet, made ballerina-courtesans seem as outmoded as the convoluted pantomime, or *mimika*, then being inserted into ballets of the Imperial Theater. An alternative to all that Petipa-inspired gaudiness had recently appeared in the form of Sergei Diaghilev (1872–1929), the Russian-born leader and impresario of Les Ballets Russes, a company mainly composed of Imperial Theater ballet stars, who welcomed the opportunity to moonlight in an enterprise that was thoroughly avant-garde. Diaghilev urged his motley crew of artists to astonish him with new creations, and they eagerly obeyed. The former Imperial dancer Vaslav Nijinsky produced groundbreaking choreography in the form of *Le Sacre du printemps* (The Rite of Spring), inspired by the original dissonant score of the same name by Igor Stravinsky (1882–1971) and featuring equally revolutionary set and costume designs, consisting of folkloric tunics and boots, by the Russian mystic and artist Nicholas Roerich. *Le Sacre du printemps* represented a turning point in the history of ballet: in it Nijinsky eschewed the expressive pointe work and graceful lifts that had characterized ballet at the Imperial Theater. His modernist ballet was grotesquely flat-footed and emotionally raw in depicting a savage pagan ritual of human sacrifice meant to ensure a season of new growth. *Le Sacre du printemps* was itself something of a victim, being booed off the stage by the outraged audience that had attended the much-hyped premiere at the Théâtre des Champs-Élysées in Paris on the night of May 29, 1913. The angry crowd threw rotten vegetables at the dancers, who could not hear the music for the volume of yelling erupting in the auditorium; Nijinsky had to shout their counts to them from the wings. When it was over, *Le Sacre du printemps* had ushered in a new era of ballet experimentation that would continue through the rest of the century, driven by the accomplishments of Les Ballets Russes.

There was method in this ballet madness. Once a premiere entertainment, ballet in the early years of the twentieth century found itself having to compete with new mass-media forms of culture, like the relatively recent invention of the cinema, creating a demand for novelty. Ballet became more visually opulent and sensational (as seen in the Diaghilev troupe) at the same time as it was becoming more strictly a business enterprise, unsubsidized by state largesse. Ballerinas at this time had to develop a new set of skills, enabling them to dance the nineteenth-century classics as well as the experimental extravaganzas of Les Ballets Russes. Part of being modern was preserving past works but revitalizing them with new sensations: original music, visually arresting set and costume design, unconventional choreography, and energized dancing. In reviving classicism (the leading minds of Les Ballets Russes all professed a deep and undying love for Petipa's *The Sleeping Beauty*), Diaghilev encouraged an Orientalist approach (they were Russians, after all), which appeared to audiences (who lapped it up) as both decadent and fresh. The troupe as a whole, abetted in no small way by Léon Bakst's pseudo-Oriental costumes and exotic set designs, came to embody a palpable eroticism that only served to fuel the popularity of Les Ballets Russes. Several of its star dancers emerged as sex symbols, among them Nijinsky, who was Diaghilev's lover and the company's resident mad genius; stirred by his pantherine presence on the stage, groupies—both men and women—would gather at the stage door to grab at Nijinsky's clothes, wanting a piece of him.

At this time, the male dancer rivaled the female as an object of desire. But ballerinas of the day had not lost their sexual appetite. Backstage affairs continued apace. Ballerinas like the exotically beautiful Ida Rubinstein (1885–1960) matched Diaghilev's skill at manipulating the press by serving up intimate details of their love life for public consumption. Born into a wealthy Russian-Jewish family, which later bankrolled productions in which she starred, Rubinstein first came to audiences' attention dancing the title role of *Cléopâtre* and the female lead in *Schéhérazade*, opposite Nijinsky, during the Paris season of 1909. Provocatively for being both a woman and a non-Christian, in 1911 she danced the title role in Claude Debussy's *Le Martyre de Saint Sébastien*, a mystery play created to show off her also remarkable acting talents. She was sexually and professionally independent and actively cultivated an erotic persona. Her lovers included Walter Guinness, the Anglo-Irish heir to the Guinness brewing fortune. With the Italian nationalist poet Gabriele d'Annunzio and the bisexual American painter Romaine Brooks, Rubinstein formed a *ménage-à-trois*.

Sex also blossomed within the confines of the company. The ballerina Lydia Lopokova (1892–1981), a favorite of Fokine, had a fling with the married Stravinsky before moving beyond the ballet to take up with the English-born economist John Maynard Keynes, whom she eventually married, ending her days as a baroness.[8] Another Fokine ballerina (she was his lover) was the dark-haired beauty Tamara Karsavina (1885–1978), who originated roles in several of his ballets, among them *Petrushka* (1911), *The Firebird* (1910), and *Le Spectre de la Rose* (1911). Her range in lovers was just as diverse; they included the notorious Hollywood lesbian Mercedes de Acosta and the British diplomat Henry James Bruce, whom she later wed, settling down in Hampstead Heath, where she became the teacher of British ballerina Margot Fonteyn (1919–1991).

Kschessinska was only briefly a member of Les Ballets Russes; she preferred the ballets of the old regime, the Petipa classics. Her taste in lovers was equally influenced by the Imperial school. She was a ballerina steeped in the aristocratic traditions of Russia past; a former aide-camp once described her as representing "what Russian society was, and ought to be. Order, punctiliousness, symmetry, work well done everywhere... Whereas those horrible modern ballets—Russian ballets, as you call them in Paris—a dissolute and poisoned art—why, they're revolution, anarchy!"[9]

Kschessinska was out of step with the times, and dangerously so, as observed by Maurice Paléologue, the French ambassador to Russia, who, in his memoirs, described an event he witnessed in 1916 that sealed the ballerina's fate as an artifact of a lost era. It had been a long, cold winter and food and fuel had been in short supply. But by dint of her being the tsar's mistress, Kschessinska did not have to suffer. Paléologue described in outraged detail seeing four military trucks filled to the brim with coal, courtesy of the tsar, which arrived at the dancer's mansion at a time when the French embassy had been denied the necessary provisions to see its operations through the season. Even commoners were reportedly astounded by the sight of such a prized commodity being lavished on a woman who, in essence, was only a dancer. Overnight, the Mighty Mathilde became known as the Mighty Kutcha—the whore. When the

Revolution erupted the following October, a vengeful mob was quick to descend first on Kschessinska's house, in search of the ballerina who symbolized the decadence and nonchalant privilege of the ruling class. If they had found her, they most certainly would have hanged her. But she had escaped to Paris, via the Côte d'Azur, fearful for her life and that of her bastard son. She ended up as a ballet teacher who could barely earn a living. While fleeing the Bolsheviks, Kschessinka had squandered her precious jewels on a roulette table in Monte Carlo. As for her precious palace, symbol of her reign as one of ballet's last great courtesans, it was taken over by the Bolsheviks; in an ironic twist of fate, Kschessinska's pleasure dome was handpicked by the revolution's ruthless leader, Vladimir Lenin, who occupied it next, addressing the masses on the street below from the ballerina's ornately decorated balcony and using her sunken bathtub as a giant ashtray.

Kschessinska was among the last of her kind, largely because society had irrevocably changed: mass democratization and the emancipation of women, among other social movements, rendered aristocratic privilege and concubinage increasingly unacceptable. The overt sensuality and bejeweled glamor of the old-style ballerina was being swept aside by a new asceticism and factory-like discipline in ballet.

The idea of the ballerina as chaste and obedient, a fullfledged devotee of the dance, had been established by a fellow Russian, the great Anna Pavlova (1881–1931), who approached ballet as something akin to a religion; she was fiercely devoted to it, to the point of self-sacrifice, literally dancing herself to death. Pavlova gave her all to her art. She married but remained childless. She lived by her own saying: "God gives talent. Work transforms talent into genius." Agnes de Mille, the pioneering American dancer and choreographer, met Pavlova once and described her as a victim of her own desire to meld with the essence of her dance: "What was gross had been burnt and wasted off her. She had kept no part of her body that was not useful to her art, and there was about her the tragic aura of absolute decision."[10]

Pavlova came from humble origins; she was the daughter of a washerwoman, and her father was unknown. She had learned early that success depended on a fighting spirit. She was nine when she attended her first ballet at the Mariinsky, *The Sleeping Beauty*, and was instantly smitten by the onstage fantasy. To the young Pavlova, the ballet represented a world of beauty and transformation. She wanted badly to become a part of it and, according to her biographer, Keith Money, had to overcome the doubts of the examiners at the Imperial Ballet School, who at first refused her entrance, believing her too small and sickly. Pavlova worked for two years to make her body more pliable and strong and was finally accepted at age ten, making her older than the other girls in her ballet classes but also more determined.[11] She became a *première danseuse* when she was only sixteen.

Once Pavlova was accepted into ballet, she became utterly focused on spreading its gospel of discipline and rarefied beauty to the masses, becoming something of a ballerina-missionary who made a career of performing one-night stands across the globe; her signature role was *The Dying Swan*, a solo created for her in 1907 by Fokine, and from 1910 until 1931, she logged over 350,000 miles over six continents performing this poignantly beautiful role, a eulogy of feathers, as the head of her own classical ballet touring company.[12] No town was ever too small as long as it had a stage where she could share the magic that had first entranced her. Pavlova was the world's first international ballerina superstar, loved and admired by all those who saw her. In America, which had barely seen ballet before, her performances were hailed as "ocular opera." "Everywhere our dancing was hailed as the revelation of an un-dreamed of art," Pavlova said."[13] Her dancing was perceived as existing beyond the here and now; Pavlova had that elusive something, an inner glow and gravitas, which enabled her to turn even the most basic of ballet steps into a kind of personal prayer. Audiences were reportedly spellbound by her; Russian critic André Levinson said of Pavlova that she was the embodiment of emotion saturated by form and of form saturated by emotion.[14] That limpidness shone most brightly in classic ballets like *Giselle* and *La Bayadère*, in which she danced Nikiya, Kschessinska's own role. When briefly she danced with Diaghilev's troupe in Paris in 1909, performing opposite Nijinsky, she performed only work from the old repertoire, nothing avant-garde. She cultivated roles in which she appeared as a dragonfly, butterfly, snowflake, or swan, phenomena associated with lightness and flight, to which her diaphanous dancing style was suited.

That Pavlova was a ballerina possessed became tragically clear when she contracted pneumonia while on tour in The Hague and yet insisted on dancing even when doctors told her to rest. She danced *The Dying Swan*, and the role ultimately killed her. She died of double pleurisy just three days later, on January 23, 1931. She was fifty years old.

Yet, Pavlova appears to have been in control of her fate; certainly, for the most part, she called the shots as far as her own career was concerned. During her lifetime, Pavlova had been an astute ballet entrepreneur, carefully stoking the fire of her own legend by attaching her name to any number of commercial enterprises, from face creams to silk stockings; a light and frothy dessert bears her name today. Pavlova had been her own boss, dictating not only what she would dance but also where and when and how, driving herself even if her frailty could barely sustain the effort. After her, ballerinas the world over would pay her homage by adopting her *Dying Swan* solo, imitating her fluttery dancing style, which had been preserved on film. But what they would not be able to recreate was the business model that Pavlova had created to ensure her autonomy as a ballerina entrepreneur. In her wake, ballerinas would come to lose control over their own careers in subordinating themselves to the new star of twentieth-century ballet—the choreographer. Typically male and sometimes doubling as an impresario, the choreographer had begun nudging the ballerina from center stage during the Diaghilev era. But after Pavlova, the choreographer's dominant role in the art became more apparent. A Svengali-like figure, the choreographer demanded that the ballerina become his inferior, a docile handmaid serving his artistic needs more than her own. Strangely, and at a time when the rest of the world was starting to embrace women's rights, the ballerina almost unquestioningly obeyed, subsuming her will to the choreographer's in ways unprecedented in the history of ballet.

The choreographer who almost single-handedly brought about a cataclysmic change to the status of the ballerina in modern times was George Balanchine (1904–1983), an undisputed genius of twentieth-century ballet who also is responsible for some of its more negative aspects. While he was ballet-master-in-chief of New York City Ballet, Balanchine intensified the tyranny of artistic director and sparked the epidemic of eating disorders arising from his preference for lean and leggy ballerinas. Balanchine claimed to idolize ballerinas and publicly called them his muse. But behind the scenes, he subtly and systematically degraded them, denying them sex (unless it was with him) and sustenance, both in the form of food and domestic fulfillment. If his ballerinas married or had babies, he grew angry and was known to shun them. If they did not capitulate to his sexual advances, he was known to have them banished from ballet. He was a god-like figure to whom scores of ballerinas completely devoted themselves while submitting to his tyranny. As the zealots became teachers themselves, the almost unattainable Balanchinean feminine ideal took root and flourished in all corners of the world where ballet is performed—despite its now proven deleterious effects on ballerinas' health and well-being. This remains Balanchine's legacy, as much as his repertoire of brilliantly crafted, vibrantly musical works.

Born Georgi Melotonovich Balanchivadze in St. Petersburg, the son of a respected Georgian composer who bestowed on his son, one of two, the gift of music, Balanchine was the fiendishly prolific progenitor of ballet's neoclassical style. He created works not only for Les Ballets Russes but also Hollywood, Broadway, and the circus after moving to the West in 1933 at the request of wealthy American philanthropist Lincoln Kirstein, with whom he would eventually form New York City Ballet.

Balanchine had formulated his ideas carefully throughout a lifetime of meticulous study and association with some of the leading creative minds of his day. He was old enough to have experienced the heady days of the Imperial Ballet School, where he had been a student; the ballerina Karsavina was one of his favorites, and it is said that as a boy he loved watching her. However, Balanchine had been too young to decamp from Russia on his own when the Bolsheviks took over. He ended up being partly schooled in the Soviet system, which influenced his emerging choreographic style as much as did Petipa's ballets under the tsar.

In the Soviet Union as a young man, Balanchine was inspired by Constructivist theories and the idea that art could be stripped clean of emotional encumbrances to make it more a reflection of pure energy. He approached ballet as a formalist, seeing it as a distinct and autonomous art form that was expressive not in a literary sense but through its own physical movement, its own centuries-old style.[15] As such, Balanchine's ballets emerged as non-narrative vehicles for showcasing the ballet's new machine-age aesthetic. In ballet terms, this involved manipulating the body to make it move faster, sharper, and higher, with more musical complexity and breadth. In his predominantly abstract or plotless works, he used intricate interlacings of bodies to create sculptural effects, an approach influenced by the Soviet avant-garde dance artist Kasyan Goleizovsky in the Soviet Union. "I did not imitate him," Balanchine once told an interviewer, "but he gave me a desire to do something, a desire to move. He started to move differently."[16]

Balanchine made the ballerina symbolic of his new direction in ballet, even redesigning her image according to his own idea of what the ideal female dancer should look like: tall, with long legs, highly arched and flexible feet, narrow hips, long arms, and a small head. The look quickly became iconic, replacing all past images to the point that all ballerinas who have come since bear his stamp: "[When] you think about dancers—long-legged, slender girls who move as quickly as delight," observed American dance critic Joseph Mazo, "you are thinking about Balanchine. He invented them."[17] The prototype was said to have been Ballets Russes dancer Felia Doubrovska (1896–1981), with whom Balanchine had worked, casting her as the Siren in the original production of his 1929 Diaghilev ballet, *The Prodigal Son*.[18] Doubrovska described Balanchine's approach to ballet as an art that spoke with the legs: the accent was on pointe work, which only the ballerina could perform.[19]

"Ballet is woman," Balanchine famously declared. But it wasn't really a compliment. Balanchine wanted to control women, to make them look, move, feel, be as he wanted. A more accurate statement would have been "Ballet is Balanchine," because under his direction, the art became his. The ballerina would be stripped of the independence she might previously have enjoyed; the ballet master demanded of his ballerinas total devotion bordering on self-sacrifice. Any progress ballerinas might have made while under his watch was tied to Balanchine's own desires as a heterosexual male and machine-age artist. "If you marry a ballerina," Balanchine once told an interviewer, "you never have to worry about whether she's running around with somebody else or anything like that. You always know where she is—in the studio, working."[20] Ballerinas who did strive for a life outside ballet were punished; the Canadian-born ballerina Patricia Wilde, a vivacious dancer for whom Balanchine created principal roles in *Scotch Symphony* (1952), *Swan Lake* (1951), and *Raymonda Variations* (1961) when she danced with New York City Ballet from 1950 to 1965, says that when she dared wed, on the eve of the master's staging of *The Nutcracker*, Balanchine punished her by refusing her a wedding night: "After rehearsal, I *did* tell him. He was fine about it," Wilde recalls. "Then he said that he would need me for rehearsals that evening between seven and nine. I was taken aback but came to rehearsal anyway. In the meantime, my husband and my in-laws were having dinner and waiting for me. This, after all, was my wedding night. Anyway, I was rehearsing and nine o'clock came around. Mr. B. wasn't looking at the clock. He asked me to do incredible things, like *entrechat-six* from pointe to pointe, *tours en l'air*, and one incredibly difficult variation which had no end. We finished at ten o'clock. I rushed to join my wedding party. But you know, Mr. B. didn't call me again for two weeks. That rehearsal was his wedding present to me!"[21]

Ballet demanded a ballerina's allegiance to her art to the exclusion of everything else; perhaps it made sense for the day. New York City Ballet in the 1950s and 1960s was frequently on tour, sometimes on the road for five months at a time, making domesticity difficult, if not impossible—especially when dancers' salaries ran on average $85 a week. Joysanne Sidimus, a native New Yorker, danced in the New York City Ballet from 1958 to 1962. Today she works as a répétiteur licensed to stage Balanchine ballets around the world through the Balanchine Trust, an organization that enshrines and perpetuates the choreographer's genius through careful presentation of his work. She says that Balanchine never understood why a dancer would want a life outside ballet anyway; married women were expected to devote their lives to their husbands and families— it was the social norm. "So it's not so much that Balanchine was a dictator," she continues. "Society itself made it very difficult for ballerinas to get married. I remember meeting guys and then it would come down to one sentence: 'Marry me and give up dancing.' But how could I? It was my life."[22]

But was it society, or was it Balanchine? In the 1960s and 1970s, when the master's influence on ballet was keenest, North America was being rocked by the women's liberation movement. Everywhere, women were burning their bras, but within the confines of Balanchine's ballet company, they were being told to park their brains at the stage door and submit themselves to his rule. Certainly, Balanchine could not be called a feminist choreographer for putting women on pedestals of high choreographic art. The act itself suggested that he, and he alone, was in control.

"We are under the dictatorship of one man, whom we adore and respect," said Toni Bentley, an Australian-born dancer who wrote about her experience dancing under Balanchine from November 1980 to February 1981 as a New York City Ballet corps de ballet dancer, "and his every whim is our law, no questions asked."[23]

After Balanchine, it can be argued, the ballerina was no longer a real-time woman but a translucent cipher serving the vision of a hyper-possessive heterosexual male who, while claiming to love women, deemed them inferior, in need of controlling. "Man is a better cook, a better painter, a better musician, composer," Balanchine said. "Man is stronger, faster, why? Because we have muscles, and we're made that way. And woman accepts this. It is her business to accept. She knows what's beautiful. Men are great poets, because men have to write beautiful poetry for woman—odes to a beautiful woman. Woman accepts the beautiful poetry. You see, man is the servant—a good servant. In ballet, however, woman is first. Everywhere else the man is first. But in ballet, it's the woman. All my life I have dedicated my art to her."[24]

Becoming a Balanchine ballerina meant learning not only a whole new repertoire of complex and difficult moves but also how to subordinate her will to the dictates of the master machinist, the guy tightening the screws, so to speak, on the art of classical dance. The choreographer preferred this image of himself as a manual laborer who tinkered with the female body to create ballets universally celebrated for their clockwork precision and locomotive speed. People who called him a genius were soon set straight: "I am not a genius, I am a craftsman," Balanchine said. He was equally disparaging of being called an artist: "Only God creates; I assemble."[25]

Balanchine's so-called blue-collar approach to ballet reduced the ballerina to the status of a mechanical appendage that could be manipulated to drive the art form forward. It perhaps explains how a celebrated Balanchine ballerina like Patricia McBride, when she was at the height of her powers as a dancer with New York City Ballet, ended up being (unironically) described by a leading New York critic as "having dispensed with all angles in her body" to the point that she appeared "to be dispensing with her body as well, with recalcitrant flesh."[26] Shy of calling them robots, such Balanchine ballerinas appeared more like widgets than flesh-and-blood women, a product of the assembly line. It's an interpretation supported by dance anthropologist Judith Lynne Hanna, who calls modern ballet as interpreted by Balanchine "protechnology in its emulation of the machine's precision, economy, and speed."[27]

Balanchine emphasized the technical in his ballets, telling his ballerinas not to feel, just dance his steps without question. Many dancers who worked under Balanchine report that he was succinct about what he wanted: "Don't think, dear, do."[28] The movement, he said, would be its own source of emotion, according to Balanchine ballerina Sara Leland in a 1972 interview: "Mr. B. depends on the movement itself to bring out the quality he wants in a ballet, he does not try to develop 'expression' in the dancers. It is there, he tells us, in the choreography—we have only to dance the choreography to express it."[29] His ballerinas mostly did as they were told. "First of all, dancers are very obedient," remarked Vera Zorina (1917–2003), the Ballets Russes dancer who was Balanchine's wife, his second, and the star of the commercial dance spectaculars Balanchine created for Broadway in the 1930s.[30] "Dancers don't go about making a fuss."[31]

Balanchine might have believed himself to be acting in accordance with his times in creating works stripped to their essence, but his notion of the ballerina as a selfless being in servitude to her art was more a recasting of the nineteenth-century Romantic ideal that modern ballet was said to have moved away from; the identity of the ballerina in the twentieth century was predicated on a deep-rooted notion of self-sacrifice: "A great modernist artist, Balanchine created his art on the bodies of his ballerinas, whom he convinced to starve themselves toward his own vision of beauty,"[32] observed one ballet scholar. Emaciation and enslavement to an ideal were the methods by which the ballerina would succeed under his watch. In this regard, Balanchine's modern ballerina was no different from the fragile heroine of *Giselle*, the fluttering Sylph in *La Sylphide*, or Emma Livry's combustible butterfly in *Le Papillon*: she was equally meant to be an ethereal and ephemeral being, an object of unrequited desire.

"As dancers we spent enormous amounts of time working in front of mirrored walls in brightly lit studios where our physiques were on constant public display," said ballerina-turned-scholar Susan Young. "Relentless critical self-assessment of the body and a concomitant drive to suppress the physical evidence of female maturation—breasts, hips, fleshy curves—were not only tolerated but professional requirements. In this context, remaining physically prepubescent fed into the practical, that is, biomechanical—requirements of the female dancer. This is because a *ballerina* seeks to present the illusion of weightlessness, of occupying as little space as possible in order to suggest a chaste and unattainable woman-child. She is a creature of the air, not the earth."[33]

Creating that illusion of weightlessness during the Balanchine era was not just a matter of technique but of extreme thinness. While he liked women of all shapes and sizes—from the diminutive Japanese-Canadian soloist Sono Osato to the statuesque Native American ballerina Maria Tallchief (another of his four dancer wives)—Balanchine felt no shame in describing his ideal female body as "like toothpick."[34] He made thinness a visible marker of the moral worth of the modern ballerina and seemed most to admire those ballerinas who could conform to his exacting principle—"that long-legged thing," as Zorina called it.[35]

On the surface, Balanchine's ballet appeared female centered, but it was, in fact, responsible for institutionalizing an image of the female dancer achievable only through the utmost deprivation, bordering on torture. Ballerinas routinely went under the knife to enhance their onstage line. Gelsey Kirkland had her earlobes trimmed and her nose tweaked; she also had silicone implants inserted into her lips, breasts, and ankles, the latter to enhance her onstage line. Ballet is a visual art, and dancers are always made aware of how they look, practicing before mirrors all day long, a habit that makes them hyperaware of their bodies and also hypercritical. Dancers often experience pressure to conform to a certain look, especially when the right body gets the right roles, a truism as valid in Balanchine's time as it is today.

But more prevalent than plastic surgery in emulating the Balanchine ideal is self-starvation in the form of eating disorders like anorexia nervosa and bulimia, which ballerinas routinely engage in to bring themselves down in size. Dancers have been known to subsist on coffee and soft drinks, amphetamines and lettuce. If they eat anything more substantial, they stick their fingers down their throats to make themselves disgorge their food. Self-induced vomiting introduces a host of other problems: corrosive stomach acids that eat away at the esophagus and the enamel of the teeth, weakened bones that make dancers prone to stress fractures and other injuries. Still, some dancers think it's better to eat nothing at all: "We don't eat food," says Bentley in her ballet memoir, A *Winter Season*. "We eat music."[36]

How small did the Balanchine dancer need to go to make herself favorably noticed? Kirkland, one of the greatest American dancers of her generation, makes it explicit in her explosive memoir, *Dancing on My Grave* (1986), in which she discusses Balanchine's demand for an emaciated aesthetic:

> He halted class and approached me for a kind of physical inspection. With his knuckles, he thumped on my sternum and down my rib cage, clucking his tongue and remarking, "Must see the bones." I was less than 100 pounds even then. Mr. B did not seem to consider beauty a quality that must develop from within the artist; rather, he was concerned with outward signs such as body weight. His emphasis was responsible in part for setting the style that led to some of the current extremes of American ballet. I allowed him to use me to that end by trusting his advice. He did not merely say, "Eat less." He repeatedly said, "Eat nothing."[37]

Many dancers have since willingly followed that dictate, sparking an epidemic of eating disorders in ballet that continues to rage today. "Anorexia nervosa is believed to have increased in the past several decades, due to the new cultural ideal of the angular thin woman," reports one medical study, based on data collected by experts in the field of eating disorders over the last twenty-five years.[38] "This has been attributed to the marked influence of the choreographer, George Balanchine."[39]

Test cases involving ballet students since the 1970s, when the Balanchine effect on the health of ballet dancers first started being recorded by the medical establishment, show that female ballet dancers generally ingest fewer calories than controls of the same age, height, and weight: average intakes of 1,000 calories have been reported, though some highly active female ballet dancers have been known to consume as few as 600 calories a day.[40] The recommended daily intake for people four years or older is 2,000 calories, according to the U.S. Department of Health and Human Services.

Ongoing research on female ballet dancers and eating disorders shows that professional female ballet dancers today are "at a much higher risk for reporting eating disorders than are non-athletic women or even adolescent dance students."[41] The prevalence of anorexia nervosa in ballet dancers is significantly higher than in the normal population.[42] On average, professional female ballet dancers weigh more than 20 percent below their ideal weight for their height.[43] The demand for dieting and slimness is more intense for them than for "other females in a western cultural environment."[44] Ballet school students are seen as "a population at high risk" and "an endangered group,"[45] who often cannot even recognize that they are ill.

This goal of thinness, this skeletal ideal, was and continues to be exceedingly harmful to ballerinas' health. Poor nutrition creates brittle bones, which can lead to injuries, the bane of a ballerina's existence, and possibly early retirement. It also diminishes dancers, stunting their development as women and turning them into sexless waifs. "If you take a girl at twelve years of age and keep her below about 17 percent body fat," observed Dr. Lawrence M. Vincent, a physician and former dancer who studied anorexia in student ballerinas in New York, "she won't menstruate. Puberty is arrested, her hypothalamic function is suppressed, and she has low estrogen levels. Estrogen, of course, affects breast and hip development. These girls go into a puberty-holding pattern. The claims of ballet mistresses that they can pick out a future ballet body are false; they're simply selecting late developers and, with the help of poor nutrition, keeping them that way. It's almost as if ballet had created a new species of woman: low estrogen and androgynous."[46]

The emphasis on thinness in female ballet dancers was an artistic imperative that penetrated the ballet world with alarming ferocity, producing underfed dancers with jutting hip bones and prominent clavicles everywhere classical ballet is practiced. Balanchine's acolytes helped institutionalize the ideal and the eating disorders that are the direct result of its pursuit. "In the first half of the century, ballet dancers were not especially thin, although they certainly were athletic," observes dance scholar Wendy Oliver, a specialist in dance and women's studies. "Since the advent of George Balanchine's company, the New York City Ballet, the American female ballet dancer has been slimmer than ever before. As is now legend, Balanchine favored a slim-hipped, long-legged look that has since become the standard for ballerinas in most companies."[47]

Dancers who never even danced with Balanchine have ended up suffering the consequences of Balanchine's impact on twentieth-century ballet, though few are willing to talk about it. The point is driven home by Deborah Bull's 2011 book, *The Everyday Dancer*, a first-person account of the author's former life as a principal ballerina with the Royal Ballet. Now creative director of the Royal Opera House, Bull devotes only one page to an eating disorder "that affected half of my career" but seven to the rituals used in preparing her toe shoes. "The art of ballet, so predicated on physical denial," writes a reviewer, "is described here by a writer whose loyalty to its customs operates as a kind of veil over its everyday pain."[48]

Eating disorders are linked to mental illness, which might explain why dancers are generally reluctant to speak openly about their own experiences, fearing further stigmatization by their art. But the problem is real. A dancer like Kirkland, among the first to sound the alarm back in the 1980s, is more the rule than the exception. What marks her as different is her bravery in going public with what, to a large extent, remains a forbidden topic, especially in ballet itself. It is only very recently that the subject of anorexia, bulimia, and other eating disorders in ballet is being publicly aired. A Dance U.K. conference on eating disorders that took place in London in April 2012 was pronounced by the press as radical for just that reason. Attending the conference was the Royal Ballet's outgoing artistic director, Monica Mason, who underscored the prevalence of the disease in ballet today: "Any director who said they have never had an anorexic dancer," she told the BBC, "would have to be lying."[49]

One of those anorexics was Rachel Peppin, a former principal dancer with Birmingham Royal Ballet, who suffered from an eating disorder for twenty years. To keep her weight down, she over-exercised, strictly monitored her daily caloric intake, and ingested the occasional laxative to maintain what one critic gushingly called her waif-like appearance. She equated extreme thinness with success in ballet until company doctor, Victor Cross, did a series of body scans as part of his 1993 research into the bone density of ballet dancers with eating disorders. They revealed that she had the spine of a seventy-year-old woman, even though, at the time, she was just twenty-three. "I always thought osteoporosis was something that happened to elderly women," she told an interviewer.[50] But after seeing for herself how her eating disorder was ravaging her body, she entered into a rehabilitation program and today, almost twenty-years later, is a recovered anorexic with healthy bones.

A more poignant example of the debilitating effects of eating disorders on ballerinas is South African ballerina Beverly Bagg, who won a scholarship to study at the Royal Ballet School in England. When she first moved to London in 1975 at age seventeen, she had never been away from home before. She was on her own in a new city in a new country, not even sure of how to cook for herself. "So I gained a little weight, and I was thrown out of the *pas de deux* class and wasn't allowed to come back until I slimmed down," she says, thirty-six years later.[51] But Bagg wasn't given any guidelines. After putting herself on a self-devised diet of chewing gum and coffee, she winnowed her weight down and then down some more. She stands five feet two inches inches tall, and her ideal performing weight is 115 pounds. But she had starved herself down to 81 pounds and was sure she would die: "It was very scary," Bagg says.

A friend in the school called her parents in South Africa and told them to take her home. With their help, Bagg slowly recovered her body mass and went on to dance with the Frankfurt Ballet and with South Africa's Pact Ballet, a prominent sixty-member troupe, where, in 1984, she became a principal dancer, performing all the lead roles in classics like *Swan Lake* and *The Sleeping Beauty*. By all appearances, she was a ballerina at the top of her profession, luxuriating in its benefits. But, inside, Bagg never stopped feeling like that ballet student of old, continually punishing herself for not being perfect.

"The general view is that it is so glamorous being a ballerina. You're so lucky, people used to tell me. It's such a gorgeous profession. It looks so easy. And yet, there is a dark side to being a dancer that people don't see, and it's nurtured and perpetuated by history," Bagg says. "It's hard to explain to people how much I suffered as a dancer. Even though I was a ballerina, a principal dancer in a major company, I don't remember ever being happy. I always felt this pressure to be better than I was. I never felt good enough. I believed that I didn't dance well at all, and that I was totally unworthy being a ballerina."

Bagg's dancing career lasted fifteen years before she suffered a nervous breakdown and was hospitalized. She was put on medication and released, somewhat wobbly but no longer in danger of hurting herself. She quit dancing professionally soon after.

If these stories look as if they belong to another era, it is sobering to note that today's blogosphere is clogged with the angst-ridden confessions of young ballet dancers tormented by the ideal of extreme thinness—thirty years after Balanchine's death in 1983 of Creutzfeldt-Jakob disease, a neurological ailment said to have been triggered by rejuvenation treatments featuring animal glandular products. "I just want to be thin, fragile, weightless. I'm 17 and fat. Disgusting. I'm trying to change all that. Heres [sic] to being the thin girl in ballet," writes one typical ballet blogger.[52] Another young ballerina blogger obsessively lists all the food she eats, together with its calorie count, and posts downloaded images of skeletally thin professional ballerinas who inspire her, among them the Russian-born Alina Somova of the Mariinsky (or Kirov) Ballet.[53]

The young American dancer Heidi Guenther was also afflicted by eating disorders but did not live to write about them. In June 1997, the twenty-two-year-old corps de ballet dancer employed by the Boston Ballet suffered a fatal heart attack after developing an eating disorder. She was five feet three inches tall and weighed ninety-three pounds when she died, a well-liked dancer whom no one seemed capable of helping, even as they saw her withering away before their eyes: "I don't think they could have helped her," said former ballerina Traci Hennessey at the time. "Once someone says they want to lose weight its set in their minds. When people tell them, 'You're too thin,' that feels good to them because they're achieving their goal...To tell you the truth, I'm surprised there haven't been more deaths."[54]

The problem started when then artistic director Anna-Marie Holmes told Guenther she should lose some weight because she was looking "a little pudgy."[55] Allegedly, she had been five pounds over her ideal dancer's weight.[56] Guenther embarked on a series of ruthless diets that blossomed into an eating disorder, which Holmes became aware of. She asked Guenther to stop and eventually offered her professional help, but Guenther refused. The family later sued the Boston Ballet and its artistic director, claiming that their daughter had died after she was threatened with non-renewal of her contract if she did not slim down. But the courts dismissed the claim when an autopsy ruled the cause of death to be an irregular heartbeat with no known link to anorexia.[57]

The case nevertheless brought to light some of the pressures put on modern-day ballerinas to reduce their weight beyond what is considered the societal norm, often at their peril. It also underscored the power and influence directors continue to wield over their dancers.

Few ballerinas, in fact, ever protested against the tyrannical hold Balanchine had over them. Balanchine was, if not their surrogate husband, their big daddy, the father figure many dancers felt compelled to respect: "We are all his children. But his adult children, his working, dancing, performing children," Toni Bentley writes. "His power over us is unique."[58] Those who have eagerly jumped to Balanchine's defense include Suzanne Farrell, the American ballerina with whom Balanchine fell in love and for whom he created many ballets. Among them was his full-length *Don Quixote* (1965), in which he played a lovesick

Don to Farrell's unattainable Dulcinea, a ballet that in many ways was true to his own life at that time—a man in pursuit of a dream disguised as a woman. "I'd kill myself for a man, but I ain't gonna kill myself for a woman," said Farrell around the time of Balanchine's death in 1983. "I think it works well that way also. It's not that a woman couldn't... be president, but I think it works better if it's a man with a very powerful woman behind him."[59]

But such selfless devotion bred a sense of malaise among Balanchine's dancers. Gelsey Kirkland underwent years of therapy to help her cope with the loss of self she felt during her Balanchine years; she also became a drug addict, later confessing that cocaine helped quell the hunger pains and kill the desire for food. It also made her dance faster, contributing not only to her superstardom but also to her breakdown. Kirkland, and other ballerinas who have likewise suffered, prove that dancers are not the creatures of lightness audiences like to think they are: "They are often miserably unhappy people," Kirkland says. "How can you possibly deny yourself all those things you deny yourself in order to dance, and put your body through all that you do, and still be happy?"[60]

But it has been hard to shake off the expectation of denial imposed on ballerinas since the dawning of the Balanchine era. Dance critics have eagerly participated in keeping the ballerina down, attacking her for committing human transgressions like gaining weight, for instance, a practice that has continued into the twenty-first century. A powerful and influential voice during the Balanchine years, *New Yorker* dance critic Arlene Croce was one of the master's most devoted acolytes and a principal guardian of the myth that Balanchine could do no wrong. In her highly regarded dance writings, she preached the gospel of thin, admiring the way Balanchine used dieting as a form of social control. In her essay, "Balanchine's Girls," published in her book *Afterimages*, Croce praised Balanchine for taking the American woman, "whose athleticism, independence, and intelligence are a challenge to the female role in ballet," and taming her. Balanchine, Croce said, had succeeded in getting "American girls to stop thinking and start dancing."[61]

"In one sense," continued Croce, "New York City ballerinas are like nuns: they're a sisterhood. They survive in an atmosphere of an aesthetic style that happens to exist nowhere else in the world, that absorbs modern tensions and transcends them; and they put up with untold miseries because they know it's the only way to look the way they want to look—ravishing like mortal goddesses, yet reachable."[62]

It was a lie, of course. The dancers didn't want to look like goddesses; Balanchine wanted them to look like goddesses, or celestial handmaids, who would aggrandize his own image as a god, Apollo of the dance. It was a megalomaniacal pursuit that, as far as dancers' health and well-being were concerned, ended up causing more damage than good.

"The ballet is a purely female thing," Balanchine once said. "It is a woman, a garden of beautiful flowers, and man is the gardener."

Cutting her off at the stem.

5

LABORING UNDER AN ILLUSION
THE BALLERINA AT WORK TODAY

THERE IS AN enduring perception that ballerinas live on air, unfettered by earthly concerns, and so they are not in need of special protections. As artists specializing in wordless dance, ballerinas appear voiceless and are expected to be silent—an image exploited by their employers, who generally overwork and underpay them, confident that they won't speak up or fight back. Ballet exacts docility from the dancer to achieve its superhuman feats; blind obedience to ballet's rules is necessary in an art that contorts the body through early and methodical exercise to achieve the essential ninety-degree turnout from the hips. When dancers do speak out, the repercussions are often swift and career damaging.

The dancers of American Ballet Theatre in New York learned this firsthand when in 1979 they voiced concern over the small salary and benefit increase presented to them as part of contract negotiations. The dancers rejected the offer, and management responded by locking them out. With nowhere else to ply their trade, the situation was dire. Ballerinas took to the streets, carrying placards, drawing public attention to their plight. They also spoke to reporters and went on television, demonstrating that ballerinas could indeed speak and that what they had to say about their workplace conditions—one ABT dancer described their situation as nothing short of slavery—was deserving of attention. For outsiders, it was their first glimpse of how the ballet world really worked: "the long hours, low pay, paltry benefits, and occupational hazards."[1] The crisis ended ten weeks later when management finally conceded to some of the dancers' demands, granting them improved wages and workplace conditions. "The starting salary for a corps dancer went from $235 a week to $495 a week by the end of the three-year contract; a fourth-year corps dancer, who earned $285, now [made] $420; and a tenth-year soloist, who used to earn $422, now earn[ed] $610."[2]

It looked as though the dancers had empowered themselves. But within three years, back at the bargaining table for a new round of contract negotiations, it looked as though they would lose the ground they had earlier gained. In 1982, ABT ballerinas again took to the streets and marched en masse in the New York City Labor Day Parade, asserting their status as workers with rights. It was startling to see them out on labor's front lines, dressed in their short classical tutus, faux tiaras, and running shoes and holding aloft a banner declaring them full-fledged members of the American Guild of Musical Artists. Still, crowds of onlookers cheered them on. To at least one observer, the appearance of dancers in the Labor Day Parade was a sign that ballet was itself marching into a new enlightened era of fair labor practices. But that was an illusion worthy of the stage. Within a few weeks of that event, ABT's ninety-two dancers were again locked in a dispute with management over their collective rights as workers. A new contract was on the table, which the dancers were refusing to sign because it failed to meet their demands for increased pay. The company was crying poor, and when the dancers' union asked to check the books, management refused it access. The dancers then filed unfair labor practice charges against ABT, prompting management to cancel the company's season at the Kennedy Center for the Performing Arts in Washington in October 1982. The dancers demonstrated outside New York's Lincoln Center, their home base, and demanded that at the next round of bargaining their artistic director come to the table to negotiate directly with them.

Mikhail Baryshnikov had assumed directorship of the New York–based company in 1980 after an inspired period dancing under Balanchine at New York City Ballet, following his high-profile defection from the Soviet Union in the summer of 1974. Almost immediately, the Russian-trained dancer, among the best of his generation, began alienating other dancers in his charge. Baryshnikov was perceived as more interested in his own career than those of his fellow dancers. He was at the time a much sought-after guest artist and movie star who was also preoccupying himself with choreography—with lackluster results. Baryshnikov's lack of attention to dancers' needs was especially acute where ballerinas were concerned. He was known to fire them at will for not being young or thin enough. Baryshnikov demanded discipline from his dancers and used putdowns in the classroom to put ballerinas in their place, and that place was beneath him (in more ways than one). If Baryshnikov felt that dancers did not jump to attention as he commanded, he simply let them go.

Among the casualties of Baryshnikov's shoot-from-the-hip approach was his ex-girlfriend and frequent dancing partner, Gelsey Kirkland, then with a new beau, whom he dropped from the company after she failed to show up for a rehearsal. Taking her place was an ingénue ballerina, Cynthia Harvey, who showed she had the spunk to stand up to him. "Working for Baryshnikov is brutal," it was reported in *People* magazine in 1981, the year Harvey first ascended the company hierarchy. "But that hasn't intimidated Cynthia Harvey, the 23-year-old brunette he has chosen as his new partner. While rehearsing a tender pas de deux recently, he instructed her to 'whisper something sweet in my ear.' As the music swelled, she murmured, 'Can I have a raise?' She didn't get one (her salary is $500 a week), but she has Misha's number. 'When he's dancing with you,' she reports, 'he really stares into your eyes. I just look right back!'"[3]

Baryshnikov promoted another young dancer but only after he ordered her to lose ten pounds, fix her teeth, and change her name. The five-foot-five-inch Susan Jaffe agreed to everything he asked—save for the name change—winnowing her weight down from 112 to 102 pounds during a summer subsisting on iced tea: "I had to go in every two weeks," she said, "and the management would look at me to see if I was getting thinner."[4] Jaffe ended up becoming one of Baryshnikov's star dancers, gladly filling the hole created by Baryshnikov's sidelining of two other ABT star ballerinas, Leslie Browne and Marianna Tcherkassy who were then (*gasp!*) entering their thirties.

But not everyone wanted to dance ballet Misha's way. Baryshnikov's fellow defector from the Soviet Union, Natalia Makarova, stormed out of ABT shortly after Baryshnikov took over, citing artistic differences. Meanwhile, the Dutch-born Martine van Hamel complained to the press that the company felt lost under Baryshnikov's direction; at least that was how she was feeling after Baryshnikov started reducing the number of her roles she could dance, presumably because at forty she was no longer of much use to him: "It's not an ideal situation," van Hamel said at the time. "There has been disappointment at Baryshnikov's lack of involvement in the company, but it's difficult to find the ideal director."[5]

Baryshnikov also locked horns with leading American-born ballerina Cynthia Gregory, another dancer then entering the prime of life; Gregory was already on Baryshnikov's bad side for having openly questioned, in 1975, ABT's preference for Russian-born dancers at the expense of homegrown talent. The defectors got more money and press than the American dancers at the time; Gregory wanted an even playing field. Baryshnikov never forgot the dancer's outspokenness, and once he became her artistic director was said to have retaliated by reducing the number of roles she could perform in a season, essentially rendering her redundant. In 1985, their ongoing backstage battles started leaking into the press, and Gregory was soon seen licking her wounds. She was nearing forty and knew she had only a few years left on the stage. She was forced to eat crow to safeguard what was left of her career: "I know the performing isn't going to last," she said at the time. "I give myself a good four more years, then that'll be it." To make the best of those years, dancing roles that were challenging, stimulating, and satisfying, Gregory made her peace with Baryshnikov, agreeing to dance less at ABT and more with other companies: "In the past, I've gotten in trouble because I'm too outspoken," the ballerina said. "So, I think it's better to keep my mouth shut."[6]

Baryshnikov left ABT in 1989, after promoting a new generation of young ballerinas to take the place of those whom he considered old for having turned forty. But despite Baryshnikov's departure, ageism within ballet has remained firmly in place. National Ballet of Canada ballerina Gizella Witkowsky was told to step down as principal dancer after a twenty-year relationship with the Toronto-based company after she turned thirty-eight. Artistic director Reid Anderson pushed her into early retirement, saying he felt she was ready. But the ballerina was not anywhere near ready and made that clear in an embittered interview she gave at the time: "Even though I'm 38, I'm totally healthy, and in peak form as an artist," Witkowsky said while fighting back tears. " It's not like I'm asking for ten more years. Just a couple at my peak. That's all."[7] Her pleas fell on deaf ears.

But by today's ballet standards, Witkowsky might even be considered lucky for having retired at age thirty-eight. She had a longer career than most ballerinas. A Dance/USA study published in the late 1990s showed that the average age of retirement for ballerinas had fallen to twenty-nine, down from forty. That seems grossly unfair, considering how long and hard ballerinas train for their careers, starting in childhood and pursuing their dance studies often to the exclusion of everything else, including a high-school education. For ballerinas, their bodies are their currency, the alpha and the omega of what they do. Their art demands youthfulness and vigor to execute it correctly and with élan. One of the biggest tragedies about ballet is that just as dancers are coming into their own as artists, they are often released from their responsibilities as professional company members precisely for having grown mature. "Seniority in a ballet company does you some good only if you can conceal it," as the American dance critic Marcia Siegel has observed. "This means that a dancer's experience and maturity have no value in the coin of [her] profession. Older dancers make good teachers, coaches, choreographers, but they cannot use their years on the stage, except in lesser roles."[8]

But why does today's ballerina have a shorter shelf life? A main reason is ballet itself: the art is increasingly more

strenuous and demanding on the body, resulting in more
career-ending injuries. Salaries have also dropped substan-
tially in recent years. According to the U.S. Bureau of Labor
Statistics, the median hourly wage of dancers was $12.22 in
May 2008. Dancers who work with performing arts companies earned a median income of $15.30 per hour.[9] Ballet is a
low-paying job and it is hard for many dancers to sustain their
lifestyle, especially in big cities where rents and food prices are
generally high. In the dance capital of New York, for instance,
it is not uncommon for professional dancers to wait on tables
by day to afford the luxury of dancing on a theater stage at
night. As dancers mature, they find they are less willing and
able to carry the financial burden associated with their profession, and so they quit before they turn thirty to find a better life
for themselves.

Contributing to the low income levels for dancers is an
increased influx of female dancers. Dance academies yearly
are churning out far more ballerinas than there are jobs, resulting in a highly competitive culture and marketplace. Bridgett
Zehr is a principal dancer with English National Ballet in London, and she says that ballerinas' opportunities to dance have
diminished in recent years. "It's a different generation than it
was in the 1970s or 1980s," Zehr observes. "Ballet seemed easier back then if you were a ballerina because at least you had
guesting opportunities. People were willing to pay big money
to see you because you were in demand. But today, especially
for women ballet dancers, the guesting opportunities have
practically dried up. It's the men who are more sought after
because they are more rare; there just are fewer of them to go
round and so they get to dance more."[10]

Although only twenty-seven years old, Zehr is already pan-
icked about the end of her career and is intensively exploiting
her capabilities, knowing they are short-lived. Born in Sarasota,

Florida, to a former dancer and her construction worker partner (since divorced), Zehr comes from an impoverished
background. She has risen through the ballet profession on the
back of scholarships, which she worked devotedly to achieve,
but is prone to injuries, having several times broken bones in
her ankles and her metatarsals, which has put her on crutches
and away from the ballet stage for months at a time. She knows
firsthand that a ballet career is fragile and easily felled and
so has made a habit of company hopping, moving from the
Houston Ballet to the National Ballet of Canada and now the
English National Ballet, maximizing her chances at having a
fruitful career. "The career is so short," she says, "and I can't stay
in one place, knowing it will soon be over."

Inspiring her is her sister who, before quitting ballet at age
sixteen, was also a scholarship student, having trained hard.
Rachel Zehr was reportedly as lithe and innately musical as
Bridgett but she was unable to find her place as a ballerina and
committed suicide. "She could have been so much but she
didn't take the opportunities she should have taken," Zehr says.
"Instead of being depressed I want to do something out of my
comfort zone. I want to do what she couldn't, in a way."

Job security is not part of the job description for women
entering ballet. Stateuniversity.com, a U.S. academic and career
counseling website, is blunt in informing prospective dancers that the profession isn't as pretty as it looks: "Dancing is
very difficult, strenuous work, and the hours of rehearsal can
be tedious and exhausting. Most dancers remain in the field
only because they love to dance and would not be happy in
any other occupation."[11] Even leading dancers in major ballet
companies live precariously. If age and injury don't get them,
then there's always the fear that a career will be cut short at the
whim of the artistic director.

A native of New Westminster, British Columbia, who had previously danced with the Stuttgart Ballet, Reid Anderson cut a swath through the National Ballet of Canada after assuming the directorship in 1989. At least six dancers lost their jobs, apparently for reasons having to do with artistic discretion—often code for not being to the director's liking. One dancer who got the axe, apparently for having done nothing more than look voluptuous, was principal dancer Kim Lightheart, who was fired for having big breasts—of that she was sure. As a naturally curvy ballerina—a Raquel Welch among Twiggys—Lightheart had early in her career rejected the fetish of flat-chestedness that had grown popular during the Balanchine era; encouraging her was the National Ballet's previous artistic director, the Danish-born Erik Bruhn (1928–1986), one of the finest *danseurs nobles* of the twentieth century, who repeatedly urged her to be proud of her body, telling her she looked like a woman. But Anderson preferred the stick look and soon was dropping Lightheart from performances, including one scheduled for her hometown of London, Ontario. The stress only made things worse. Lightheart gained weight, growing to 112 pounds, seven pounds heavier than her ideal weight of 105, prompting management to intensify their criticisms of her body. When she was fired, she was angry because she felt she did not get any support; she also, for a period, felt lonely and unloved. Lightheart had trained long and hard for ballet since childhood, but then in a moment she was out. Pleasing the eye of one master, she shone; displeasing another, she withered and was banished from the stage, every ballerina's worst nightmare.[12]

But even artistic directors can get the blues. Patricia Neary was a gifted dancer before she became a ballet teacher and then director of several of the world's leading ballet companies, including Geneva Ballet, Zurich Ballet, and La Scala Ballet. A Balanchine protégée, Neary had all the right attributes: long legs, loose hips, musical sensitivity. But she also had a big mouth, at least where the ballet world is concerned. When she became artistic director of the fledgling Ballet British Columbia in 1989, the wiry blonde, who had hip replacement surgery before the age of forty as a result of her dancing, was characteristically outspoken when describing the real world of ballet to a reporter who had come to interview her about her new top job. Her troupe was then on a Canadian tour and Neary was in a hotel room surrounded by cans of peas, a jar of instant coffee, and a growing pile of artificial sweetener packets. She had no money, she said, and was struggling to live on the $30 per diem the company allotted her while on tour.[13] When members of her board of directors read that Neary had lifted the veil on the unglamorous life of the ballet dancer, they soon after gave her the boot. Neary was out of Ballet B.C. within a year, punished for speaking out.

Outspokenness, body image, and ageism were the main issues affecting ballerinas post-Balanchine. They all seemed to come to a head in the case of Kimberly Glasco, the American-born ballerina fired in December 1998 for daring to speak out on behalf of fellow dancers about working conditions at the National Ballet of Canada, where she had been a much loved principal dancer, one of only four in the company. It was a devastating blow that precipitated an abrupt end to a brilliant international career launched when Glasco had won the silver medal for overall dancing excellence at the 1981 Moscow International Ballet Competition, one of her profession's most esteemed events. Born in 1960 in Eugene, Oregon, into a working-class family, she had been with Canada's largest classical dance troupe for eighteen years (she had left briefly to dance with American Ballet Theatre, returning to the National Ballet of Canada in 1983), rising steadily through the ranks following her graduation from the Toronto-based National Ballet School in 1979. A dark-haired beauty with a clean, solid grasp of balletic technique—a 24-karat ballerina—she had, before her dismissal, performed majestically in the company's fall season, dancing, to laudatory reviews, the notoriously difficult role of Nikiya, the spectral heroine of Petipa's nineteenth-century crystalline classic, *La Bayadère*.[14] She was, from all appearances, at the peak of her powers. "At this point in my career, I feel fantastic," said Glasco, who was thirty-eight at the time. "I am not ready to retire."[15] But James Kudelka, the celebrated Canadian-born choreographer who also trained at the National Ballet School before becoming a National Ballet dancer himself, thought otherwise.

He had been the company's artistic director since 1996 and had frequently cast Glasco prominently in his ballets, including as recently as the fall of 1998, when the company made a long-awaited return to New York City, presenting mostly Kudelka ballets, which Glasco had performed to widespread critical acclaim.[16] But less than six weeks later, in a December 1 meeting in his office lasting all of five minutes, Kudelka abruptly informed Glasco that her services were no longer needed.[17]

Kudelka told Glasco that he would not be renewing her three-year contract when it expired at the end of June. Until then, for the remainder of the season, he would cast her in nothing save one performance of *Manon*, a ballet about an eighteenth-century Paris courtesan, which she would dance in April in Montreal, far from her devoted fan base in Toronto. It would be her final performance.

Kudelka had given Glasco six months' notice as required by the company's collective agreement, but she felt he had fired

her without cause. Soon after that meeting, she launched a lawsuit for wrongful dismissal, which seized the attention of the
ballet world. Ballerinas rarely complain about their employers or their working conditions; they seem almost incapable of
speaking out against abusive practices within their profession,
let alone contemplating litigation. This is what makes Glasco
noteworthy: she represents a rare example of a ballerina who
staged a rebellion in the name of justice.

That she is remarkable in this respect is borne out by the
fact that, throughout ballet history and continuing to today,
there is scant evidence of ballerinas ever fighting back against
exploitation within the art form. There's even less evidence of
ballerinas fighting back successfully.

Star Bolshoi ballerina Anastasia Volochkova was twenty-
seven when she was fired in September 2003 for failing to
sign a reduced contract; management had said she was too big
for her partners to carry. The highly publicized contract dispute attracted the attention of Russia's Labor Ministry and
its Culture Ministry, generating a turf war between the two
authorities over the dancer's body and rights.[18] Even though
she was eventually reinstated to the Bolshoi in November
2003, and paid an estimated $9,000 in lost wages, Volochkova
was not given roles and had to leave the company to find work
elsewhere.[19]

Vienna State Opera soloist Karina Sarkissova was also
twenty-seven when she lost her job in 2010 for appearing
nude in the Austrian men's magazine Wiener and in Penthouse.[20]
The Sarkissova case illustrates how ballerinas, even today, are
subject to a higher moral standard than that applied to other
women. She fought to get her job back and won when she was
able to show that her artistic director, Manuel Legris, had himself posed nude for a series of erotic photographs involving

both men and women that were published in books in the 1980s while he was a star dancer with the Paris Opéra Ballet.[21] Sarkissova fought her case in the court of public opinion in the form of an open letter published in the local press rather than through the judicial system. She got her job back after successfully showing that the Vienna State Opera, and to some extent Viennese society, had been guilty of naked prejudice by having automatically sided with the male artistic director over the female ballet dancer.

Barbara Moore was fired from her position as principal dancer of the Alberta Ballet shortly after having a baby in 2000, at age thirty-two. Then director Mikko Nissinen said the reason was not because she left ballet to have a child but because he did not think she suited his vision for the company. After she launched a lawsuit, Moore and the Alberta Ballet reached a financial settlement through mediation, the terms of which were never disclosed. After Nissinen left the company to take over the Boston Ballet in October 2002, his successor, Jean Grand-Maître, invited Moore back to the company as a coach, a job she performed briefly before leaving to have a second child. She never danced professionally again.

By comparison, Glasco's case is unique. She did not wage her battle quietly behind the scenes, as Moore had done, but publicly, in the courts. In suing her employer, the National Ballet of Canada, Glasco launched a celebrated legal battle, which yielded a series of unprecedented legal successes. For eighteen intense months, from December 1998 to July 2000, she was the world's most controversial ballerina, with the eyes of her profession keenly fixed upon her. She was fighting for her rights against a company that, in an attempt to belittle her, called her an aging ballerina who couldn't accept the inevitable: "I don't think her work was as strong lately," said Kudelka in a newspaper interview, hitting the ballerina where it would hurt most. "Dancers want to dance forever, and I don't think that they can."[22]

In Canada in 2005, dancers were still close to the bottom of the pay scale for professional artists, earning a median employment income of $19,767, down from the $26,912 reported in 2000, according to the most recent census data compiled by Statistics Canada.[23] In the United States, the situation is similar: full-time dancers had a median income of $25,000 in 1999, based on the most recently available national data from the Census Bureau.[24] Salaries can vary. According to the Canadian Ballet Agreement with the National Ballet of Canada, 2010–2013, weekly incomes can range from $884 for a member of the corps de ballet to $1,362 for a principal dancer. Not all dancers are paid a fifty-two-week salary, however, causing annual incomes to fluctuate greatly. Only principal dancers and dancers with more than a six-year association with the company qualify for a yearly salary. Those with fewer than six years have unpaid leaves from the company, mostly during the summer months. Glasco was one of the highest paid dancers of her day, having successfully negotiated her own contract above scale. Kudelka made an issue of her earning as much as she did. In the same interview, Kudelka also criticized Glasco's annual salary, which, at around $96,000, was far above the industry average for ballerinas. Kudelka said that Glasco didn't merit the cost. She was a classically trained ballerina excelling in tutu roles; as such, Kudelka claimed that she was something of an anachronism, incapable of moving with the times: "I just wish people [meaning Glasco] would be more realistic about the fact the world is changing," he said.

Kudelka's stated plan was to replace Glasco with four younger dancers at $24,000 apiece for the cheaper-by-the-dozen corps de ballet; Kudelka would also terminate four other senior dancers who, like Glasco, drew high salaries; their names were not disclosed. His objective, he added, was the creation of a new generation of National Ballet dancers who could dance every ballet in the National's mixed repertoire, particularly his own contemporary works. Except, and it should be noted, Glasco was a versatile artist. She danced classic and contemporary ballets, including Kudelka's own. A few weeks before her firing, in fact, she had received glowing reviews for performing his work, in which he had personally cast her, during an important company tour to New York City.

Chief among them was his new version of *Swan Lake*, with sets and costumes by frequent collaborator Santo Loquasto, which Kudelka was eager to unveil for the upcoming 1999/2000 season. The budget for the ballet had been set at an estimated $1.75 million, an exorbitant sum for a company then struggling with a $3-million deficit, the highest incurred by the National during its then forty-eight-year history.

At the time, morale was at an all-time low, as Glasco well knew. In 1997, her peers had elected her as one of two representatives authorized to speak on behalf of her fellow dancers at National Ballet board meetings, and in that capacity she suggested the dancers were increasingly losing confidence in the company as a result of dwindling finances.[25] The chief problem was reduced wages for more work. As a cost-saving measure, management was proposing to reduce the dancers' paid work weeks to thirty from fifty-two, essentially laying them off for five and a half months without pay. This the dancers, as a whole, found unacceptable.

Glasco made more money than the majority of her colleagues and so wasn't herself at risk of financial ruin should the National Ballet start laying off dancers; her concern was for colleagues who would suffer if their salaries were cut. She presented their concerns about wages and the terms of their employment in two Dancers' Reports the board requested from her in 1997—the first in May, the second in June. During these meetings, she openly questioned the financial cost of mounting a new, expensive production of *Swan Lake*, positioning it as a gross misplacement of priorities that would result in reducing dancers' wages. Glasco cited the example of Kudelka's relatively new 1997 version of *The Nutcracker*, which had cost the company close to $2 million, but which in its first season had resulted in a $560,000 loss.[26] Besides, the company already had a *Swan Lake* in its repertoire as staged by Bruhn, which it had been performing for years and to critical acclaim—it wasn't broken so it didn't need fixing. In any event, Glasco said that dancers' salaries shouldn't be sacrificed for company expenditures on new, even superfluous, ballets at a time of severe belt tightening. She pleaded for fiscal responsibility, pointing out that the orchestra represented a larger percentage of the payroll than did the dancers, so why did they have to take the fall?

Glasco appears to have had an impact. The board decided that as a result of losses sustained by *The Nutcracker*, all future new productions would have to be self-financed, their budgets secured separately from regular fundraising efforts. Kudelka threatened to quit as artistic director if he didn't get his ballet, and the board reversed its decision.

Even though he ultimately got his way—the ballet would have its world premiere in May 1999—Kudelka was obviously smarting from having to fight for what he considered his right to plan ballets as he pleased—but especially *Swan Lake*, which he had been contemplating for three years prior to the Glasco fiasco, as the ensuing melee came to be known.[27] When he summoned Glasco to his office in December 1998, following yet another October board meeting at which the budget for *Swan Lake* had again been on the agenda, he made his feelings clear. He fired her, telling Glasco that her lack of support for his ballet showed that she did not support him as artistic director.

Kudelka had delivered a death sentence, but Glasco refused to simply fade away like Giselle or any of the other frail heroines from the nineteenth-century ballets for which she was internationally known. Uncharacteristically for a ballerina, Glasco fought back. She filed an unfair labor practice complaint with the Ontario Labour Relations Board, claiming reprisals as a result of her advocacy work on behalf of other dancers, and took her case to arbitration, hiring one of the country's top lawyers to represent her.[28] Glasco also sued in the courts for libel and slander (the National Ballet had publicly called her "deadwood" and repeatedly insinuated that she was a liar) and filed a complaint with the Ontario Human Rights Commission alleging age discrimination.

At thirty-eight, Glasco was considered old for a working ballerina. But there were plenty of examples of ballerinas who had successfully defied the odds: Margot Fonteyn at the Royal Ballet danced until age fifty-nine; the enormously gifted Soviet ballerina Ekaterina Maximova, a Bolshoi alumna married to the male dancer Vladimir Vassiliev, danced until she was sixty; the Italian-born Alessandra Ferri retired in 2007 at age forty-four; in 2010, illustrious French ballerina Sylvie Guillem was still on her toes at the ripe age of forty-six. The National Ballet of Canada's history also includes senior ballerinas of its own, among them Karen Kain, one of her country's most popular dancers, who retired from dancing in 1997 at the age of forty-six; Kain's former colleague and fellow principal dancer Veronica Tennant danced until she was forty-one, quitting the stage in 1989. Glasco was young in comparison with some of these ballerina stalwarts; she felt she had many good years left in her. Even her coaches and teachers thought so, among them fabled Canadian ballet mistress Betty Oliphant: "I think that Kim has many more years of dancing," the founder of the National Ballet School said in an interview at the time of Glasco's dismissal. "She is a fine classical dancer who has also danced well in contemporary ballets. For me she is one of the superb artists of her generation."[29]

The issue at hand was really the right of a ballet dancer to speak out about working conditions. But the National Ballet deftly shifted the focus to the role of the artistic director in the twenty-first century, which suddenly became the all-important issue.

The National's lawyers argued before the courts that the very future of ballet itself depended on artistic directors having ultimate authority over a company and its dancers; there could only ever be one authority in ballet, and it belonged to the person at the top of its hierarchy, hurt feelings be damned. "I can only quote Nureyev," said National Ballet of Canada founder Celia Franca who had publicly thrown her weight behind Kudelka. "'Celia! Ballet must be autocrat!' There has to be one person. The artistic director is the one who has to make the choice and take the blame. You can't have a democracy in a ballet company."[30]

Pending a full hearing of the merits of the case, Glasco's lawyers had applied to the arbitrator for interim reinstatement, arguing that a ballerina prevented from dancing for any length of time risked losing her artistic skills, reputation, and even identity. Glasco by this time had turned thirty-nine and didn't have many years left to dance. She couldn't move to a new company because the National Ballet had effectively seen to it that no one would hire her; Kudelka himself had publicly declared her as a ballerina past her best-before date.[31] "There was no way I could go to another company and find work elsewhere," says Glasco. "I was labeled a troublemaker. I was regarded as the bull in the china shop that is ballet. But I wasn't. I was just the mouse that squeaked."[32] Much legal wrangling ensued, and although Kudelka was ultimately required by the arbitrator to take the ballerina back, he steadfastly refused.

The case held the nation riveted; ballerinas were suddenly being talked about in ways they hadn't been since the nineteenth century, when society was glued to their every move, both on and offstage. The Glasco story amply demonstrated that there seemed no limit to the public's fascination with the backstage realities underlying the ballerina's idealized image. The case did feel curiously old-fashioned, especially with regard to the national debate involving the rights of the ballerina versus the role of the artistic director. Glasco was the underdog, the David fighting the Goliath of not just a government-funded cultural institution but also an art form with a history of female oppression committed in the name of art. For that, she should have been celebrated. But a great many observers saw fit to chastise her for not knowing her place. A headline on a story about Glasco at the time referred to her as "an uppity ballerina."[33]

Her behavior, not her grievance, was frequently commented on, the expectation apparently being that ballerinas are supposed to remain as mute and malleable as they were in the Romantic era, no matter what abuses they might be suffering in the workplace. Glasco was accused of lacking class, as if by fighting for her rights she had somehow violated the ballerina's unspoken code of displaying courtly manners at all times. "Anyway, she shouldn't have done that. I mean who's going to keep somebody in the company who is a nuisance?" said Franca of Glasco at the time. "It has nothing to do with how old you are—38 years of age is okay, and you can go on. Now, I don't know what's going to happen to Kim Glasco, because I don't think she's been using her head. I mean, what a silly thing, to publicly go against your boss. If you don't like the job you're in, then get out and get a new one. I don't think any dancer should expect to change the direction of a company."[34]

This, then, became the issue: the insistence of artistic directors that they have autocratic powers and should not be held accountable to the law. The expectation that they, like everyone else in society, be subject to labor and human rights laws that prohibit discrimination based on freedom of association, as much as discrimination based on sex, race, creed, or color, was anathema to them. That Glasco might have been fired for non-artistic reasons seemed, to them, to be beside the point. Her cries of injustice were drowned out by the self-righteous outrage of artistic elites who wanted to maintain the despotic rule of artistic directors at all costs, even if that meant terminating a dancer without cause.

But it wasn't so much art itself that the artistic directors and their vocal supporters wanted to defend; it was an antiquated mindset. Astonishing for a group calling itself artistic was their utter lack of open-mindedness on this count. They wanted the arts to be run as they always had, with little regard for employees' rights. Glasco, the one in the starchy old tutu and a tiara on her head, was herself advocating for reform. In asking that the ballerina, for once, be respected as a working woman with rights in addition to significant talents, she was moving with the times and faster than those lining up to oppose her, despite Kudelka's claims to the contrary.

Yet, Glasco had her supporters. Her fans rallied to create a national booster club, the Bring Back Kimberly Glasco Network, spearheaded by ballerina Svea Eklof, formerly a principal dancer with the Royal Winnipeg Ballet, the Alberta Ballet, and the Ballet du Grand Théâtre de Genève, together with Julie Houle, formerly a soloist with the National Ballet of Canada. Their view, shared by the network's approximately five hundred supporters, was that ballerinas were vulnerable to exploitation and entitled to the protection of labor and human rights laws governing the rest of society.

Vanessa Harwood was a top-notch ballerina who had performed with the National Ballet as a principal dancer from the 1970s until her retirement from the stage in 1985 at age thirty-eight, and she had been handpicked by Rudolf Nureyev as one of his dancing partners and also by photographer André Kertesz as one of his subjects. She drew attention to the role played by senior ballerinas like Glasco in maintaining the high standards of the art form. "First of all, I am glad that someone in ballet is finally earning a decent living. I never did," Harwood said, referring to Glasco's higher-than-average salary, which had been negotiated by the company just three years earlier in an effort to keep her from straying into the arms of another, more international, ballet troupe. "And second, you can bring in lots of apprentices at $200 a week, but when an audience is paying $75 a ticket, they don't want to see children, they want to see artists. If you want to see children, go to the National Ballet School. The tickets are a lot cheaper and the performances quite fine."[35]

Lois Gochnauer, a former National Ballet dancer who had gone on to serve as senior advisor on violence against women in the U.S. State Department, took a broader feminist perspective; she described what was happening to Glasco as a form of abuse: "I don't know about in Canada, but in the U.S. there are laws preventing an employer from terminating a woman from her place of employment because of age. It's discrimination against women."[36] (Mandatory retirement has since been abolished in Canada.)

The negativity surrounding the ballet was getting to be too much to bear. The National Ballet went to the courts and arbitration five times and with four different sets of lawyers and lost on every occasion.[37] It was time to throw in the towel. On July 20, 2000, the case was settled. Glasco was given a substantial monetary settlement, said to be worth $1.6 million, in exchange for waiving her right to return to the National Ballet. The company's insurers, American Home Assurance Co. and Chubb Insurance Co., picked up the tab and also paid the legal bills, said to be in excess of $1 million. The National Ballet issued a press release that read like a formal apology for wrongs done Glasco by management:[38]

> Ms. Glasco is an outstanding ballerina in both classical and contemporary ballets who has many years left in her career as a principal dancer. She is a widely acclaimed artist of unique abilities who has performed a broad range of ballets and will continue to do so in the future. Neither the National Ballet's original decision not to renew Ms. Glasco's contract nor any subsequent public statements regarding the matter by the Ballet's representatives were intended to reflect in any way on Ms. Glasco's fine qualities as a dancer. The National Ballet regrets any adverse effects caused to Ms. Glasco.[39]

Glasco had won, and won big. But she did not go back to the stage, and for her supporters that made the victory bittersweet. Glasco had decided of her own volition not to return. She said later that she feared an adverse reaction from her peers if she returned. Indeed, some of her colleagues had gone public about wanting to distance themselves from her: "We tried to close ranks and protect her at first," said principal dancer Jennifer Fournier in an interview at the time. "We didn't want to hurt her. But now this has gotten to the point where it is doing serious damage to the company and to relations between the dancers."[40] Few, it seems, can tolerate an outspoken ballerina.

But although her fellow dancers showed little appreciation for her efforts on their behalf, the arbitrator's decision, which was subsequently upheld by the courts, established an important precedent: the right of a dismissed ballerina, where dismissal is based on non-artistic reasons, to reinstatement as well as damages.

But not all ballerinas have been willing to take advantage of the precedent, fearing reprisals. Andrea Boardman, a long-time principal dancer with Montreal's Les Grands Ballets Canadiens, was forcibly removed from her position by company director Gradimir Pankov around the same time that Glasco lost her job. Like Glasco, she was thirty-eight and had been with her company for twenty years. A popular dancer, Boardman wasn't ready to retire and was crushed when her director made the decision for her. Friends within the company urged her to fight for her job as Glasco had done, but Boardman thought other-wise: "I did not want to split the company and force people to take sides," she said in a 2001 interview, presumably taking a swipe at Glasco in the fashion typical of dancers as a vulnerable, oppressed, and victimized class of women. "I have no patience with the diva mentality."[41] Boardman went on to have a second career dancing in Montreal choreographer Edouard Lock's La La La Human Steps troupe. Lock had come to her after he heard of her split from Les Grands Ballets, eager to work with a dancer with a dynamic stage presence. Displeasing one director, she had been banished; pleasing another, she was brought back into the fold.

It all goes to show just how subjective and arbitrary ballet can be.

Here are two more examples. In 1988, then directors of the National Ballet of Canada, Valerie Wilder and Lynn Wallis, fired American-born soloist Summer Lee Rhatigan for having a tall, big-boned, and muscular body, saying her look was no longer in line with their vision for the company. Rhatigan eventually moved on to the English National Ballet, among other companies, where how her body looked was never a problem but rather a plus. She later became director of the San Francisco Conservatory of Dance, never having lost her love of dance. Sometimes the sting of body criticism can be mitigated when both sides—director and dancer—are able to reach a mutually satisfactory plan for handling a perceived problem. This is the case of Morgann Rose, a naturally muscular ballerina with the Washington Ballet whose athletic shape has frequently brought her into conflict with her artistic director. "I've been with Washington Ballet 10 years and every year we've had a conversation about my body," she said.[42] Those conversations, she continued, usually ended up with her being told to "lean up" or "lose five pounds." Frustrated, she eventually sat down with her director to determine a plan of action. By asking specific questions—and demanding clear-cut answers— she discovered that, in fact, he didn't want her to be thinner; he wanted her muscles to look lengthened so that she'd fit in with the rest of the women in her troupe. Rose then came up with a workable solution that not only safeguarded her career but saw her advancing to perform lead roles in company programs as recently as March 2012. "Lean and lengthen are different," she said. "Lean means lose weight; lengthen means lengthen—and I can totally do that. You can do certain exercises and hold your upper body in a way that will help change the look and line of your muscle."

These are ballerina stories with happy endings, mainly, it seems, because these dancers kept quiet about the injustices they were enduring in the workplace, ensuring for themselves a future in dance. Because, like it or not, ballerinas who do speak out are ostracized. It isn't fair, and it shouldn't happen,

but it does. Repeatedly. A recent case involves Italian-born ballerina Mariafrancesca Garritano, who was fired from La Scala
in Milan in February 2012 for publicly claiming that her company, and its school affiliate, coerced dancers into severe eating
disorders like anorexia and bulimia in pursuit of an unattainable female ideal. Speaking to the British paper the *Observer* in
December 2011, the thirty-three-year-old ballerina told stories
of fellow dancers being rushed to hospital to have food forced
into them and of others who had become infertile, as a result
of unnaturally low body weights, and who were depressed. She
described the ballet world as "an anorexic emergency" that has
already claimed many lives.[43] Garritano cited statistics, saying
seven in ten dancers at the La Scala Academy in Milan have
had their menstrual cycles stop, one in five have anorexia, and
many are unable to have children. She also said she had lost
her period between the ages of sixteen and seventeen, when
she had dropped below ninety-five pounds, and added that
the bone fractures and intestinal pain she currently suffers is
a result of the strict dieting she imposed on herself as a young
dancer following the dictates of her profession. Her teachers
had called her "Mozzarella" and "Chinese dumpling" when she
was a plump adolescent. She starved herself as a result, hoping to gain their approval. Other girls, she said, would resort to
breast reduction operations to keep their slim frames: "They're
crazy," Garritano added, "I am a woman first, then a ballerina."

Garritano was speaking as part of an interview for a book she
had just written called, appropriately enough, *La verità, vi prego,
sulla danza!* (The Truth, Please, About Ballet!). For that she got
herself terminated; La Scala accused her of willfully damaging
its brand.

The initial story positioned her as a well-intentioned
whistle-blower: "The chance of getting fired has crossed my
mind, but I love La Scala, I care about it, and that's why I really

hope things can change."[44] But others in the blogosphere have been quick to lambaste the dancer for breaking ballet's code of silence, accusing her of working out a personal issue and, worse, biting the hand that feeds her. Garritano's supporters, however, say that she is telling the truth: ballet has a long history of eating disorders and she should not have been fired without an investigation.

But the point is that skinny is already well out of the closet. It's no longer ballet's dirty little secret. Ballet companies have started recognizing the widespread problem of eating disorders within their ranks. The goal for many now is to eradicate eating disorders from the ballet world, as announced by Canada's National Ballet School, a forerunner of the trend. Even La Scala says it's changed, claiming that the rampant eating disorders Garritano describes are a thing of the past. Garritano's own experience with anorexia nervosa, it adds, happened fifteen years ago, when ballet was still enslaved to a skinny ideal. "Management at the dance corps completely changed six years ago," said a theater spokesman.[45]

The culture *has* changed, artistic directors and dancers finally agree. Endorsing this view are other ballerinas, Garritano's dancer colleagues, who are speaking up, issuing collective statements that they resent being depicted as victims: "There is no anorexia emergency, and whoever is part of our world knows that well."[46]

How true a statement that is will be explored in the next chapter. In addition to being recognized as workers, ballerinas today increasingly want it known that their art is also something more than a job. As the British sociologists Bryan Turner and Steven Wainwright have written in their study of the corps de ballet, the ballet company "is more than a site of work...[it is] a calling rather than an occupation...designed to produce a distinctive 'personality' or self."[47] Ballet, in other words, is not just something you do; it is what you are. Whether they are primas or members of the corps de ballet, ballerinas seek acknowledgement that they are whole persons, and women, too, with a variety of attributes and desires. They want increased autonomy within their profession, even if, reluctantly, ballet is acquiescing to their demands, dancing with them into the future.

6

CHANGES AFOOT
THE BALLERINA
OF THE FUTURE

BALLERINAS TODAY ARE healthier than they used to be, as a result of a growing awareness of what the body needs to function at optimum levels of athletic performance. Enlightened directors and teachers of ballet are developing a new generation of curvier ballerinas in the understanding that scrawny dancers are weak dancers, unable to keep up with the accelerated pace and heightened athleticism of today's ballets.

Ballerinas of the twenty-first century tend to be more muscular and less emaciated than they have been in the recent past. Anorexic chic is no longer in vogue. "Bodies are more athletic looking and more womanly, shapely with curves as a result of muscle mass," says Beverly Bagg, the South African ballerina now employed as the ballet mistress for Canada's Alberta Ballet. "The technical demands are such that a ballerina today can't be thin anymore; she has to have muscle mass in order to facilitate performing to the new athletic standard. She can't fulfill her obligations as a dancer if she doesn't have the power. That's why holistic training is important; it creates a more capable instrument, a more empowered dancer."[1]

Joysanne Sidimus has staged ballets all over the world. Over the last forty years she has personally witnessed the ballet evolve into a more responsible and socially aware endeavor, repositioning ballerinas' needs closer to the center of the art: "We've come a long way, baby," Sidimus says. "I am not saying that anorexia no longer exists—you and I know that it does— but companies just aren't allowing it, anymore. If there are dancers who are overly anorexic they are encouraged to get help, leave until they can get it together again. And the schools are changing: they now have psychiatrists, social workers, nutritionists—the works—on staff, teaching young dancers what it means to be healthy and helping them stay that way. It really is a different world."[2]

American-born Svea Eklof, who danced with the Royal Winnipeg Ballet, today coaches young dancers at Toronto's George Brown College, a feeder school for Ballet Jörgen in Toronto. She concurs that the culture is changing—and ballerinas along with it. "There are extreme regulations in place," Eklof says. "In dance schools in the United States a teacher can't even say the word *weight*. It's not allowed. It's a result of an attitude change, I think. People have begun to understand that girls between fifteen and eighteen are at the heaviest period of their lives because of hormonal changes within their own bodies. They have to have a little plumpness in order to grow into women. So that's better understood now, and I think that's good for the art form as a whole."[3]

The dancers now being created as a result of this shift in focus "are not sticks anymore," Eklof continues. "Lean and mean is now seen as better than thin and frail and constantly having stress fractures. It also makes better sense for the art form as well as companies worried about their bottom line. If you have dancers unable to dance because they get injured all the time as a result of brittle bones caused by poor nutrition then you can't operate your business. So the thinking today is more take better care of the talent and the talent will take care of you, which is a good thing, of course, all around."

To keep up with the growing demands of their profession, ballerinas today have to take better care of their bodies. It is no longer acceptable, or prudent, to abuse them, as in the second half of the twentieth century, when eating disorders and substance abuse among ballet dancers were on the rise. The new generation of ballerinas shows sinew, not bone. Some, like the Royal Ballet's Tamara Rojo and the New York City Ballet's Sara Mearns, to name just two new contemporary dancers making a name for themselves, show rounded hips and breasts. It's a brave new look, and Mearns says it's a sign of empowerment. "I think that ballerinas today are going from strength to strength."[4]

But for every giant step forward, ballet takes two steps back.

In December 2010, the *New York Times* dance critic, Alastair Macaulay, in his review of the New York City Ballet's annual performance of *The Nutcracker*, took umbrage that the lead ballerina was fleshier than the ballerinas he had been used to seeing in his many decades as a seasoned dance observer. In print, he accused the ballerina dancing the role of Sugar Plum Fairy as having eaten one sugarplum too many, a cheap shot ostensibly meant to shame the dancer for having veered away from the skinny norm.[5] Jenifer Ringer, the ballerina in question, a working mom, had, in fact, been battling an eating disorder for years; her curvier body was a result of her having shucked old and dangerous eating habits in favor of new, healthier ones. The critic's jibes could have set her back. But it was a sign of the times that her public rushed to her defense, writing letters of protest to the paper and clogging the blogosphere with complaints about ballet's tyranny of thin. It was evidence that the public was all for a curvier, healthier aesthetic. Ringer showed herself to be equally in step with the times, appearing unfazed by the negative scrutiny of her body; she knew it to be an antiquated mindset, a relic of ballet past without relevance or currency. Ringer told Ann Curry on the *Today Show* that ballet no longer felt a need to demand and reward thinness: "If you are too thin really you can't do the job," she said with poise and aplomb. "You're weak. You can't do the job. You can't perform it well."[6]

Helping the ballerina perform well—and stay healthy—is science. It might seem a strange dance partner for her to have, but, as Jeffrey Russell, an assistant professor of dance medicine at the University of California, Irvine, points out, without science, ballet couldn't exist: "Without the physics of muscular force there would be no movement, without biochemistry there would be no muscular activity; you need food to create the energy needed for your body to perform as a dancer. If you take science away, you've taken away life itself."[7]

At the dance research lab he has been operating out of the university's engineering wing since 2010, Russell applies these rudimentary scientific principles to enhancing the life of ballet dancers as experienced on the stage. The aim, he says, is "to develop dancers to be better at what they do." Although his clinic cares for dancers hurt as a result of their jobs, the primary focus is on injury prevention. "It's a lot easier to maintain something than it is to fix it," he says, using the analogy of a car, which runs better if it gets regular lube jobs instead of being driven into the ground. "When it breaks down, it's harder to get it moving again. So it's better to anticipate the problems than let them happen in the first place."

Russell views injuries as the biggest problem plaguing ballet as a career choice. "That must mean something is wrong," he says. As is often the case, it takes an outsider to question what, to the initiated, has become accepted practice. "So let's study what's going wrong so we can reduce the number of injuries that come as a result of a dancing career."

Russell works with a research group of eighteen students, and he isn't the first health practitioner to devote his energies to helping ballet dancers. Many professional dance companies today are staffed with physiotherapists and other health-care workers who help ballet dancers stay in optimum condition. Russell cites the New York City Ballet, the San Francisco Ballet, the Mariinsky (or Kirov) Ballet, the Alvin Ailey American Dance Theater, and the Birmingham Royal Ballet in England as companies where dance medicine is practiced. But Russell is the only dance scientist he knows of working within a university setting, alongside community-based dance programming. At UCI, there are over two hundred fledgling ballet dancers, and they constitute Russell's main area of study. But his reach also extends into the community; he uses Twitter to advertise his particular area of expertise. He's a New World doctor working to help an Old World profession keep in step with the times. Why hadn't anyone thought of it before? "By and large, people don't consider dancers as athletes," Russell says. "There is a complete lack of understanding among the general population about what ballet dancers do. People look at them up on the stage and don't see the effort. They seem beautiful and not really working hard. Dance isn't in people's consciousness the same way that professional sport is. The rigors of what they do and the injuries they sustain just aren't that well publicized."

Russell owes his unique perspective on ballet to not having a dance background. He is, by profession, a certified athletic trainer, one of those guys seen running to help an injured football player on prime-time TV. He was working in a sports medicine clinic at Mississippi's Belhaven College, tending to injured basketball and football players, when a slip of a dancer came in among the jocks desperately seeking his help for a damaged Achilles tendon. He had never treated a ballerina before, but he brought her back to full functioning after a series of therapeutic treatments, including body-strengthening exercises. She told her friends, and soon one ballerina turned into a trickle that became a flood of dancers, all seeking his help. They were mostly young people, community as opposed to professionally trained, left to fend for themselves. Their bodies were a mess, and many weren't even out of their teens. Their plight inspired him to switch professions. He moved to England to pursue a PhD in dance medicine, which he received in 2008.

Russell did his thesis on the wearing of pointe shoes by ballerinas, specifically the cruel damage they inflict, including tendon damage and sprained ankles. At the forefront of dance science, Russell developed an MRI method for evaluating the ankles of female ballet dancers standing on their toes. The scans shed light on the weight-bearing anatomy of female dancers, affording doctors and scientists a rare glimpse at how pointe shoes impact bones, joints, and soft tissue.[8] Together with scientists in England, Russell analyzed the images, comparing them to dancers' own descriptions of their pain. "I wanted to know the demands of ballet on the ankle and the foot. What are the stresses imposed by the pointe shoe?" It was a breakthrough study, which not only showed "how the musculoskeletal system responds to dance" but also furthered "progress toward the ultimate goal of reducing injuries."[9]

"After examining the MRIs of ballerinas, I can tell you that dancing on pointe is not at all good for the ankle," Russell says. "But the pointe shoe is not going to go away. It would alter the art of the ballerina far too much. So what we can do is help dancers dance to the best of their ability within the confines of ballet and not be sidelined by injury."[10]

It's a radical objective—and also a tricky one. Ballet dancers are slow to give up past practices; their art form is rooted in tradition. Ballet history is passed down from one generation of dancer to another, thereby maintaining its classical lineage. But there is an unforeseen problem with older-generation dancers teaching their successors how to perform ballet as they once practiced it; their instruction often comes encased in bad habits that help perpetuate ballet as an injury-prone profession.

"There's an old-school line of thinking that physical training will ruin the ballet aesthetic," Russell says. "In terms of generations, we're still in a situation where the ones teaching the younger dancers are those who came through a system where there wasn't much being offered in the way of physical training or even healthy dance practices. In their day, you just did what you did, and if you got hurt, tough. It really comes down to you teach what you know, and if that includes suffering for your art then that's what's also being passed down. It will take a major paradigm shift for the average ballet teacher to want to teach ballet in a different way."

In other words, what often needs fixing most is a mindset. Besides dance teachers, Russell's biggest challenge remains convincing dancers to set aside time for strengthening and conditioning exercises that will help lessen the number of injuries they sustain in the course of their work. "There are only twenty-four hours in a day, and I understand that for a lot of dancers carving out time to do cross-training isn't a priority. The typical dancer is going to spend the bulk of that day perfecting the craft."

But reducing the amount of time given over to technical training in favor of core physical training actually does result in making dancers better artists. Heightened technical achievement in dancers can now be proven to be directly related to a stronger physical foundation. But that's just the tip of the pointe shoe, so to speak. Russell says more needs to be done to help ballerinas of the future become even stronger as artists and more gifted as athletes. "We're about twenty years behind sports medicine," Russell says. "In terms of research, we're still a number of years away from saying this is what we think is useful. And it will still be a difficult thing to get across to people used to working in the old way, especially because ballet has traditionally not been an area attended to by science. So it's tough. But I'm going to stick with it. It's my calling. I do see that I am making a difference. I think I am helping the ballerinas of the future."

It is a clarion call also to companies to make it their mandate to safeguard the art of ballet for future generations. It starts with a shift in perception, seeing the ballerina not as a slave to her art but as a valuable employee within the juggernaut of the professional ballet company. Such is the thinking of an enlightened troupe like the Australian Ballet. There, ballerinas are perceived as elite athletes and are treated as such.

In 2007, the Australian Ballet implemented a company-wide Injury Management and Prevention Programme aimed directly at dancers' health. The program came about as a result of ballet culture as a whole becoming more aware of medico-legal and liability issues.[11] According to the company's published mission statement, the aim is to do away with the days when ballerinas would bleed into their pointe shoes and no one would care, replacing a culture known for its abuse and neglect of dancers with one that sincerely cares about their overall health and well-being: "The Australian Ballet is committed to the health (physical and psychological) and safety of its most precious asset, the dancers. This commitment stems from the Board and extends to all levels of the company. The Australian Ballet has facilitated a change in behavior over the years, which has directly influenced the culture from one that poses a high risk to health to one that embodies health and wellbeing. As a result, the company has experienced fewer injuries, dancers are recovering faster and morale has increased."[12] Management regularly counsels dancers that injuries are not to be swept under the carpet or ignored for fear of reprisals. This concern for dancers' health is written into the company's policy: "The Australian Ballet has demonstrated to the dancers that reporting injuries does not disadvantage them in any way; on the contrary, everything is done to ensure that dancers are not restricted from their pre-injury status."[13]

But it's a two-way relationship, says Australian Ballet artistic director David McAllister, a former principal dancer with the company: "I see it very much as a shared responsibility. We have tried to build a culture within the company where the dancers are proactive about injury prevention and report any niggles early so we can treat them and avoid long-term periods away from the stage," he says. "We have also built a great collaboration between the medical and artistic teams so we have shared responsibility about workload for dancers, so that we can keep them dancing but modify their load to avoid progressing to a major injury. But you can only do this with dancers who present early and don't hide injury. They also need to make sure they are doing all the strengthening and technical coaching work and take responsibility of their own bodies; otherwise you will only be able to patch up."[14]

The Australian Ballet takes a multidisciplinary approach to injury prevention; in the wings, at the ready, is a kind of Team Ballet, composed of various physiotherapists, myotherapists, masseurs, sports doctors, rehabilitation facilitators, body conditioning specialists, psychologists, and alternative medicine practitioners doing needling and other forms of acupuncture, devoted to ensuring that all dancers are performing at peak condition. Addressing dancers' needs extends also to ordering special pointe shoes for a ballerina whose feet might be vulnerable to tendinitis or stress fractures.[15] Great care is taken to ensure that they have healthy and strong bodies, a balanced diet, and sound nutrition. Dancers are also encouraged to have open communication with management in discussing their needs and concerns.

Principal dancer Amber Scott credits the open-door policy and the access to pertinent scientific knowledge as enabling her to have a long and rewarding profession: "It's a grand statement but I believe the medical team and body conditioning programs at the Australian Ballet have been paramount in keeping me dancing professionally for the past eleven years," Scott says. "The combination of very specific treatment, body conditioning and coaching all unite in a way that educates the dancers to understand the capability of their bodies in a safe environment. The open channels of communication between all departments have been key for learning as much as possible from the medical team. This knowledge has taken away many of the fears I had about injuries. It has empowered me in my quest to maintain a long and healthy career."[16]

But even with injury prevention programs in place, accidents do and will happen. Ballerinas can pirouette into the orchestra pit, be hit by falling scenery, be dropped by their partners, or, as was common in the past, catch fire. They can also injure themselves from overuse and as a result of poor training or unsafe choreography. Injuries are worrisome because they can terminate a career before a dancer feels ready to quit. Claire Vince, a member of the National Ballet of Canada's corps de ballet from 1989 to 1992, had to stop dancing after only four years as a result of a deteriorating hip: "The cartilage on the right hip had worn out from repetitive use, " says the Australian-born Vince, who trained at England's Royal Ballet School. "Dancing was so painful for me at the end that I couldn't do *developpés*."[17] After moving back to Australia, she had hip replacement surgery. But before that, while still in Toronto, she had what she calls "a big operation on both ankles," to address os trigonum syndrome, a medical condition caused by repeated downward pointing of the toes, as is common in ballet. Surgeons had to remove excess bone from the back of Vince's ankles: "Effectively, I had to have the ankles broken, the bones removed, then go in plaster for six weeks," she says. It sounds horrific, but Vince is matter-of-fact about what she endured as a result of ballet, calling her injuries "a part of a dancer's natural term."[18]

Today pain free, Vince has a new career in public relations. But for most ballerinas, when the dancing stops, they often are at loose ends. They don't know what to do next. The pain that lingers lies within. The celebrated Canadian ballerina Evelyn Hart, formerly the prima ballerina of the Royal Winnipeg Ballet, has described the abrupt conclusion of a dancing career as a loss of identity, a loss of expression: "I feel I have no voice left."[19]

When Joysanne Sidimus stopped dancing in 1970, she plunged into a deep depression. "It was a terrible time," she says. "I went home to my mother's and went to bed for six months; I didn't get out of bed because I didn't have a reason: My whole life was falling apart."[20] Having experienced first-hand the pain and desperation endured by dancers forced to leave their professions because of illness, injury, or incompatibility with an artistic director, Sidimus soon inquired after some of her colleagues, to see how they were coping with the break from ballet. What she heard shocked her; fifteen of her former partners had committed suicide and another had been committed to the psychiatric ward at New York's Bellevue Hospital: "I wanted to do something."

In 1985, Sidimus founded the Dancer Transition Resource Centre, a forward-thinking facility in Toronto providing career counseling, legal and financial advice, grants, and other supports to dancers needing to regain their moorings after being cast adrift from the stage. Since its founding twenty-five years ago, the center has gone on to help more than ten thousand dancers move into second careers in academia, arts administration, medicine, law, graphic design, engineering, public relations, and real estate. One dancer who went through the center became a commercial pilot.

When it first opened, the center was radical for its time. "When we began, the issue was taboo for most dancers," Sidimus says. "To end a performing career was something most dancers feared and did not wish to discuss or face."[21]

The physical demands are so tough on the body and injuries in ballet are part of the job description. To withstand the wear and tear, a dancer needs youth on his or her side. The average age of retirement for ballet dancers today is twenty-nine. For modern dancers it is forty.

"More than any other professional, with perhaps the exception of athletes," Sidimus says, "dancers don't have a choice. Early retirement is built into the profession, and there's no way around it."[22] In general, Sidimus adds, dancers are forced to give up their careers at a time when most other professionals are just starting to take off in theirs: "As a psychologist who works with us at the Centre says, 'Dance is a downwardly mobile profession in an upwardly mobile society.'"[23]

David Tucker is a psychologist who worked closely with retired professional hockey players through the Phil Esposito Foundation in Toronto and served as a consultant to Sidimus when she was first establishing the Dancer Transition Centre. "The problem with professional athletes and dancers is that for all their lives they have been so focused on their careers, they don't know where to even begin looking for a new job," said Dr. Tucker at the time. "Often they feel desperate and will grab the first thing that comes along. It's important that they think these things through so as to save themselves perhaps even greater aggravation later on."[24]

The stigma is lessening, and Sidimus sees that as another sign that the ballet culture is changing in ways ultimately beneficial to the ballerina: "The whole subject is now out of the closet; people are now talking about it and they are doing something about it. If a dancer has a transition plan at the beginning of the career, knowing in advance that it is short, it takes some of the anxiety away. It helps dancers be better at what they do."[25]

Still, retirement for dancers is like death: a scary prospect. Aware that dancers are spooked by the prospect of letting go of the one thing they have trained their whole lives for, the center and its half dozen branch offices across Canada offer its dancer-clients the services of onsite psychologists, psychiatrists, and sociologists to help them through a time in their lives that can be quite disorienting.

Indeed, in ballet, as one dance writer has wryly noted, "There are few stories like that of Nora Kaye, one of the brightest stars of American Ballet Theatre, who reportedly celebrated the event by driving with her husband through the Black Forest of Germany, happily hurling her old pointe shoes through the window of their car."[26]

When Sidimus started investigating the post-dance lives of her former colleagues for her 1987 book, *Exchanges: Life After Dance*, a collection of interviews with dancers who have successfully moved on from the stage, she discovered instead that the majority were shell-shocked and destitute.[27] "Many of these people were founders of dance companies. They have the Order of Canada, and yet they have nothing to live on," Sidimus says. "There aren't hordes of them, but you would be shocked by the names."[28]

Evelyn Hart is a poignant example, as well as a reminder that more still needs to be done to safeguard the ballerinas of our time. Born in Ontario in 1956, she won the Gold Medal and the Certificate for Artistic Achievement at the International Ballet Competition held in Varna, Bulgaria, in 1980. During her years on the stage, from 1977 until her abrupt departure in 2006 as a result of arthritic ankles, Hart was internationally regarded as a consummate artist; in the 1980s, she toured Russia and other Eastern Bloc countries, where audiences and critics alike hailed her as one of the greatest Giselles of the twentieth century.

Her artistry had come at a great personal price. Hart made no secret of having approached ballet as an act of self-sacrifice; she starved herself to be what she perceived as an expression of balletic perfection and denied herself intimate relationships, including marriage. She spent most of her waking hours in the ballet studio, devoting every ounce of her being to perfecting her craft. Those who danced alongside her at the RWB during the 1980s still marvel at the single-mindedness with which Hart pursued her career, to the exclusion of everything else. "She was unique in her approach, almost neurotic but in a good sense of the word; her process didn't allow for anything else in her life," says Svea Eklof, who shared a dressing room with Hart when both were with the RWB. "She was known to say, 'You are not as deep into this [meaning ballet] as I am; that's why you took time off to have a husband and to have a baby.' She said it, and she meant it: She is the best dance artist that Canada has ever produced."[29]

But when the curtain came down on her final performance in 2006, Hart, then fifty, was suddenly unemployable. Although she was a recipient of the Order of Canada, she had no assets other than a highly disciplined body blessed with a rare degree of musicality. She tried acting but didn't have the articulation.[30] She applied for a job in a bridal salon, making and selling the fanciful headdresses that she used to craft as part of her onstage costume but was turned down for lack of experience.[31] Save for a handful of students who have come to her privately for coaching, Hart's own profession has been reluctant to hire her as teacher or coach; the perception within her industry is that Hart represents an old-school, tunnel-vision approach to ballet, which is contrary to the new emphasis on life-work balance that many of today's ballet institutions say they want to instill in their students. Certainly, to see Hart is to see a woman ravaged by her profession—thin, alone, and invisible in a crowd now that her dancing career has ended. This is an artist who, just years earlier, had full houses leaping to their feet, cheering and showering her with roses. That she has been so abandoned by her profession and by society is a great scandal. Had she lived in another era, her selfless devotion to ballet might have been lauded. But today, she is no doubt one of the dancers Sidimus is talking about: a jilted female not unlike Giselle, a ghost of her former self.

Sidimus says she has been lobbying for years to get funding for artists like Hart, dancers she calls "national treasures," urging Canada to provide for them in retirement as other countries have done for their senior dance artists. It would be respectful, at the very least, to create for ballerinas who have given their lives to their art the respect of a position worthy of their experience and training, a chair within a university dance program, for instance, where they could pass their artistry on to the next generation. Shunning dancers because they are old and put out to pasture is a shameful way for any nation to treat its artists. "There's something about a dancer in transition that is exceptionally difficult and painful and different from anyone else in transition," Sidimus says.[32]

Previously, the ideal in ballet was to pretend that you would keep on dancing until you dropped—as Anna Pavlova and Rudolf Nureyev did. While romantic, this image of the swooning dancer, shackled to the art, no longer cuts it in today's climate of economic restraint. "The average annual salary in Canada is still under $14,000 for a dancer," Sidimus says. "They can rarely put enough money aside to live on while they study something else for a second career."[33]

Sometimes a dancer has to leave dance because of an injury that never quite heals.

"In the past twenty years I've seen a lot of heartbroken people," former National Ballet of Canada dancer Karen Kain, now the company's artistic director, has said. "They had trained, almost killed themselves, given 150 per cent—and suddenly it was all over. There was nothing for them. I've seen nervous breakdowns when people's dreams were shattered. There were people who came into the company with me, and I've seen them fall apart."[34]

Leanne Simpson was one of those dancers, devastated when the dancing was over. The former ballerina with the Alberta Ballet and Les Grands Ballets Canadiens who quit dancing in 1988 said in an interview, "I was very depressed. After five months, I called the Transition Centre."

Through the center, Simpson received counseling and then went to university, where she chose a new career, teaching in an arts school. To help her, the center gave her grants that helped cover expenses for two years of her post-dance training. "I feel much better now," Simpson said. "I still miss performing, but I feel that I fit into the real world now."[35]

Mary Jago-Romeril sees many dancers like Simpson in her position as a national representative of the Dancer Transition Resource Centre, a position she has held since 2002. From her vantage point, she is able to see how dance has changed since she was a principal dancer with the National Ballet of Canada, from 1966 until her retirement from the stage at age thirty-eight in 1984. During her illustrious career, the British-born, Royal Ballet–schooled ballerina was celebrated as one of the Fabulous Five, a group of top-ranking female dancers, each of whom had been handpicked in the 1970s by guest artist Rudolf Nureyev to dance as his partner in his extravagant and costly version of *The Sleeping Beauty*. The others in this pack of elite ballerinas were Nadia Potts, Vanessa Harwood, Veronica Tennant, and Karen Kain, all of whom toured with Nureyev as part of their National Ballet duties, an experience that inspired camaraderie among the dancers: "In my day, being in a ballet company was like family," Jago-Romeril says. "You looked out for each other."[36]

Touring isn't as common for ballet companies anymore; the costs have grown prohibitive, and few companies can afford it. As a result, today's dancers don't get to play the field as much as Jago-Romeril once did; they have tended to become more specialized, dancing full-out only a few times during a performance run, not every night, as Jago-Romeril used to, under her stage name, Mary Jago. She wonders if that is why she is seeing an increase in injured ballet dancers. "There's not enough consistency," Jago-Romeril says. "Dancers no longer get to dance every day, which puts them at greater risk of hurting themselves."

Although it is definitely beneficial to commit resources to helping dancers cope with the inevitability of injuries in the course of their profession, perhaps a more effective approach for companies to take would be to address the problem of injuries at its root, get dancers more exercised, expose them regularly to performance opportunities, large or small, so as to keep them resilient. This would require a rethinking of how ballet is organized and produced. There's innovation now in choreography. How about a similar level of innovation applied to ballet administration? But there are no easy solutions. How do you get dancers to dance more, when ballet companies in general struggle to make ends meet? How do you keep them from being injured when taking physical risks is a key component of the profession? How do you strike a balance? Jago-Romeril doesn't pretend to have the answers, but she does express concern that the current emphasis on experimentation in ballet puts dancers at a greater risk of injury, especially when their bodies haven't been trained to perform the new multi-step, hyper-frenetic, acrobatic-style creations being produced by some of today's cutting-edge choreographers. "What we have noticed today," continues Jago-Romeril, "is that choreographers are pushing dancers more than they did in previous years. In my day it was basic classic. Today's choreographers are emphasizing a contemporary approach, and actually I feel sorry for the dancers performing it: Ballet is now very hard."

But on the bright side, and partly as a result of diminished touring opportunities that have turned ballet dancers from nomads into people who can lay down roots, Jago-Romeril says that there's a greater acceptance of the need for dancers to balance their workload with a life outside the studio. She cites the example of the National Ballet, where several principal dancers in the company over the past decade have started families, while still pursuing a full-time dancing career. These new-generation ballerinas are now taking advantage of paid maternity leaves and job protection. "And that's a huge step forward," Jago-Romeril says. "Today's dancers have families if they want them, they have children. I think that's important because it puts a different focus on your life, it's not all about ballet. Human beings need balance," Jago-Romeril concludes, "no matter what they do for a living."

The advancement of workers' rights has liberated women in all professions, including ballet, where pregnancies among professional dancers are increasingly common. Increased wages combined with guaranteed paid maternity leaves as required by law have provided incentives for dancers to want to start families while still pursuing a dance career. These relatively recent changes in labor law and general societal attitudes have brought artistic directors on board in giving ballerinas leave to have babies in the understanding that their jobs will be waiting for them when they are done. "For me it's a miracle," says Sidimus who, at seventy-three years of age, is a member of ballet's all-or-nothing generation, having waited until her dancing days were over, at age forty, to have a child. "In my era it was a much more isolated view. You were expected to be a ballerina and not anything else. Today when I look at a dancer like [National Ballet of Canada's] Sonia Rodriguez, a principal dancer who is also a mother of two, I really do wonder how she manages to do it all."[37]

It's not entirely a mystery. Advances in health sciences like nutrition and body conditioning have enabled dancers to fully recover their dancing form after childbirth. Cross-training involving Pilates, yoga, and weight lifting has also helped ballerinas cope with the demands pregnancy places on their bodies, enabling them to stay supple and dance well into the last trimester. Some ballerinas claim that motherhood has made them better dancers, physically, mentally, and emotionally: "I feel stronger," said Julie Kent, the American Ballet Theatre ballerina who, in 2004, posed pregnant on the cover of *Dance Magazine*, dressed in flowing white chiffon and a skintight white leotard that showed off the voluptuousness of her rounded figure. She was thirty-three. "Motherhood has changed my priorities and impacted my performance," Kent continued. "It has liberated me and broadened my perspective. I don't apply as much pressure on myself and I have blossomed."[38]

Motherhood, muscle building, and healthy weight gain are changes directly affecting the ballerina's body, making it feel more in balance. But ballet is not composed of just one body; it is also a social body, a tightly knit network of human relationships where imbalances have for a long time been allowed to proliferate unchecked, in the mistaken belief that to change one aspect of ballet is to change the culture as a whole, killing in it what has long been regarded as beautiful. This is especially true with regard to racial imbalances within the ballet culture. For centuries, and continuing into the present day, ballet has widely been regarded as a white, elitist, European pursuit. Its symbol is the *ballet blanc*, literally the white ballet, an ethereal dance performed by white women in white dresses and pointe shoes pretending to be ghosts or swans or something equally vaporous. But society today is rapidly diversifying, especially in immigrant-rich North America, and this image of a white ballet is deeply unreflective of the social composition.

Ballerinas of color, especially black ballerinas, tend to be rare. The thought is that audiences won't readily accept a black Giselle or a black Aurora, thinking she is too obviously cast against type. It's a ridiculous premise: ballet is theater and theater is make-believe. Of course a black ballerina isn't Giselle: it's a role. But there's another prejudice at work: black women on the stage are perceived as naturally earthy and robust; they are not the airy sylphs more easily embodied by their white counterparts. There perhaps is a reason for this: scientific research demonstrates that black ballet dancers typically have not fallen prey to the anorexia epidemic that swept the ballet world during the Balanchine era. According to one study, black female ballet dancers had a more consistently positive body image than white female ballet dancers, leading to the conclusion that anorexia nervosa is "a disorder of the white upper-middle-class, where a premium is placed on the pursuit of thinness."[39]

Misty Copeland supports the statistic. A ballerina of African-American descent, she says that she never suffered from an eating disorder, even while her teachers and her white classmates chided her for being big—"big" being relative given that the dancer stands five feet two inches and weighs a mere hundred pounds. "I never had an issue with an eating disorder," says Copeland, a rising star at American Ballet Theatre who is also the first black ballerina soloist in a major company in decades. "I can't imagine dealing with that or having to speak up about it," she continues. "But I'm definitely not fat; I just have a different body type than all the rest. I am thin, but I have muscles and I have curves and I have a breasts—I'm a size 30D."[40]

Her curves allow Copeland to stand out on stage, which ultimately is a good thing: "I think it has given me an advantage," she says. "It has allowed me to develop as an individual, which is often hard to do for ballet dancers. From a young age we are groomed to be in a corps de ballet, all trained in the same technique and expected to look the same. I tried as a student to be the dancer others wanted me to be but I found that it was better for me to be me; it's what has enabled me to become a soloist and, hopefully, it will help me become a principal dancer, which is my goal."

But to get ahead, Copeland says that she has to work extra hard to appear worthy of promotion: "My skin color was never before a factor for me," says Copeland, one of six children born to a single mother who raised her kids in Los Angeles after moving there from Kansas, the dancer's birth city. "I only saw my color when I started to dance. Still, I was a dancer. I wasn't a black dancer. It wasn't until I moved to New York City and joined ABT was it talked about. I wasn't aware it was an issue. And then I looked around me—and oh my gosh—there were no other black ballerinas but me. I still wouldn't have thought it mattered, but then I watched as others were promoted ahead of me, given roles that I could easily have done but wasn't allowed to. And that's when I realized that my natural talent wasn't enough. As a black woman I have to work three times harder. I have so much to prove. I'm extremely exhausted. I've been doing this now for eleven years."

But her hard work and tenacity are paying off. In December 2011, Copeland received word that Russian choreographer Alexei Ratmansky, said to be the most important choreographer working in ballet today, had cast her as the lead in his new production of Firebird, which had its world premiere in Los Angeles, Copeland's hometown, in April 2012, to glowing reviews. "I'm ecstatic," the dancer says. "Ballet will never be perfect, but for me this is about as good as it gets."

Another indication that ballet might be moving in new directions is the increased popularization of ballet as entertainment. These days the art born in the courts of kings is showing up at the movies, on the fashion runways, and in rock and rap music videos by the likes of Kanye West, whose 2010 single, Runaway, came with a thirty-four-minute promotional film featuring ballerinas aggressively stabbing the ground with their pointes: "I was just moved by the classic dance," the rapper told MTV News, "I just wanted to crash it against the pop music."[41]

As a black ballerina trying to break down barriers herself, Copeland understood what the pop star was after, saying in an interview that by mixing ballet with pop music, West was making classical dance "relatable to the audience that's viewing those videos." The expectation was that it would increase audiences for ballet, one of the reasons Copeland agreed to dance in the 2009 fever-dream video for the single *Crimson and Clover* by Prince. Copeland was also the featured ballerina in the pop star's *Welcome 2 America* tour, which played Madison Square Garden and New Jersey's mammoth Izod Center in the early part of 2011. Copeland says working with Prince was both a career and a confidence booster: "It signaled my growth as an artist; it made me more visible to others as a role model."[42] Her bravura style of dancing was readily accessible to stadium audiences for whom *ballet* remains a foreign word. Copeland lured them in. "I think that there's so much history when it comes to classical ballet—it's not going to change overnight… [but by] inviting people in and exposing them to the fact that classical ballet doesn't have to be uptight… I'm hoping that change can happen."[43]

"Classical ballet needs great interpreters," says Sylvie Guillem, the former *étoile* of the Paris Opéra Ballet and principal guest artist of London's Royal Ballet, the ballerina other ballerinas still look to for inspiration—a YouTube darling. "It can't be done in a mediocre or average way, even if danced very well. Like it or not, ballet comes from the past; we have to drag it from the past into the present, and if it is not danced intelligently, not danced with beauty, the people will no longer come, and ballet will not survive into the future."[44]

But ballet is not breaking with its past; it is renewing itself, while at the same time drawing inspiration from a long tradition of classical dance. Embodying that feeling of continuity and regeneration in ballet today is former ballet star Gelsey Kirkland, among the first to lift the veil on the art of the ballerina as a punishing life of self-deprivation and self-sacrifice in the name of beauty. To many observers, Kirkland is the poster girl for all that is wrong with ballet—eating disorders, injuries, insecurity, exploitation, and a dissolute lifestyle. Kirkland lived it all—and more. She altered her anatomy to make herself more closely approximate the ideal ballerina. The sad irony is that Kirkland was already a rare specimen of balletic excellence— and a beauty as well. A dancing prodigy who entered New York City Ballet in 1968, at the tender age of sixteen, after being trained by George Balanchine at his School of American Ballet, Kirkland was born with the requisite long-limbed body type, the swan neck, the hyper-flexible feet. Her speed, grace, and agility survive in films and videos of her earlier performances, especially the 1977 film version of Balanchine's *The Nutcracker*, in which she dances opposite her former onstage and offstage partner, Mikhail Baryshnikov.

Often referred to as the female Nijinsky for her genius for dance, this American-born ballerina was one of the great ballet artists of the twentieth century. Ballet patrons who remember her when she was at the peak of her powers shake their heads and speak of her as the ballerina who squandered her talents. They want to think of her as one of the neurotic pinheads of the Balanchine era, a malcontent who exaggerated ballet's dark side as an act of morbid self-promotion. They see her as twisted and irreparably disconnected from ballet as an art of beauty and transcendence. But the opposite is true. After dancing in the trenches of ballet, Kirkland has emerged, scarred but wiser, and is today channeling her remarkable gifts into her own Gelsey Kirkland Academy of Classical Ballet, which she founded in New York in the fall of 2010, at age fifty-eight, to train young dancers for a professional dancing career.

Located on Broadway, in Manhattan's industrial TriBeCa district, the dance school perches incongruously over a dusty fabric shop and next to scaffolding emblazoned with graffiti. It's only a subway ride away from Lincoln Center, where

Kirkland once ruled as one of America's reigning ballet super-stars, but in many ways it is light years away from the life she once knew. She runs the school with her husband, Michael Chernov, an Australian-born former dancer and Broadway actor, who trained at the National Ballet and Theatre School in his native Melbourne. The interior walls are covered in framed oversized vintage posters from the Diaghilev era; another image, of Kirkland dancing opposite Baryshnikov in Balanchine's *The Prodigal Son*, serves as a computer screen saver. There are four studios spread over 8,000 square feet of high-ceilinged space, in addition to an exercise room teeming with workout machines and balls and bands for core training. The Russian-based training is rooted in the Vaganova method of teaching ballet, a combination of French lyricism and Italian virtuosity as developed early in the twentieth century by former Imperial Ballet dancer-turned-pedagogue Agrippina Vagonova. Each day begins with a morning yoga-inflected stretch class using mats on the floor. This is followed by classes in ballet technique and also, unusual for a ballet school, voice and drama.

The emphasis in her pedagogical approach is on storytelling through dancing. Abstract ballet, such as Kirkland knew in her Balanchine ballerina days, is not the objective. Kirkland wants her sixty-four registered students to learn how to move from the heart, to connect with audiences emotionally as artists using their bodies expressively, not as athletes performing acrobatic tricks. The divide between expressiveness and pyrotechnics has existed in ballet for centuries, at least since Camargo, the technician, and Sallé, the poet, ruled the stage. Kirkland has no doubt as to which rival she supports. In conversation, she uses words like *pure* and *truth* to emphasize that her training is less image oriented, more focused on inner states of being.

"You can't drive the body from its form," she says. "There are other ways of creating a stage life."[45] She wants her students to connect to the inner core of ballet and not be distracted by the allure of the superficial attractions of the art, a lesson she must have learned herself the hard way. One technique used at the school is to have students dance in the studio with the mirrors covered, getting young dancers to concentrate on what it feels like to dance, rather than on how it looks to somebody else. It is the opposite of how Kirkland and other ballerinas of her generation learned their craft, and she is determined that her students don't make the same mistakes. Taking her place in the studio on a busy Manhattan morning, Kirkland is dressed head-to-toe in black, over which is layered a button-down shirt flapping around her small, birdlike body. She moves silently around her cavernous academy, looking as if she could suddenly take flight. Kirkland covers most of her face with large Jackie O–style sunglasses; her fine auburn hair is tied back in a chignon. When she opens her mouth to speak the words come out nasally and in staccato bursts, pushed through the cushiony contours of distorted lips, a reminder of her days as a tortured artist. It's her reputation as a complex ballet genius that draws students to her from across the United States. They choose her academy over larger and more prestigious schools like Juilliard or Kirkland's own alma mater, School of American Ballet, because they believe she has something valuable to teach them, no matter how negative her own past experiences of ballet.

"I am inspired by her," says Jacqueline Wilson, a twenty-one-year-old dance student, who traveled halfway across the country to study with her ballerina idol. "I grew up with a blown-up poster of her on my bedroom wall. She represents ballet to me."[46] In Kirkland's morning technique class, Wilson takes her place at center floor in front of the watchful eye of Kirkland, sitting like a Buddha on the edge of a stool at the front of the studio. The dancers come in all shapes and sizes—tall, short, svelte, muscular. Kirkland is easily the tiniest person in the place; her waiflike look definitely marks her as senior, her body having been shaped by the eating disorders that have plagued her profession. But she has moved beyond the tyranny of that aesthetic. During a lunch of a homemade sandwich laced with onions—"You're not bothered by the smell, are you?" she asks, betraying the kindness that those who know her say is one of her most unsung attributes—Kirkland explains that the point is no longer to create dancers who all look the same. It's about creating dancers who are unique, with something of their own to say. She had learned the hard way the mistake of trying to conform to someone else's idea of what a ballerina should look like and is now passing on the benefit of that experience to her own students. In one of her studio's classrooms, in fact, a curtain has been drawn over the mirror to get the dancers to find meaning within themselves, not in a reflected image. "A perfect body can be dead as a doornail," chimes in Chernov, allowing his wife another bite of her brown-bagged meal. She sits beside him, nodding in agreement. "The idea is to get people out of ballet's image orientation," he adds. "The ideal," says Kirkland, swallowing, "is to explore what's true."

Back in the classroom, Kirkland provides an insight into what she means. Perched slightly forward on her stool, ready to pounce, she watches her dancers in ominous stillness as strains of Tchaikovsky fill the air from the accompanist in the far corner. "Draw the line on the way out, open the door," she shouts above the music, her hand beating time on one thigh. But the dancers are having difficulty understanding. She leaps up from where she has been sitting to give an impromptu demonstration. The once famous body pulls up and lengthens. All the weight is pushed forward onto the balls of the feet, and she rises slightly into the air. She opens her chest wide, her arms blossoming into an elegant *port de bras*. Her head is slightly tilted; her eyes are raised. "To the king," she says. And then she bows slightly to this imaginary being in the room, looking down from on high.

It's an extraordinary gesture. In that moment, all the minutes, the hours, the months, the years, the decades, the centuries go whizzing by. We are no longer in traffic-clogged Manhattan, with the horns blaring outside the window, the graffiti spray-painted on the wall, a pretzel cart on every corner. We have gone back in time to the opulent court of Louis xiv, where this glorious art of ballet first flourished more than four hundred years ago.

Kirkland provides a link, a ballerina who through her own training, stage experience, and tortured past is showing the way for how the art can proceed from a troubled history into a more hopeful future—a ballet survivor.

"There's a lot of rigidity that frees you," Kirkland says. "There are ways of using tradition to move forward and not sideways. It's about knowing what matters, and following the right path."

In Kirkland's hands, the catastrophes that have befallen ballerinas through time have been channeled into catharsis.

EPILOGUE

IT'S HARD, it's injurious, and the pay stinks. So why would anyone in their right mind commit to ballet as a career when the heartache and the hazards are so clearly spelled out in advance? The average ballerina now blazes out by age thirty, often with little to fall back on. If the motivation is glory, the result of being in the spotlight before a paying audience, that feeling of being on top of the world is always short-lived. The next day, no matter how high she soared the night before, the ballerina comes crashing back down to earth in the form of the daily ballet class. There, the aches and pains of a sometimes recalcitrant body remind the dancer that she is like Sisyphus, rolling the boulder of human weakness up an ideal hill, only to have it come crashing down, mocking her effort and making her start all over again. It seems a thankless task, riddled with deprivations.

On the surface, the ballerina appears in control. But in reality, she is controlled—by teachers, directors, and choreographers (most often men), and by societal expectations regarding her role as a representative of divinely patterned grace here on earth, as well as by ballet itself, an art with centuries of built-in rules and regulations. The brute backstage reality of the ballerina contrasts sharply with her image as a cultural icon of idealized femininity: the worm within the butterfly. The difference between the public image of the ballerina as embodying ethereal exotic glamor and romance and the crassly physical circumstances she endures has been there since the beginning and is intrinsic to an art form where difficult movements (indeed difficulties of any kind) must appear effortless, even natural.

BUT AMERICAN-BORN BALLERINA Caroline Richardson, who danced with the Frankfurt Ballet under the direction of choreographer William Forsythe, says that nothing in life compares to dancing ballet. It's "this sacred space," a place literally set apart from the mundane, where deep inner change and freedom can be experienced. "Dance for me was the most intimate experience I had of spirit and truth. It had so much depth to it, no matter how lonely it was. It felt powerful to me. There was a great sacrifice of the self, but with the intention of being able, ultimately, to move out of the self towards truth and peace and sacredness, towards a refuge of the soul."[1]

The former soloist with the National Ballet of Canada is today an award-winning choreographer for experimental film and video, new-fangled media light years away from the special effects used in the Romantic ballet spectacles performed by Marie Taglioni, one of the first ballerinas to represent ballet as an inspirational art form. And yet now, in the twenty-first century, Richardson likewise exalts the art of the ballerina as a liberation of the spirit: "It was a blazing sword of truth that I knew I could use to cut through the pettiness of the world outside, and let the people in, to feel the power also inside them." To ballerinas like Richardson, achieving transcendence through dancing ballet is what justifies the hardships, a sentiment many dancers share.

Other ballerinas have described the hidden motivation to dance—what the audience often doesn't see—as experiencing an unbearable lightness of being. Being on stage for many dancers also represents a rare opportunity to inspire pleasure in people, not just the evaluative judgment of the ballet studio. Some dancers point to the intense, yet liberating, physicality of dancing as the reason they do it. Recalled one ballerina who had retired from the stage, "There was a physical aspect to dancing which was wonderful because you burn yourself out, you sweat yourself to dance, and you feel like you are light, clean… burned to the essentials… very pacified, and very… content."[2]

But there's something else about ballet, and that is the ballerina herself as a figure of power. It's why women love to do ballet and watch ballet, easily outstripping men as audience members. Despite the known pitfalls of eating disorders, low pay, injuries, and the specter of sexual exploitation, women and girls continue to flock to ballet in droves. The ballerina on stage and in the spotlight is an idealized extension of themselves. She is the ultimate feminine, a creature both beautiful and strong, the embodiment of grace and music and light. To one observer, "It was a virtuoso way of being a woman. It required discipline, expertise. No movement, no expression, no position of the limbs was without precise definition and timing. You sculpted with your body; to dance was to be simultaneously medium, instrument and artist. The dancer commanded respect and awe. The word 'commanded' was operative. She appeared to control situations and interactions as well as herself... Even a wimpish dance role like Giselle cannot help but display the female in the vigorous and active expression of her own desires."[3] It's a Utopian vision of the ballerina that inspires not just ballet dancers but also ballet lovers in wanting to support an art form that, behind the scenes, can be brutally punishing. It's not that those of us who cherish ballet want to turn a blind eye to its dark side. More, the intention is to show that the darkness, in the end, has not overwhelmed the brilliance of the art.

Ballerinas will probably always have to endure pain and suffering to attain ecstasy, transcendence, intoxication, flow (or whatever other term describes such peak experiences). They won't likely ever go away. As with any other physically demanding performing art or sport, the motto "No pain, no gain" applies. Ballerinas are conditioned from a young age to accept self-sacrifice as an integral part of the art form. They learn to work through the pain, from childhood until the end of their days as dancers, numbing the pain with drugs and other means. After their performances, they reach for buckets of ice in which to soak their swollen, gnarled, and bleeding feet, seeking relief from the agonies of having danced in pointe shoes. The expectation is that they will tolerate their pain stoically, and in silence. If a ballerina dares speak up, she risks ostracism. One of ballet's great sources of shame is how often ballerinas are mistreated and then expected to carry on, as if nothing bad has happened. It's a pattern of negative behavior that is part and parcel of the unnaturalness of ballet. Bodies aren't made to stand perfectly still on one leg to six bars of music, but ballerinas are taught how to perform such physically taxing feats without strain and without a whimper. Pain is denied—or at least its expression is. An art form founded on a stifling of discomfort has produced a culture where deprivation and degradation are allowed to flourish because they are seen to yield superhuman results.

But those performing such antigravitational illusions have had to compromise themselves as individuals. Ballerinas, in particular, have been expected to subsume their wants and needs to keep ballet flourishing. They give their all and then in the end, when the curtain falls on their last performance, they are pushed out into the cold, soon forgotten. The ballerina's life, seen from afar, looks like a balancing act on the edge of a precipice, fraught with danger and the understanding that one false move and, *splat*, it's finished. Such is the gritty behind-the-scenes world of the ballet. One scholar has called the ballet world a "fairly perverse social order,"[4] whose perversities are often defended as beauty, even by the victims themselves. The end justifies the means, according to Suki Schorer, a former New York City Ballet dancer under George Balanchine and, later, a leading teacher at the School of American Ballet. She was once asked why a student jumped without putting down her heel—wouldn't that cause tendinitis? "Yes," Schorer smiled, "when people come into this company they get tendinitis—but it's *beautiful*."[5]

Yet *some* of that thinking has changed. Ballet shows evidence that it is catching up with the twenty-first century in becoming more sensitive to dancers as individuals with constitutionally protected rights. Ballerinas are having babies; they are even gaining weight to protect their bodies from repetitive injuries and prolong their careers. Science is bellying up to the *barre* to help dancers become more recognized as the elite athletes they are. There's more job protection and, in some companies, better wages. But as the ballerina progresses, so does the art form. Choreography today is more athletic and acrobatic than it was even twenty years ago. This is putting the ballerina before a new set of risks: one step forward, two steps back.

Really, you wonder how she manages to rise above it all.

Ballet will always require the utmost dedication . However, the scandal and exploitation in which ballet history has so often been wrapped can be, and are, being shaken off. A more empowered generation of dancers and a more enlightened ballet-going public will no longer tolerate such unnecessary depredations. The ecstasy, whether experienced by the performing ballerina on stage, or vicariously, by an adoring audience on whose energy the dancers feed, will always be the reason and justification for keeping the flame of ballet going. And the ballerina will continue to be at the center of it all— the ideal, the driving force, the embodiment of beauty, grace, and hope.

The symbol of perfection.

NOTES

PRÓLOGUE

1. *Je redanserai*, Vidéo INA. www.Ina.fr/art-et-culture/arts-du-spectacle/video/CPF04006930/je-redanserai.fr.html (accessed February 17, 2012).

2. Janine Charrat, Facebook, http://fr-fr.facebook.com/pages/Janine-Charrat/134001929998865, viewed February 17, 2012.

CHAPTER 1: THE FEMINIZATION OF BALLET

1. Rayner Heppenstall, "The Sexual Idiom," from "Apology for Dancing," in *What Is Dance?*, ed. Roger Copeland and Marshall Cohen (New York: Oxford University Press, 1983), 274.

2. Steven P. Wainwright and Bryan S. Turner, "'Just Crumbling to Bits'? An Exploration of the Body, Ageing, Injury and Career in Classical Ballet Dancers," *Sociology* 40 (2006): 241.

3. Quoted in Joann Keallinohomoku, "An Anthropologist Looks at Ballet as a Form of Ethnic Dance," in *What Is Dance?*, 544.

4. Evan Alderson, "Ballet as Ideology: 'Giselle,' Act II," *Dance Chronicle* 10, no. 3 (1987): 292.

5. Susan Au, *Ballet & Modern Dance* (London: Thames and Hudson, 1988), 18.

6. Julia Prest, "Dancing King: Louis XIV's Roles in Molière's Comédies-ballets, from Court to Town," *Seventeenth Century* 16, no. 2 (2001): 285.

7.   Jennifer Homans, *Apollo's Angels: A History of Ballet* (New York: Random House, 2010), 13.

8.   Mary Clarke and Clement Crisp, *Ballerina: The Art of Women in Classical Ballet* (London: BBC Books, 1987), 18.

9.   Natalie Lecomte, "The Female Ballet Troupe of the Paris Opera from 1700 to 1725," in *Women's Work, Making Dance in Europe before 1800*, ed. Lynn Matluck Brooks (Madison: University of Wisconsin Press, 2007), 117.

10.   Quoted in Edmund Fairfax, "The 'Fair Sex' and Its Style," *The Styles of Eighteenth Century Ballet* (Lanham, MD: Scarecrow Press, 2003), 221.

11.   Wendy Hilton, *Dance and Music of Court and Theater* (New York: Pendragon Press, 1981), 276 ff.

12.   Homans, 15.

13.   Phillip E. Hammond and Sandra N. Hammond, "The Internal Logic of Dance: A Weberian Perspective on the History of Ballet," *Journal of Social History* 12, no. 4 (Summer 1979): 595.

14.   Molière, *The Middle Class Gentleman* (English translation, *Le Bourgeois Gentilhomme*), Act I, Scene I. Kindle edition.

15.   Pierre Rameau, *The Dancing Master*, trans. Cyril W. Beaumont (New York: Dance Horizons Republications, 1970): 31.

16.   Carlo Blasis, *Code of Terpsichore* (London: James Bulcock, 1828), 94–95.

17.   Au, 23.

18.   The invention of opéra-ballet is also attributed to French composer and musician André Campra, whose *L'Europe galante* of 1697 is considered one of the first known works in the genre.

19.   Frederick H. Martens, "The Attitude of the Dancer Toward Music," *The Musical Quarterly* 4, no. 3 (July 1918): 441.

20.   Clarke and Crisp, 18.

21.   Lecomte, 99.

22.   Clarke and Crisp, 18.

23.   Lecomte, 100.

24.   Lecomte, 99.

25.   Hammond and Hammond, 595.

26.   Roger Copeland and Marshall Cohen, "The Dance Medium," in *What is Dance?* (New York: Oxford University Press, 1983), 104–5.

27.   Régine Astier, "Françoise Prévost: The Unauthorized Biography," in Brooks, ed., *Women's Work*, 142.

28. André Cardinal Destouches, as recorded in a letter to Antoine de Grimaldi, Prince of Monaco, quoted in Lecomte, 110.

29. Claude Conyers, "Courtesans in Dance History: Les Belles de la Belle Époque," *Dance Chronicle* 26, no. 2 (2003): 220.

30. Lecomte, 106.

31. Astier, 142.

32. Astier, 143.

33. Astier, 158; footnote in reference to "Histoire de la demoiselle d'Azincourt, danseuse de l'Opéra écrite par elle-même, 1743," in the Bibliothèque Nationale, Paris.

34. Quoted in Astier, 143.

35. Quoted in Astier, 142.

36. Astier, 142.

37. Lecomte, 107.

38. Astier, 107.

39. Lecomte, 106.

40. Lecomte, 107.

41. Robert Greskovic, *Ballet 101: A Complete Guide to Learning and Loving the Ballet* (Montclair, NJ: Limelight Editions, 1998), 20.

42. Karen Eliot, *Dancing Lives, Five Female Dancers from the Ballet d'Action to Merce Cunningham* (Chicago: University of Illinois Press, 2007), 9–11.

43. Quoted in Victoria Huckenpahler, "Confessions of an Opera Director: Chapters from the *Mémoires* of Dr. Louis Veron, Part II," *Dance Chronicle* 7, no. 2 (1984).

44. Quoted in Astier, 131.

45. Lecomte, 103.

46. The *courante* is a sixteenth-century French court dance in compound time; the *musette* is a popular dance from the time of Louis XIV and Louis XV performed to the drone of a bagpipe.

47. Quoted in Astier, 125.

48. Astier, 141.

49. Manuscript 3137, also known as *Mémoire pour l'Ambassadeur de Malte contre Mademoiselle Prévost, Factum*, which was hidden for almost three hundred years in the Arsenal Library of Paris until its discovery earlier this century by the ballerina's biographer, French dance scholar Régine Astier. Much of its contents are revealed in Astier, 123–159.

50. Roughly equivalent to about $25,000 in today's money.

51. Astier, 133–34.

52. Astier, 133.

53. Astier, 128.

54. Astier, 128–29.

55. Astier, 129.

56. Lecomte, 107.

57. Lecomte, 125.

58. Quoted in Astier, 137–38.

59. Susan Au describes the *entrée* as structured like a ballet *mascarade*, with an opening *récit* or song, followed by dances. Au, 16.

60. Quoted in Cyril W. Beaumont, *Three French Dancers of the Eighteenth Century* (London: C.W. Beaumont, 1934), 12.

61. Ivor Guest, *The Paris Opera Ballet* (Alton, UK: Dance Books, 2006), 17.

62. Quoted in Fairfax, 223.

63. Lillian Moore, *Artists of the Dance* (New York: Thomas Y. Crowell, 1932), 27.

64. Lincoln Kirstein, *Four Centuries of Ballet: Fifty Masterworks*, 99.

65. Régine Astier, "Marie-Anne Camargo," in *International Encyclopedia of Ballet*, ed. Martha Bremser (London: St. James Press, 1993), 229–30.

66. Quoted in Fairfax, 229.

67. Quoted in Fairfax, 219.

68. Moore, 30–31.

69. Prudhommeau, 80.

70. Ibid.

71. Prudhommeau, 81.

72. Parmenia Migel, *The Ballerinas* (New York: Macmillan, 1972), 32–33; Prudhommeau, 80.

73. Quoted in Moore, 25.

74. Prudhommeau, 80.

75. Sarah McCleave, "Dancing at the English Opera: Marie Sallé's Letter to the Duchess of Richmond," *Dance Research* 17, no. 1 (Summer 1999): 32.

76. Quoted in David Charlton and Sarah Hibberd, "'My Father Was a Poor Parisian Musician': A Memoir (1756) Concerning Rameau, Handel's Library and Sallé," *Journal of the Royal Musical Association*, 128, no. 2 (2003): 177.

77. Charlton and Hibberd, 31.

78. Quoted in Moore, 29.

79. Migel, 19.
80. Sarah McCleave, "Marie Sallé, a Wise Professional Woman of Influence," in Brooks, ed., *Women's Work*, 163.
81. McCleave, "Marie Sallé," 164.
82. McCleave, "Marie Sallé," 170.
83. Quoted in McCleave, "Marie Sallé," 168.
84. Migel, 25.
85. Quoted in McCleave, "Marie Sallé," 166.
86. Sallé appeared at Versailles in late 1745, in March 1746, and February–March 1747, dancing in Rameau's *Les fêtes de l'Hymen et de l'Amour*, among other ballets. She also danced at the palace at Fontainebleau in 1752–53. See Charlton and Hibberd, 161–199.
87. Charlton and Hibberd, 177.
88. Quoted in McCleave, "Marie Sallé," 168.
89. Prudhommeau, 81.
90. Marie-Françoise Christout and Lucienne J. Serrano, "The Paris Opera Ballet," *Dance Chronicle* 2, no. 2 (1978): 135.
91. *La Guimard* (Paris, 1893; reprinted Geneva, 1973).
92. Migel, 75.
93. Moore, 51.
94. Migel, 73.
95. Moore, 52.
96. Ivor Guest, "Luminaries of the Opera Ballet in 1770," in *The Ballet of the Enlightenment: The Establishment of the Ballet d'Action in France, 1770–1793* (London: Dance Books, 1996), 36.
97. Moore, 52.
98. Maureen Needham Costonis, "Marie-Madeleleine Guimard," in *International Dictionary of Ballet*, 624–27.
99. Migel, 74.
100. Quoted in Guest, "Luminaries" 38.
101. Migel, 75–77.
102. Moore, 54.
103. Her daughter died young, aged just sixteen, and her loss was Guimard's only moment of tragedy.
104. Guest, "Luminaries," 36.
105. Guest, "Luminaries," 36.
106. Migel, 78.
107. Quoted in Moore, 53.

108. Moore, 53.

109. Quoted in Migel, 83.

110. Karl Toepfer, "Orgy Salon: Aristocracy and Pornographic Theatre in Pre-Revolutionary Paris." *Performing Arts Journal* 12, 2/3 (1990): 115.

111. Quoted in Toepfer, 115.

112. Toepfer, 116.

113. Quoted in Migel, 72.

114. Migel, 116.

115. Migel, 80.

116. Guimard wrote an affectionately gossipy letter to her banker friend in 1789 when she was briefly in London, in which she recounts in comic detail how she has to fight to get the money owed her by management of London's opera house, which had just burned down, sending her 350-guinea contract up in smoke. See Ivor Guest, "Letters from London: Guimard's Farewell to the Stage," *Dance Chronicle*, 18, 2 (1995): 207–15.

117. Migel, 83.

118. Moore, 56.

119. Moore, 55.

120. Toepfer, 116.

121. Migel, 88.

122. Migel, 88.

CHAPTER 2: PIMPS, POVERTY, AND PRISON

1. Edmund Fairfax, "The 'Fair Sex' and Its Style," in *The Styles of Eighteenth-Century Ballet* (Lanham, MD: Scarecrow Press, 2003), 238.

2. Molly Engelhardt, "Marie Taglioni, Ballerina Extraordinaire," *Nineteenth-Century Gender Studies*, 6.3 (Winter 2010). www.ncgs-journal.com/issue63/engelhardt.htm.

3. Laura Leivick, "Through Which She Is Seen: Bodies and Ballet," in *The Threepenny Review* 2 (Summer 1980), 30.

4. Quoted in Huckenpahler, no. 2, 201.

5. Quoted in Huckenpahler, no. 2, 222.

6. Susan Griffin, *The Book of the Courtesans* (New York: Random House, 2001), 166.

7. David Jordan, *Transforming Paris: The Life and Labors of Baron Haussmann* (New York: The Free Press, 1995), 257.

8. Quoted in Jill DeVonyar and Richard Kendall, *Degas and the Dance* (New York: Harry Abrams, 2002), 66.

9. Quoted in Mari Kalman Meller, "Exercises in and Around Degas's Classrooms: Part l," *The Burlington Magazine* 130, no. 1020 (Special Issue on Degas, March 1988): 213.

10. DeVonyar and Kendall, 21–22.

11. DeVonyar and Kendall, 24.

12. DeVonyar and Kendall, 35.

13. Quoted in Huckenpahler, 200.

14. Huckenpahler, no. 2, 221.

15. Quoted in Huckenpahler, no. 2, 198–228.

16. Théophile Gautier, "Le Rat," in *Quand On Voyage* (Paris: Michel Lévy Frères, Libraires Éditeurs, 1865), 329. Author's translation.

17. Gautier, 331. Author's translation.

18. Quoted in Richard Kendall with contributions by Douglas W. Druick and Arthur Beale, *Degas and the Little Dancer* (New Haven, CT: Yale University Press; Omaha, NB: Joslyn Art Museum): 10.

19. Quoted in DeVonyar and Kendall, *Degas and the Dance*, 120.

20. Quoted in Huckenpahler, no. 2, 211.

21. Quoted in Huckenpahler, no. 2, 218–19.

22. The work is called *Ces demoiselles d'Opéra par un vieil abonné.*

23. Quoted in Kendall, 19.

24. DeVonyar and Kendall, 120.

25. Kendall, 15.

26. Quoted in Martine Kahane, "Enquête sur la Petite Danseuse de quatorze ans de Degas—Le modèle," in *La Revue du Musée d'Orsay* 7 (Autumn 1998), Paris: Reunion des Musées nationaux and Musée d'Orsay. Revision and translation published in *Degas Sculptures: Catalogue Raisonné of the Bronzes*, edited by Joseph S. Czestochowski and Anne Pingeot (Memphis: The Torch Press and International Arts, 2002): 106.

27. Quoted in Kendall, 65.

28. Quoted in Kendall, 17.

29. Alexandra Carter, "Blonde, Bewigged and Winged with Gold: Ballet Girls in the Music Halls of Late Victorian and Edwardian England," *Dance Research: The Journal of the Society of Dance Research* 13, no. 2 (Autumn–Winter 1995), 35.

30. Huckenpahler, no. 2, 217.

31. Huckenpahler, no. 2, 211.

32. Quoted in Engelhardt.

33. At the time of the unveiling, she was fifteen; Degas had originally planned to show the sculpture a year earlier, at the Fifth Impressionist Exhibition, held in the spring of 1880, but had failed to complete it on time.

34. Kahane, 103.

35. Ibid.

36. Ibid.

37. Ibid.

38. Kendall, 15.

39. Quoted in Kendall, 21.

40. Quoted in Zoë Blackler and Ben Hoyle, "Little Dancer Points to Sensational Discovery of Degas Sculpture Hoard," *The Times*, November 28, 2009, T1.

41. Quoted in Kendall, 21.

42. Kendall, 21.

43. Quoted in Jill DeVonyar and Richard Kendall, "The Class of 1881: Degas, Drawing, and the Little Dancer Aged Fourteen," *Master Drawings* 41, no.2 (Summer 2003): 151.

44. Blackler and Hoyle, T1.

45. De Vonyar and Kendall, "The Class of 1881," 160.

46. Kendall, 10.

47. Quoted in Paul Trachtman, "Degas and His Dancers," *Smithsonian* (April 2003): 91.

48. DeVonyar and Kendall, *Degas and the Dance*, 119.

49. Kendall, 16.

50. Kahane, 105.

51. Ibid.

52. DeVonyar and Kendall, "The Class of 1881," 154.

53. DeVonyar and Kendall, "The Class of 1881," 159.

54. Lillian Browse, *Degas Dancers* (London: Faber and Faber, 1949), 62.

55. Quoted in Kendall, 15.

56. Quoted in Kahane, 106.

57. Kahane, 106.

58. Ibid.

59 Carol Pardo, "La Petite Danseuse de Degas," *DanceView* 20, no. 4 (Autumn 2003): 34.

CHAPTER 3: BONFIRE BALLERINA

1. Maurice Quatrelles L'Épine, "Une Danseuse française au xixe siècle, Emma Livry," *Bulletin de la Societé de l'histoire du théâtre, revue trimestrielle* (November–January 1908–1909): 10. All translations from the French in this chapter by Cameron Tolton.

2. Lillian Moore, "The Tragedy of Emma Livry," *Dance Magazine* (June 1952), 38–39.

3. Quoted in Parmenia Migel, *The Ballerinas* (New York: Macmillan, 1972), 233.

4. Ivor Guest, *The Ballet of the Second Empire: 1858–1870*, (London: Adam and Charles Black, 1953), 2.

5. Nathalie Yokel, "Légendaire Emma Livry," *Danser* 195 (January 2001): 22.

6. Quatrelles L'Épine, 14.

7. Chassiron also built a large collection of Japanese and Chinese artifacts which are displayed today at the Orbigny-Bernon Museum in La Rochelle.

8. Friedrich Engels, "Introduction," in *On the Twentieth Anniversary of the Paris Commune* in Karl Marx, *The Civil War in France* (1891). www.marxists.org/archive/marx/works/1871/civil-war-france/postscript.htm.

9. Quoted in Gilson MacCormack, "Emma Livry," *The Dancing Times* (September 1928): 613.

10. Yokel, 23.

11. Quatrelles L'Épine, 22.

12. Quatrelles L'Épine, 20.

13. Lillian Moore, "Emma Livry," *Artists of the Dance* (New York: Thomas Y. Crowell, 1932), 156.

14. Sarah C. Woodstock, "Archives of the Dance: Later Dance Holdings of the Theatre Museum," *Journal of the Society for Dance Research* 8, no. 1 (Spring 1990): 62–77.

15. Ivor Guest, "Emma Livry 1842–1863," *Dance Gazette*, 174 (June 1980): 52.

16. Quatrelles L'Épine, 30.

17. Quatrelles L'Épine, 34.

18. Quatrelles L'Épine, 30.

19. Quoted in Quatrelles L'Épine, 32.

20. Quatrelles L'Épine, 32.

21. Quatrelles L'Épine, 32.

22. Quatrelles L'Épine, 42.

23. Victoria Huckenpahler, "Confessions of an Opera Director: Chapters from the *Mémoires* of Dr. Louis Véron, Part II," *Dance Chronicle*, 7, no. 1 (1984): 78.

24. Huckenpahler, no. 1, 80.

25. Fanny Johnstone, "Women: Dressed to Kill," *The Guardian*, October 20, 2006, 18.

26. Mary Grace Swift, "Dancers in Flames," *Dance Chronicle* 5, no. 1 (1982): 1.

27. Ivor Guest, *The Ballet of the Second Empire*, 30.

28. Quoted in Judith Hatcher, "Trials, Troubles and Temptations in a Dangerous Era—Ballet Dancers in the nineteenth Century—Abstract," *Dance Magazine* (January 1999). http://findarticles.com/p/articles/mi_m1083/is_1_73/ai_53501128/. December 12, 2011.

29. Quoted in Quatrelles L'Épine, 27.

30. Quatrelles L'Épine, 27.

31. MacCormack, 615.

32. "Ces Demoiselles de l'Opéra," in *Bulletin*, 28. The nineteenth century was filled with examples of artists dying before their time, not only on the stage as Clara Webster had done but as a result of consumption, which claimed the lives of Polish composer Frédéric Chopin and the English poet John Keats, Romantic artists both. An entire school of art grew up around consumption as a metaphor for the artistic life, with victims of the disease said to have been consumed from within, by a surfeit of passion and poetic feeling. Molded in the Romantic tradition, Emma would have been aware of the metaphors surrounding death at that time. Death by fire to her was perhaps only death by consumption of a different sort.

33. Joel Fish, an internationally recognized burn specialist who treats pediatric burn victims at Toronto's Hospital for Sick Children, says that while lemon juice might today seem a primitive, if not barbaric, form of treatment, those caring for Emma knew what they were doing: "The most common bacteria associated with burn wounds is

pseudomonas," Dr. Fish says. "It's got a specific smell, very sweet, and one of the treatments is an acidic-based application, so the citrus juice probably neutralized the odor and helped infection from setting in."

The lemon juice may also have helped Emma live as long as she did after the accident, despite sustaining burns to 20 to 40 percent of her body. Those burns, Dr. Fish surmises after analyzing the evidence, were also deeper than the original doctors suspected: "A flame has the same temperature today as it had in the Romantic era, and flesh is still flesh no matter what year it is. She was badly burned, and had she been much younger or older, she might not have survived. But she was young and strong enough to allow the wounds to heal secondarily, this is, on their own."

34. Paul d'Ambert, *Le Nain jaune* (August 1, 1863).
35. D'Ambert, *Le Nain jaune*.
36. The people had loved Emma as much as those at court; they were incensed that the Paris Opéra kept its doors open on the night of her funeral and wrote letters to newspapers holding the institution accountable for her death.
37. *Le Moniteur universel* (August 3, 1863).
38. Quatrelles L'Épine, 43.
39. Quatrelles L'Épine, 39.

CHAPTER 4: STRIVING AND STARVING FOR ATTENTION

1. Jennifer Homans, *Apollo's Angels, A History of Ballet* (New York: Random House, 2010), 247.
2. Homans, 254.
3. Alexander Pushkin, *Eugene Onegin*, trans. Vladimir Nabokov, revised edition (Princeton: Princeton University Press, 1975), 103.
4. Lynn Garafola, *Legacies of Twentieth-Century Dance* (Middletown, CT: Wesleyan University Press, 2005), 26.
5. Mindy Aloff, *Dance Anecdotes: Stories from the Worlds of Ballet, Broadway, the Ballroom, and Modern Dance* (New York: Oxford University Press, 2006), 118.
6. Jeffrey Taylor, "The Dancer, the Tsar, and the Boy Who Believed He Was the Romonov's Lost Heir," *Express on Sunday*, July 30, 2006, 58–59.
7. Quoted in Aloff, 206.

8. See Judith Mackrell, *Bloomsbury Ballerina: Lydia Lopokova, Imperial Dancer and Mrs. John Maynard Keynes* (London: Orion Publishing, 2009).

9. Quoted in Jennifer Homans, *Apollo's Angels: A History of Ballet* (New York: Random House, 2010), 320–21.

10. Quoted in Laura Leivick, "Through Which She Is Seen: Bodies and Ballet," in *The Threepenny Review* 2 (Summer 1980), 30.

11. Keith Money, *Anna Pavlova: Her Life and Art* (New York: Alfred A. Knopf, 1982).

12. "Anna Pavlova Dies at Height of Fame," *New York Times*, January 23, 1931. www.nytimes.com/specials/magazine4/articles/pavlova1.html.

13. Quoted in Walter Sorrell, "The Diaghilev Era," in *The Dance Anthology*, ed. Cobbett Steinberg (New York: New American Library, 1980), 396.

14. Quoted in Anna Kisselgoff, "Inseparable from a Swan," review of Keith Money, *Anna Pavlova: Her Life and Her Art, New York Times*, January 2, 1983.

15. David Michael Levin, "Balanchine's Formalism," in *Salmagundi*, 33/34 (Spring–Summer 1976): 216.

16. Marilyn Hunt, "The Prodigal Son's Russian Roots: Avant-Garde and Icons," in *Dance Chronicle* 5, no. 1 (1982): 27.

17. Adrienne L. McLean, *Dying Swans and Madmen: Ballet, the Body, and Narrative Cinema*. (New Brunswick, NJ: Rutgers University Press, 2008), 230.

18. Hunt, 41.

19. Hunt, 28.

20. Quoted in Marvin Mudrick, "The King and His Queens," *Hudson Review* 38, no. 3 (Autumn 1985): 524.

21. Quoted in John Gruen, *The Private World of Ballet* (New York: Viking Press, 1975), 96–97.

22. Interview with the author, February 24, 2012.

23. Toni Bentley, *Winter Season: A Dancer's Journal* (New York: Random House, 1982), 34.

24. Quoted in Gruen, 284.

25. Barbara Millberg Fisher, *In Balanchine's Company: A Dancer's Memoir*. (Middletown, CT: Wesleyan University Press, 2006), 26.

26. Quoted in Suzanne Gordon, *Off Balance: The Real World of Ballet* (New York: McGraw-Hill Book Company, 1983), 209.

27. Quoted in McLean, 230.

28. Suki Schorer and Russell Lee, *Suki Schorer on Balanchine Technique* (New York: Alfred A. Knopf, 1999), 28.

29. Quoted in Levin, 224.

30. Camille Hardy, "Bringing Bourrées to Broadway: George Balanchine's Career in the Commercial Theater," *World Literature Today* 80, no. 2 (March–April, 2006): 16–18.

31. Quoted in Gruen, 62.

32. Jessica R. Feldman, "Fifth Position," in *Callaloo* 17, no. 2 (Spring 1994): 571.

33. Susan Young, "From Ballet to Boxing, The Evolution of a Female Athlete." in *My Life at the Gym*, ed. Jo Malin (Albany: SUNY Press, 2010): 45.

34. McLean, 230.

35. Gruen, 65.

36. Bentley, 16.

37. Gelsey Kirkland, with Greg Lawrence, *Dancing on My Grave* (New York: Doubleday Books, 1986), 55–56.

38. Linda H. Hamilton, J. Brooks-Gunn, Michelle Warren, "Sociocultural Influences on Eating Disorders in Professional Ballet Dancers," *International Journal of Eating Disorders* 4, no. 4, (1985): 466.

39. Hamilton, et. al., 467.

40. C. Martin and F. Bellisle, "Eating Attitudes and Taste Responses in Young Ballerinas," *Physiology & Behaviour* 46, no. 2, (1988): 223.

41. Hamilton et. al., 466.

42. Daniel le Grange, Jason Tibbs, Timothy D. Noakes, "Implications of a Diagnosis of Anorexia Nervosa in a Ballet School," *International Journal of Eating Disorders* 15, no. 4 (1994): 370.

43. Hamilton et. al., 465.

44. Le Grange, et. al. 370.

45. T. Tölgyes and J. Nemessury, "Epidemiological Studies on Adverse Dieting Behaviours and Eating Disorders Among Young People in Hungary," *Social Psychiatry and Psychiatric Epidemiology* 39 (2004): 647.

46. Quoted in Gordon, 154–55.

47. Wendy Oliver, "Reading the Ballerina's Body: Susan Bordo Sheds Light on Anastasia Volochkova and Heidi Guenther," *Dance Research Journal* 37, no. 2 (Women's Health in Dance, Winter, 2005): 46–7.

48. Fleur Darkin, "The Everyday Dancer by Deborah Bull—review, *The Observer*, October 9, 2011. www.guardian.co.uk/stage/2011/oct/09/everyday-dancer-deborah-bull-review.

49. Quoted in Alistair Smith, "Seven Days On Stage: Dance World Puts Spotlight on Anorexia," *Guardian*, May 4, 2012, http://www.guardian.co.uk/stage/2012/may/04/seven-days-stage-dance-anorexia-ballet.

50. Quoted in Matthew Lawrence, "The Complicated Truth About Eating Disorders in Ballet," *Dancing Times*, March 5, 2012, http://www.dancing-times.co.uk/features/item/830-thecomplicatedtrutheatingdisordersinballet.

51. Interview with author, November, 11, 2011.

52. http://ballerina-thin.tumblr.com/.

53. http://preppypinkballerina.blogspot.ca/.

54. Quoted in Oliver, 39.

55. Oliver, 49.

56. In an interview with *Dance Magazine*, Holmes said that two and a half years before Guenther's death, "when she first came to the company, she was a little chubby, and the artistic staff sat with her and asked her to lose five pounds." The next season, Guenther had the shape they wanted, but she continued to grow thin and Holmes asked the company's nutritionists to monitor her. She died while visiting her family in California. Susan Walker, "Ballet Shows Its Muscles" *Toronto Star*, November 22, 1997, 1.

57. Lisa Lipman, "Boston Ballet Case Dismissed," *Associated Press*, March 12, 2001.

58. Quoted in Gordon, 127.

59. Quoted in Ann Daly, "The Balanchine Woman: Of Hummingbirds and Channel Swimmers," *Drama Review*: TDR, 31, no. 1 (Spring 1987): 16.

60. Quoted in Gordon, 183.

61. Quoted in Gordon, 208.

62. Quoted in Gordon, 209.

CHAPTER 5: LABORING UNDER AN ILLUSION

1. Quoted in Suzanne Gordon, *Off Balance: The Real World of Ballet* (New York: McGraw-Hill Book Company, 1983), 185.

2. Gordon, 189.

3. Barbara Rowes, "Baryshnikov Picks a New Partner with Classic Grace, Cynthia Harvey," *People*, January 12, 1981.

4. Aimee Lee Ball, "Swan's Way, ABT's Susan Jaffe in her Championship Season," *New York*, June 5, 1989, 40–44.

5. Kate Regan, "This Ballerina Is No Fragile Swan," *San Francisco Chronicle*, November 10, 1985, 35.

6. Deirdre Kelly, "Gregory Finds Don Quixote Hurts So Good," *Globe and Mail*, November 6, 1985, C9.

7. Deirdre Kelly, "Ballerina Sees Silver Lining in Exit," *Globe and Mail*, December 18, 1995, C1.

8. Marcia B. Siegel, "Growing Old in the Land of the Young," *Hudson Review* 29, no. 2 (Summer 1976): 250.

9. Occupational Outlook Handbook (OOH), 2010–11, "Dancers and Choreographers," www.bls.gov/oco/ocos094.htm#earnings (accessed March 9, 2012).

10. Interview with the author, September 16, 2011.

11. "Dancer Job Description." http://careers.stateuniversity.com/ pages/105/Dancer.html#ixzz1oe8pblj2 (accessed March 12, 2012).

12. Deirdre Kelly, "Body Politics," *Saturday Night*, February 1992.

13. Deirdre Kelly, "New Director Sees Changes Afoot for Ballet B.C.," *Globe and Mail*, November 29, 1989, C13.

14. Deirdre Kelly, "National Ballet Report Card: Dancers Superb, Choreography Uneven," *Globe and Mail*, November 27, 1998, C8; Gary Smith, "Rex Harrington a True Ballet Star," *Hamilton Spectator*, November 27, 1998, C8.

15. Deirdre Kelly, "Glasco Considers Legal Action After Dismissal from National Ballet," *Globe and Mail*, December 19, 1998, C2.

16. Jennie Schulman. "National Ballet of Canada," *Back Stage*, October 30, 1998.

17. Kimberly Glasco, "Why I Took A Stand: Performing Artists Need Protection from Arbitrary Action and Abuse of Authority, Says Dancer Kimberly Glasco," *Globe and Mail* July 21, 2000, A11.

18. Olga Sobolevskaya, "Anastasia Volochkova: A Perfect Scandal," RIA *Vesti* 3 (October 2003). http://english.pravda.ru/society/stories/ 09-10-2003/3866-volochkova-0/ (accessed November 2, 2011).

19. "Weight of the Law Lifts Swan Lake Star Back to Starlight," *Adelaide Advertiser*, November 28, 2003, 3.

20. "Ballerina Fired for Nude Photos in Men's Magazine," *Canadian Press–Broadcast Wire*, October 8, 2010.

21. Cynthia R. Fagen, "Naked Ballerina Exposes Boss," *New York Post*, October 17, 2010, 18.

22. Kelly, "Glasco Considers Legal Action."

23. Statistics Canada 2006 Census. Employment Income Statistics in Constant (2005) Dollars, Dancers. www12.statcan.ca/census-recensement/index-eng.cfm (accessed March 8, 2012).

24. U.S. Census Bureau, "Earnings by Detailed Occupation: 1999: United States: Females," www.census.gov/hhes/www/income/data/earnings/call2usfemale.html (accessed March 8, 2012).

25. In the Matter of an Arbitration: Kimberly Glasco and The National Ballet of Canada and Canadian Actors' Equity Association, 27.

26. In the Matter of an Arbitration, 23.

27. Urjo Kareda, "The Black Swan," *Toronto Life*, May 1999, 63–69.

28. There would be five separate hearings in all, excluding the main case, which was not even heard: the majority dealt with Glasco's bid for temporary reinstatement, with the National Ballet seeking to appeal, and were heard by a variety of judges plus an arbitrator, making the case, at times, hard to follow.

29. Deirdre Kelly, "Is Glasco Really Too Old to Dance? Ballet Experts Divided Over Kudelka Decision," *Globe and Mail*, December 24, 1998, D1.

30. Deirdre Kelly, "Putting Primas in Their Place: The National Ballet of Canada's Founder Says the Current Bitter Battle There Is a Typical Result of Many Dancers' Blind Egos," *Globe and Mail*, January 11, 1999, C1.

31. Deirdre Kelly, "Ruined Reputation Ends Chances of Work: Lawyer," *Globe and Mail*, May 11, 2000, A25.

32. Interview with the author, December 12, 2011.

33. Paul Bunner, *Alberta Report*, May 8, 2000.

34 Kelly, "Putting Primas in Their Place," C1.

35. Deirdre Kelly, "Ballerinas Talk Back. Flexing Some Muscle: While Retirement Has Always Been Hotly Debated, More Dancers Are Refusing to Accept the Traditional Role as Passive Observers of Their Destiny," *Globe and Mail*, December 31, 1998, D1.

36. Kelly, "Ballerinas Talk Back," D1.

37. 1. Justice Winkler to stop the members' meeting; 2. arbitrator Christopher Albertyn, who issued the order for reinstatement; 3. Justice O'Leary, who heard the application for a stay; 4. Back to Albertyn, who upheld his original award; 5. Justice Swinton, who upheld the arbitration award.

38. Deirdre Kelly and Michael Posner, "Glasco, National Ballet End Their Marathon Pas De Deux: Dancer Wins Substantial Cash Settlement But Would Rather Be Working," *Globe and Mail*, July 21, 2000, A5.

39. Glasco v. the National Ballet, agreed public statement. www.sgmlaw.com/en/about/notablecases/ NotableCaseGlascovsNationalBalletofCanada.cf.

40. Margaret Wente, "The Glasco Fiasco (Act XVII) In Which the National Ballet's Belligerent Ballerina Triumphs in Court, But Loses Friends," *Globe and Mail*, July 4, 2000, A15.

41. Michael Crabb, "She's No Diva: At 38 Andrea Boardman Was Told Her Days with Les Grands Ballets Canadiens Were Over," *National Post*, July 31, 2001, B01.

42. Quoted in Kathleen McGuire, "When Words Hurt," *Dance Magazine*, July 2011, http://www.dancemagazine.com/issues/July-2011/ When-Words-Hurt.

43. Tom Kington, "One in Five Ballerinas at La Scala Is Anorexic, Leading Dancer Claims," *The Observer*, December 4, 2011. www.guardian.co.uk/world/2011/dec/04/ ballerinas-la-scala-anorexic-claim.

44. Quoted in Kington.

45. "No Anorexia Emergency, La Scala Ballerinas Claim," February 8, 2012. http://medicalxpress.com/news/2012-02- anorexia-emergency-la-scala-ballerinas.html.

46. Quoted in "No Anorexia Emergency."

47. Bryan S. Turner and Steven Wainwright, "Corps de Ballet: The Case of the injured Ballet Dancer," *Sociology of Health & Illness* 25, no. 4 (2003): 271–272.

CHAPTER 6: CHANGES AFOOT

1. Interview with the author, November 29, 2011.

2. Interview with the author, February 24, 2012.

3. Interview with the author, December 5, 2011.

4. Interview with the author, September 16, 2011.

5. Alastair Macaulay, "Timeless Alchemy, Even When No One Is Dancing," *New York Times*, November 28, 2010, 1.

6. John Springer, "I'm Not Fat, Says Ballerina Faulted for 'Too Many Sugarplums,'" December 13, 2010. http://today.msnbc.msn.com/id/40639920/ns/today-today_people/t/im-not-fat-says-ballerina-faulted-too-many-sugarplums/#.T2eHNNWXSI.

7. Interview with the author, November 30, 2011.

8. Laura Rico, "Keeping Dancers on Their Toes: New Technique Allows MRIs of Ballet Dancers En Pointe, Aiding Injury Treatment and Prevention," University of California, Irvine. www.uci.edu/features/2010/08/feature_ballet_100830.php.

9. Rico, "Keeping Dancers."

10. Interview with the author, November 30, 2011.

11. Sharon Verghis, "Best Foot Forward," *Sydney Morning Herald*, December 14, 2002, 30.

12. Australian Ballet, "Injury Management and Prevention Programme," 1.

13. Australian Ballet, 8.

14. Email exchange with the author, December 22, 2011.

15. Verghis, "Best Foot Forward."

16. Email exchange with the author, December 22, 2011.

17. Interview with the author, November 26, 2011.

18. Email exchange with the author, December 7, 2011.

19. Interview with the author, October 2006.

20. Interview with the author, February 24, 2012.

21. Susan Walker. "Some Signs of Life After Dance; Their Bodies Pushed to the Brink, Dancers Seek Second Careers with Help of a Local Agency," *Toronto Star*, January 31, 2008, E01.

22. Deirdre Kelly, "Kain, Hart to Perform at Fundraiser for Dancers' Centre: Budget Cuts Have Hurt the Dancer Transition Resource Centre, Founded a Decade Ago to Help Performers Make the Leap from Stage to Other Careers," *Globe and Mail*, September 30, 1996, C4.

23. Deirdre Kelly, "Kain, Hart to Perform."

24. Deirdre Kelly, "Av Paul Finds There Is Life After Dance: 'By Facing the Fact of Retirement, It's Somehow Been Less Difficult,'" *Globe and Mail*, May 11, 1985, E5.

25. Interview with the author, February 24, 2012.
26. William Littler, "Author's Digging Proves There's Life After Dance," *Toronto Star*, August 1, 1987, E3.
27. Littler, "Author's Digging."
28. Jenny Jackson, "Amid Accolades, Our Dancers Starve," *Ottawa Citizen*, January 15, 2005, G6.
29. Interview with the author, December 6, 2011.
30. Morley Walker, "A place in her Hart. Former RWB star has fond memories of Winnipeg but her life now is in Toronto," *Winnipeg Free Press*, April 17, 2008, D1.
31. Interviews with the author, October and November 2006.
32. Janice Dineen, "Dancer Transition Centre: Finding Their Feet. As They Face Retirement, Dancers Get Help to Adjust to the Strange New World Outside the Theatre." *Toronto Star*, September 1, 1990, F1.
33. Deirdre Kelly, "Kain, Hart to Perform."
34. Dineen, "Dancer Transition Centre."
35. Dineen, "Dancer Transition Centre."
36. Interview with the author, December 9, 2011.
37. Interview with the author, February 24, 2012.
38. Vicki Smith Paluch, "Motherhood Doesn't Slow Down Ballerinas," *Los Angeles Daily News*, April 24, 2005, U4.
39. Linda H. Hamilton, J. Brooks-Gunn, and Michelle Warren, "Sociocultural Influences on Eating Disorders in Professional Ballet Dancers," *International Journal of Eating Disorders* 4, no. 4 (1985): 474.
40. Interview with the author, December 16, 2011.
41. Sarah Kaufman. "Why's Ballet Showing Up in Pop Music Videos?" *Washington Post*, April 10, 2011, E02.
42. Interview with the author, December 16, 2011.
43. Kaufman, "Why's Ballet Showing Up?"
44. Interview with the author, November 17, 2010.
45. Interview with the author, September 22, 2011.
46. Interview with the author, New York City, September 19, 2011.

EPILOGUE
1. Interview with the author, November 30, 2011.
2. Quoted in Sibyl Kleiner, "Thinking with the Mind, Syncing with the Body: Ballet as Symbolic and Nonsymbolic Interaction," *Symbolic Interaction* 32, no. 3 (Summer 2009): 254.

3. Anne Summers, "On Begging to Be a Bridesmaid in a Ballerina Dress: Some Meanings of British Fashion in the 1950s," *History Workshop Journal* 44 (Autumn 1997): 230–31.

4. Evan Alderson, "Ballet as Ideology: 'Giselle,' Act II," *Dance Chronicle* 10, no. 3 (1987): 292.

5. Quoted in Alderson, 302 (in a footnote citing a review by Debra Cash of Suzanne Gordon's book, *Off Balance: The Real World of Ballet*).

BIBLIOGRAPHY

Aalten, Anna. "In the Presence of the Body: Theorizing Training, Injuries and Pain in Ballet." *Dance Research Journal* 37, no. 2 (Winter 2005): 55–72.

Albertyn, Christopher. "In the Matter of an Arbitration: Between Kimberly Glasco and The National Ballet of Canada and Canadian Actors' Equity Association. Heard in Toronto, Ontario, August 29, October 16, November, 29, December 3 and 4. Award: March 16, 2000." Ontario Labour Arbitration, No. 209, 87 LAC. (4th) 1.

Alderson, Evan. "Ballet as Ideology: 'Giselle,' Act II." *Dance Chronicle* 10, no. 3 (1987): 290–304.

Aloff, Mindy. *Dance Anecdotes: Stories from the Worlds of Ballet, Broadway, the Ballroom, and Modern Dance.* New York: Oxford University Press, 2006.

Anderson, Jack. "Preserving Nijinska's Ballets: A Family Affair." *New York Times,* August 18, 1991.

"Anna Pavlova Dies at Height of Fame." *New York Times,* January 23, 1931. www.nytimes.com/specials/magazine4/articles/pavlova1.html.

"A New Treatise on the Art of Dancing First Published in *The Lady's Magazine* 1: Volume XVI in Six Instalments (February, March, April, May, June, July 1785)." *Dance Research* 11, no. 2 (Autumn 1993): 43–59.

Astier, Régine. "Camargo, Marie-Anne." In *International Encyclopedia of Ballet.* Edited by Martha Bremser. London: St James Press, 1993.

———. "Françoise Prévost: The Unauthorized Biography." In *Women's Work, Making Dance in Europe before 1800*. Edited by Lynn Matluck Brooks. Madison: University of Wisconsin Press, 2007.

Au, Susan. *Ballet and Modern Dance*. London: Thames and Hudson, 1988.

Australian Ballet. "Injury Management and Prevention Programme." www.australianballet.com.au/res/pdfs/ InjuryManagementandPreventionProgramme.pdf.

Balanchine, George, and Francis Mason. *101 Stories of the Great Ballets: The Scene-by-Scene Stories of the Most Popular Ballets, Old and New*. New York: Random House, 1989.

Ball, Aimee Lee. "Swan's Way, ABT's Susan Jaffe in Her Championship Season." *New York*, June 5, 1989: 40–4.

"Ballerina Fired for Nude Photos in Men's Magazine." *Canadian Press–Broadcast Wire*. October 8, 2010.

Banes, Sally. *Dancing Women: Female Bodies on Stage*. New York: Routledge, 1998.

Beaujoyeulx, Balthazar. "Le Balet comique de la royne." Edited and translated by Carol and Lander McClintock. *American Institute of Musicology: Musicological Studies and Documents* 25 (1971): 90–91.

Beaumont, Cyril William. *A Short History of Ballet*. London: C. W. Beaumont, 1933.

———. "Marie Taglioni." In *The Complete Book of Ballets*. London: Putnam, 1937.

———. *Three French Dancers of the Eighteenth Century*. London: C.W. Beaumont, 1934.

———. *Three French Dancers of the 19th Century: Duvernay-Livry-Beaugrand*. London: C.W. Beaumont, 1935.

Bentley, Toni. *Winter Season: A Dancer's Journal*. New York: Random House, 1982.

Bishop-Gwyn, Carol. *The Pursuit of Perfection: A Life of Celia Franca*. Toronto: Cormorant Books, 2011.

Blackler, Zoë, and Ben Hoyle. "Little Dancer Points to Sensational Discovery of Degas Sculpture Hoard." *Times*, November 28, 2009.

Blasis, Carlo. *An Elementary Treatise upon the Theory and Practice of the Art of Dancing*. New York: Dover Publications, 1968.

Bournonville, August. *My Theatre Life*. Translated by Patricia N. McAndrew. Middletown, CT: Wesleyan University Press, 1979.

Bradshaw, Richard. "Someone Must Lead: Don't Let the Courts Program Ballet and Opera, Says the COC's Richard Bradshaw." *Globe and Mail*, May 11, 2000.

Browse, Lillian. *Degas Dancers*. London: Faber and Faber, 1949.

Bull, Deborah. *The Everyday Dancer*. London: Faber and Faber, 2011.

Bunner, Paul. "Uppity Ballerinas." *Alberta Report*, May 8, 2000. www.high-beam.com/publications/alberta-report-p5587/may-2000.

Canada Council for the Arts, News Releases, 2000. "Joysanne Sidimus Wins Canada Council for the Arts Jacqueline Lemieux Prize." Ottawa, April 8, 1999.

Carter, Alexandra. "Blonde, Bewigged and Winged with Gold: Ballet Girls in the Music Halls of Late Victorian and Edwardian England." *Dance Research: The Journal of the Society of Dance Research* 13, no. 2 (Autumn–Winter 1995): 28–46.

Castiglioni, Baldassare. *The Book of the Courtier*. Translated by Charles S. Singleton. Garden City, NJ: Anchor Books, 1959.

Charlton, David, and Sarah Hibberd. "'My Father Was a Poor Parisian Musician': A Memoir (1756) Concerning Rameau, Handel's Library and Sallé." *Journal of the Royal Musical Association* 128, no. 2 (2003): 161–99.

Chazin-Bennahun, Judith. *The Ballets of Antony Tudor: Studies in Psyche and Satire*. New York: Oxford University Press, 1994.

———. *Dance in the Shadow of the Guillotine*. Carbondale: Southern Illinois University Press, 1988.

———. "Unmasking the Body: From Lully to the Revolution." *Dance Chronicle* 33, 2 (2010): 310–19.

Christout, Marie-Françoise, and Fernande Bassan. "Les Ballets des Champs-Élysées: A Legendary Adventure." *Dance Chronicle* 27, no. 2 (2004): 157–198.

Christout, Marie-Françoise, and Lucienne J. Serrano. "The Paris Opera Ballet." *Dance Chronicle* 2, no. 2 (1978): 131–42.

Citron, Paula. "Glasco, National Ballet Settle Lengthy Feud—Ballerina Kimberly Glasco Settles Wrongful Termination Case Against National Ballet of Canada." *Dance Magazine* 74, no. 10 (October 2000): 41.

———. "Kimberly Glasco Fiasco Reaches Arbitration." *Dance Magazine* 73, no. 6 (June 1999): 31.

Clarke, Mary, and Clement Crisp. *Ballerina: The Art of Women in Classical Ballet*. London: BBC Books, 1987.

———. *The History of Dance*. New York: Crown Books, 1981.

Coeyman, Barbara. "Theatres for Opera and Ballet During the Reigns of Louis XIV and Louis XV." *Early Music* I (The Baroque Stage II, February, 1990): 22–37.

Conlogue, Ray. "Pointe of Law." *Globe and Mail*, April 24, 2000.

Conyers, Claude. "Courtesans in Dance History: Les Belles de la Belle Époque." *Dance Chronicle* 26, no. 2 (2003): 219–43.

Cooper, Elizabeth. *Le Balet de la Comique: An Analysis*. http://depts.washington.edu/uwdance/dance344reading/bctextpi.htm.

Copeland, Roger and Marshall Cohen. "The Dance Medium." In *What is Dance?* Edited by Roger Copeland and Marshall Cohen. New York: Oxford University Press, 1983.

Costonis, Maureen Needham. "Guimard, Marie-Madeleine." In *International Dictionary of Ballet*. Edited by Martha Bremser. London: St. James Press, 1993.

Crabb, Michael. "She's No Diva: At 38 Andrea Boardman Was Told Her Days with Les Grands Ballets Canadiens Were Over. She Could Have Fought the Decision, as Some Advised, But She Didn't Want to split the Company and Force People to Take Sides." *National Post*, July 31, 2001.

Croce, Arlene. *Afterimages*. New York: Vintage Books, 1979.

———. *Writing in the Dark, Dancing in the* New Yorker. New York: Farrar, Strauss and Giroux, 2000.

Cross, Samuel H. "The Russian Ballet Before Dyagilev." *Slavonic and East European Review*. American Series 3, no. 4 (December 1944): 19–49.

Dacier, Émile. *Une Danseuse de l'Opéra sur Louis XV: Mlle Sallé (1707–1756) d'après des documents inédits*. Paris: Plon-Nourrit, 1909.

Daly, Ann. "The Balanchine Woman: Of Hummingbirds and Channel Swimmers." *The Drama Review:* TDR 31, no. I (Spring 1987): 8–21.

Danilova, Alexandra. *Choura: The Memoirs of Alexandra Danilova*. New York: Knopf, 1986.

Darkin, Fleur. "The Everyday Dancer by Deborah Bull–review." *The Observer*, October 9, 2011. www.guardian.co.uk/stage/2011/oct/09/everyday-dancer-deborah-bull-review.

Denby, Edwin. *Dance Writings*. Edited by Robert Cornfield and William MacKay. New York: Alfred A. Knopf, 1986.

Desmond, Jane C., ed. *Meaning in Motion: New Cultural Studies of Dance*. Third Printing. Durham: Duke University Press, 2003.

DeVonyar, Jill, and Richard Kendall. "The Class of 1881: Degas, Drawing, and the Little Dancer Aged Fourteen." *Master Drawings* 41, no. 2 (Summer 2003): 151–62.

———. *Degas and the Dance*. New York: Harry N. Abrams, 2002.

Dineen, Janice. "Dancer Transition Centre: Finding Their Feet." *Toronto Star*, September 1, 1990.

Eksteins, Modris. *Rites of Spring: The Great War and the Birth of the Modern Age*. Toronto: Key Porter Books, 1989.

Eliot, Karen. *Dancing Lives, Five Female Dancers from the Ballet d'Action to Merce Cunningham*. Chicago: University of Illinois Press, 2007.

Engelhardt, Molly. "Marie Taglioni, Ballerina Extraordinaire." *Nineteenth-Century Gender Studies* 6.3 (Winter 2010). www.ncgsjournal.com/issue63/engelhardt.htm.

Engels, Friedrich. "Introduction." In *On the 20th Anniversary of the Paris Commune in Karl Marx, The Civil War in France* (1891). www.marxists.org/archive/marx/works/1871/civil-war-france/postscript.htm.

Escoffier, Jeffrey. "Ballet Across Borders: Careers and Culture in the World of Dancers by Helen Wulff." *Contemporary Sociology* 29, no. 5 (September 2000): 728–29.

Fagen, Cynthia R. "Naked Ballerina Exposes Boss." *New York Post*, October 17, 2010.

Fairfax, Edmund. "The 'Fair Sex' and Its Style." In *The Styles of Eighteenth-Century Ballet*. Lanham, MD: Scarecrow Press, 2003.

Farrell, Suzanne and Toni Bentley. *Holding on to the Air: An Autobiography*. New York: Summit Books, 1990.

Feldman, Jessica R. "Fifth Position." *Callaloo* 17, no. 2 (Spring 1994): 569–74.

Fisher, Barbara Millberg. *In Balanchine's Company: A Dancer's Memoir*. Middletown, CT: Wesleyan University Press, 2006.

Forbes, Elizabeth. "Offenbach's Art." *The Musical Times* 121, no. 1652 (October 1980): 629.

Franko, Mark. *Dance as Text: Ideologies of the Baroque Body*. Cambridge: Cambridge University Press, 1993.

Fraser, John, with contribution by Eve Arnold. *Private View: Inside Baryshnikov's American Ballet Theatre*. Toronto: Bantam Books, 1988.

Garafola, Lynn. *Diaghilev's Ballets Russes*. New York: Oxford University Press, 1989.

———. *Legacies of Twentieth Century Dance*. Middletown, CT: Wesleyan University Press, 2005.

————, ed. *Rethinking the Sylph: New Perspectives on the Romantic Ballet.*
Hanover, NH: University Press of New England, 1997.

————. "The Travesty Dancer in Nineteenth-Century Ballet." *Dance Research Journal* 17, no. 2 (1986): 35–40.

Gautier, Théophile. "Le Rat." In *Quand On Voyage.* Paris: Michel Lévy Frères, Libraires Éditeurs, 1865.

Gautier, Théophile, Jules Janin and Philarète Chasles. *Les Beautés de l'opéra, ou Chefs-d'oeuvre lyriques.* Paris: Soulié, 1845.

Genné, Beth. "Creating a Canon, Creating the Classics in Twentieth-Century British Ballet." *Dance Research: The Journal of the Society for Dance Research* 18, no. 2 (Winter 2000): 132–62.

Glasco v. the National Ballet. Agreed Public Statement. www.sgmlaw.com/en/about/notablecases/NotableCaseGlascovsNationalBalletof Canada.cf.

Glasco, Kimberly. "Why I Took a Stand: Performing Artists Need Protection from Arbitrary Action and Abuse of Authority, Says Dancer Kimberly Glasco." *Globe and Mail,* July 21, 2000.

Goncourt, Edmond de. *Journal; Mémoires de la vie littéraire.* Paris: Fasquelle, 1956.

————. *La Guimard.* Paris, 1893. Reprinted Geneva, 1973.

Gordon, Suzanne. *Off Balance: The Real World of Ballet.* New York: McGraw-Hill Book Company, 1983.

Green, Jill. "Somatic Authority and the Myth of the Ideal Body in Dance Education." *Dance Research Journal* 31, no. 2 (Fall 1999): 80–100.

Greskovic, Robert. *Ballet 101: A Complete Guide to Learning and Loving the Ballet.* Montclair, NJ: Limelight Editions, 1998.

Griffin, Susan. *The Book of the Courtesans.* New York: Random House, 2001.

Grimm, Friedrich Melchior, Freiherr von. *Mémoires historiques, littéraires et anecdotiques, Tirés de la correspondance philosophique et critique, adressée au Duc de Saxe Gotha, depuis 1770 jusqu'en 1790, 2. éd., rev. et corrigée.* London: Colburn, 1814.

Gruen, John. *The Private World of Ballet.* New York: Viking Press, 1975.

Guest, Ivor Forbes. "Emma Livry 1842–1863." *Dance Gazette* 174 (June, 1980): 52.

————. "Letters from London: Guimard's Farewell to the Stage." *Dance Chronicle* 18, no. 2 (1995): 207–15.

———. "Luminaries of the Opera Ballet in 1770." In *The Ballet of the Enlightenment: The Establishment of the Ballet d'Action in France, 1770–1793.* London: Dance Books, 1996.

———. *The Ballet of the Second Empire: 1858–1870.* London: Adam and Charles Black, 1953.

———. *The Paris Opera Ballet.* Alton: Dance Books, 2006.

Guest, Ivor Forbes, ed. *Gautier on Dance.* London: Dance Books: 1986.

Hall, Coryne. *Imperial Dancer, Mathilde Kschessinska and the Romanovs.* Stroud, UK: Sutton Publishing Inc., 2005.

Hamilton, Linda H., J. Brooks-Gunn, Michelle P. Warren. "Sociocultural Influences on Eating Disorders in Professional Ballet Dancers." *International Journal of Eating Disorders* 4, no. 4, (1985): 465–77.

Hammond, Phillip E. and Sandra N. Hammond. "The Internal Logic of Dance: A Weberian Perspective on the History of Ballet." *Journal of Social History* 12, no. 4 (Summer 1979): 562–608.

Hammond, Sandra N., and Phillip E. Hammond. "Technique and Autonomy in the Development of the Art: A Case Study in Ballet." *Dance Research Journal* 21, no. 2 (Autumn 1989): 15–24.

Hanna, Judith Lynne. *Dance, Sex and Gender: Signs of Identity, Dominance, Defiance, and Desire.* Chicago: University of Chicago Press, 1988.

Hardy, Camille. "Bringing Bourrées to Broadway: George Balanchine's Career in the Commercial Theater." *World Literature Today* 80, no. 2 (March–April 2006): 16–18.

Hargrove, June. "Degas' Little Dancer in the World of Pantomime." *Apollo* (February 1998): 15–21.

Hatcher, Judith. "Trials, Troubles and Temptations in a Dangerous Era: Ballet Dancers in the 19th Century-Abstract." *Dance Magazine* (January 1999). http://findarticles.com/p/articles/mi_m1083/ls_1_73/ai_53501128.

Heppenstall, Rayner. "The Sexual Idiom." In *What is Dance?* Edited by Roger Copeland and Marshall Cohen, 267–88. New York: Oxford University Press, 1983.

Higgonet, Patrice. L.R. *Paris: Capital of the World.* Cambridge: Belknap Press, 2002.

Hilton, Wendy. *Dance and Music of Court and Theater: The French Noble Style 1690–1725.* New York: Dance Books, 1981.

Holden, Anthony. *Tchaikovsky: A Biography.* New York: Random House, 1995.

Homans, Jennifer. *Apollo's Angels: A History of Ballet*. New York: Random House, 2010.

Huckenpahler, Victoria. "Confessions of an Opera Director: Chapters from the *Mémoires* of Dr. Louis Véron, Part I." *Dance Chronicle* 7, no. 1 (1984): 50–106.

———. "Confessions of an Opera Director: Chapters from the *Mémoires* of Dr. Louis Véron, Part II." *Dance Chronicle* 7, no. 2 (1984): 198–228.

———. "Confessions of an Opera Director: Chapters from the *Mémoires* of Dr. Louis Véron, Part III." *Dance Chronicle* 7, no. 3 (1984): 345–70.

Hunt, Lynn Avery. *Eroticism and the Body Politic*. Baltimore: Johns Hopkins University Press, 1990.

Hunt, Marilyn. "The Prodigal Son's Russian Roots: Avant-Garde and Icons." *Dance Chronicle* 5, no. 1 (1982): 24–49.

In the Matter of the Judicial Review Procedure Act and In the Matter of an Interlocutory Award of Arbitrator Christopher Albertyn, dated March 16, 2000, Between the National Ballet of Canada (Applicant) and Kimberly Glasco and Canadian Actors' Equity Association and Christopher Albertyn (Respondents), Heard March 29, 2000.

Jackson, Jenny. "Amid Accolades, Our Dancers Starve." *Ottawa Citizen*, January 15, 2005.

Janine Charrat Facebook Page. https://www.facebook.com/pages/Janine-Charrat/134001929998865.

Janine Charrat Returns to Ballet After Serious Burn. (Video). British Pathé. 1962. www.britishpathe.com/video/janine-charrat-returns-to-ballet-after-serious-burn.

Je redanserai. (Video). Vidéo INA. Available at www.ina.fr/art-et-culture/arts-du-spectacle/video/CPF04006930/je-redanserai.fr.html.

Jefferson, Aisha I. "Q&A: Curvy Ballerina Misty Copeland Talks Body Image." BlackVoices. March 21, 2011. www.bvwellness.com/2011/03/21/qanda-curvy-ballerina-misty-copeland-talks-body-image.

Johnstone, Fanny. "Women: Dressed to Kill." *Guardian*, October 20, 2006.

Jordan, David P. *Transforming Paris: the Life and Labors of Baron Haussmann*. New York: The Free Press, 1995.

Kahane, Martine. "Enquête sur la Petite Danseuse de quatorze ans de Degas—Le modèle." *La Revue du Musée d'Orsay* 7 (Autumn 1998). Paris: Reunion des Musées nationaux and Musée d'Orsay. Revision and translation published in *Degas Sculptures: Catalogue Raisonné of the Bronzes.* Edited by Joseph S. Czestochowski and Anne Pingeot. Memphis: The Torch Press and International Arts, 2002.

Kain, Karen. *Movement Never Lies: An Autobiography.* Toronto: McClelland and Stewart, 1994.

Kareda, Urjo. "The Black Swan." *Toronto Life* (May 1999): 63–69.

Karsavina, Tamara. *Theatre Street: The Reminiscences of Tamara Karsavina.* London: Columbus Books, 1988.

Kaufman, Sarah. "Why's Ballet Showing Up in Pop Music Videos?" *Washington Post,* April 10, 2011, E02.

Kealinohomoku, Joann. "An Anthropologist Looks at Ballet as a Form of Ethnic Dance." In *What Is Dance?* Edited by Roger Copeland and Marshall Cohen, 533–49. New York: Oxford University Press, 1983.

Kelly, Deirdre. "A Battle Every Step of the Way: Throughout Her 30-year Career, Prima Ballerina Martine Van Hamel Has Encountered and Overcome Obstacles with a Hard-Edged Determination that Prompted Mikhail Baryshnikov to Call Her, 'One Damn Tough Cookie.'" *Globe and Mail,* November 5, 1994.

———. "Av Paul Finds There is Life After Dance: 'By Facing the Fact of Retirement, It's Somehow Been Less Difficult.'" *Globe and Mail,* May 11, 1985.

———. "Ballerina Sees Silver Lining in Exit." *Globe and Mail,* December 18, 1995.

———. "Ballerinas Talk Back. Flexing Some Muscle: While Retirement Has Always Been Hotly Debated, More Dancers Are Refusing to Accept The Traditional Role as Passive Observer of Their Destiny." *Globe and Mail,* December 31, 1998.

———. "Body Politics." *Saturday Night,* February 1992.

———. "Glasco Considers Legal Action After Dismissal from National Ballet." *Globe and Mail,* December 19, 1998.

———. "Is Glasco Really Too Old To Dance? Ballet Experts Divided Over Kudelka Decision." *Globe and Mail,* December 24, 1998.

———. "Glasco Ousted from Ballet Board of Directors Jennifer Fournier to Represent Dancers." *Globe and Mail,* February 25, 1999.

———. "Gregory Finds Don Quixote Hurts So Good." *Globe and Mail*, November 6, 1985.

———. "Kain, Hart to Perform at Fundraiser For Dancers' Centre: Budget Cuts Have Hurt the Dancer Transition Resource Centre, Founded a Decade Ago to Help Performers Make the Leap From Stage to Other Careers." *Globe and Mail*, September 30, 1996.

———. "National Ballet Report Card: Dancers Superb, Choreography Uneven." *Globe and Mail*, November 27, 1998.

———. "New Director Sees Changes Afoot for Ballet B.C." *Globe and Mail*, November 29, 1989.

———. "Putting Primas in their Place: The National Ballet of Canada's Founder Says the Current Bitter Battle There Is a Typical Result of Many Dancers' Blind Egos." *Globe and Mail*, January 11, 1999.

———. "Ruined Reputation Ends Chances of Work: Lawyer." *Globe and Mail*, May 11, 2000.

Kelly, Deirdre, and Michael Posner. "Glasco, National Ballet End Their Marathon Pas de Deux: Dancer Wins Substantial Cash Settlement But Would Rather Be Working." *Globe and Mail*, July 21, 2000.

Kendall, Richard, with contributions by Douglas W. Druick and Arthur Beale. *Degas and the Little Dancer*. New Haven: Yale University Press, 1998.

Kerby-Fulton, Kathryn. "Subligny, Marie-Thérése." In *International Dictionary of Ballet*. Edited by Martha Bremser. London: St. James Press, 1993.

Kington, Tom. "One in Five Ballerinas at La Scala Is Anorexic, Leading Dancer Claims." *Observer*, December 4, 2011. www.guardian.co.uk/world/2011/dec/04/ballerinas-la-scala-anorexic-claim.

Kirkland, Gelsey, with Greg Lawrence. *Dancing on My Grave*. New York: Doubleday Books, 1986.

———. *The Shape of Love*. New York: Doubleday, 1989.

Kirstein, Lincoln. *Fifty Ballet Masterworks: From the 16th to the 20th Century*. New York: Dover Publications, 1984.

———. *Dance: A Short History of Classic Theatrical Dancing*. Westport, CT: Greenwood Press, 1970.

Kisselgoff, Anna. "Inseparable from a Swan," review of Keith Money, *Anna Pavlova: Her Life and Her Art*." *New York Times*, January 2, 1983.

———. "Three Ballerinas with the French Flair." *New York Times*, February 14, 2003.

Kleiner, Sibyl. "Thinking with the Mind, Syncing with the Body: Ballet as Symbolic and Nonsymbolic Interaction," *Symbolic Interaction* 32, no. 3 (Summer 2009): 236–59.

Koegler, Horst, ed. *The Concise Oxford Dictionary of Ballet.* Toronto: Oxford University Press, 1977.

Kurth, Peter. *Isadora: A Sensational Life.* Boston: Little, Brown, and Co., 2001.

Laver. James. *Costume and Fashion: A Concise History.* Revised, expanded, and updated edition. London: Thames and Hudson, 1982.

Le Grange, Daniel, Jason Tibbs, and Timothy D. Noakes. "Implications of a Diagnosis of Anorexia Nervosa in a Ballet School." *International Journal of Eating Disorders* 15, no. 4 (1994): 369–76.

Lecomte, Natalie. "The Female Ballet Troupe of the Paris Opera from 1700 to 1725." In *Women's Work, Making Dance in Europe before 1800.* Edited by Lynn Matluck Brooks. Madison: University of Wisconsin Press, 2007.

Lee, Carol. *Ballet in Western Culture: A History of its Origins and Evolution.* New York: Routledge, 2002.

Leivick, Laura. "Through Which She Is Seen: Bodies and Ballet." *The Threepenny Review* 2 (Summer 1980): 30–31.

Levin, David Michael. "Balanchine's Formalism." *Salmagundi*, 33/34 (DANCE, Spring–Summer 1976): 216–36.

Levinson, Andre. *André Levinson on Dance: Writings From Paris in the Twenties.* Edited by Joan Ross Acocella and Lynn Garafola. Hanover, NH: University Press of New England, 1991.

Lipman, Lisa. "Boston Ballet Case Dismissed." *Associated Press,* March 12, 2001.

Lindgren, Allana C. "'Pointe of Law': The National Ballet of Canada and Kimberly Glasco Legal Arbitration Case." Proceedings of the Twenty-Fourth Annual Society of Dance History Scholars Conference, Baltimore, Maryland, June 21–24, 2001. Stoughton, WI: Society of Dance History Scholars, 2001: 63–69.

Littler, William. "Author's Digging Proves There's Life After Dance." *Toronto Star,* August 1, 1987.

Lopatkina, Uliana, Evgenya Obratzsova, Alina Somova, Diana Vishneva, and Svetlana Zakharova. *Ballerina* (2006). DVD. New York: First Run Features, 2009.

Macaulay, Alastair. "Timeless Alchemy, Even When No One Is Dancing," *New York Times,* November 28, 2010.

MacCormack, Gilson. "Emma Livry," *The Dancing Times* (September 1928): n.p.

Mackrell, Judith. *Bloomsbury Ballerina: Lydia Lopokova, Imperial Dancer and Mrs. John Maynard Keynes*. London: Orion Publishing Co., 2009.

Magriel, Paul David. *Pavlova: An Illustrated Monograph*. New York: Henry Holt, 1947.

Martens, Frederick H. "The Attitude of the Dancer Toward Music." *The Musical Quarterly* 4, no. 3 (July 1918): 440–49.

Martin, C., and F. Bellisle. "Eating Attitudes and Taste Responses in Young Ballerinas." *Physiology & Behaviour* 46, no. 2 (1988): 223–27.

Mason, Francis. I *Remember Balanchine: Recollections of the Ballet Master by Those Who Knew Him*. New York: Doubleday, 1991.

McCleave, Sarah. "Dancing at the English Opera: Marie Sallé's Letter to the Duchess of Richmond." *Dance Research* 17, no. 1 (Summer 1999): 22–46.

———. "Marie Sallé, a Wise Professional Woman of Influence." In *Women's Work, Making Dance in Europe before 1800*. Edited by Lynn Matluck Brooks. Madison: University of Wisconsin Press, 2007.

McGuire, Kathleen. "When Words Hurt." *Dance Magazine* (July 2011), http://www.dancemagazine.com/issues/July-2011/When-Words-Hurt.

McLean, Adrienne L. *Dying Swans and Madmen: Ballet, the Body, and Narrative Cinema*. New Brunswick, NJ: Rutgers University Press, 2008.

Meller, Mari Kalman. "Exercises in and Around Degas's Classrooms: Part l." *The Burlington Magazine* 130, no. 1020 (Special Issue on Degas, March 1988): 198–215.

Migel, Parmenia. *The Ballerinas: From the Court of Louis XIV to Pavlova*. New York: Macmillan, 1972.

Molière. *Le Bourgeois Gentilhomme: Comédie-Ballet*. Paris: Larousse-Bordas, 1998.

Money, Keith. *Anna Pavlova: Her Life and Art*. New York: Alfred A. Knopf, 1982.

Moore, Lillian. *Artists of the Dance*. New York: Thomas Y. Crowell Co., 1932.

———. "The Tragedy of Emma Livry." *Dance Magazine* (June 1952): 38–39.

Mudrick, Marvin. "The King and His Queens," *The Hudson Review* 38, 3 (Autumn 1985): 520–524, 526, 528.

"National Ballet Dismisses 'Shocked' Heiress to Throne." *Winnipeg Free Press*, December 20, 1998.

Neufeld, James. *Passion to Dance: The National Ballet of Canada.* Toronto: Dundurn Press, 2011.

Neumärker, Klaus-Jürgen, Norman Bettle, Ursula Neumärker, and Oliver Bettle. "Age-and-Gender-Related Psychological Characteristics of Adolescent Ballet Dancers," *Psychopathology* 33 (2000): 137–42.

"No Anorexia Emergency, La Scala Ballerinas Claim." February 8, 2012. http://medicalxpress.com/news/2012-02-anorexia-emergency-la-scala-ballerinas.html.

Noverre, Jean Georges. *Lettres sur la danse, sur les ballets et les arts.* 4 vols. St. Petersburg: Jean Charles Schnoor, 1803–04.

Oliver, Wendy. "Reading the Ballerina's Body: Susan Bordo Sheds Light on Anastasia Volochkova and Heidi Guenther." *Dance Research Journal* 37, no. 2 (Women's Health in Dance, Winter 2005): 38–54.

Ostwald, Peter F. *Vaslav Nijinsky: A Leap into Madness.* New York: Carol Publishing Group, 1991.

Paluch, Vicki Smith. "Motherhood Doesn't Slow Down Ballerinas," *Los Angeles Daily News,* April 24, 2005.

Pappas, Nickolas, ed. *Routledge Philosophy Guidebook to Plato and the Second Republic,* 2nd Edition. New York: Routledge, 2003.

Pardo, Carol. "La Petite Danseuse de Degas." *DanceView* 20, no. 4 (Autumn 2003): 34–37.

Pepys, Tom. "Tragically." *Dance and Dancers* (February 1962): 26.

Petipa, Marius. *Russian Ballet Master: The Memoirs of Marius Petipa.* Edited by Lillian Moore. Translated by Helen Whittaker. London: Adam & Charles Black, 1958.

Plisetskaya, Maya. I, *Maya Plisetskaya.* Translated by Antonina W. Bouis. New Haven: Yale University Press, 2001.

"Poor Emma Livry." *Dance Australia* (December–January 2006/7): 65.

Prest, Julia. "Dancing King: Louis XIX's Roles in Molière's Comédies-ballets, from Court to Town." *Seventeenth Century* 16, no. 2 (2001): 285.

Prudhommeau, Germaine. "Camargo-Sallé, Duel au pied levé," *Danser* (March 1986): 78–81.

Pushkin, Alexander Sergeevich. *Eugene Onegin: A Novel in Verse.* Translated by Vladimir Vladimirovich Nabokov. New York: Bollingen Books, 1964.

Quatrelles L'Épine, Maurice. "Une Danseuse française au XIXe siècle, Emma Livry." In Bulletin de la Societé de l'histoire du théâtre, revue trimestrielle. Novembre–Janvier, 1908–1909. Paris: Impressions Artistiques L.M. Fortin & Cie., 1909.

Rameau, Pierre. The Dancing Master. Translated by Cyril W. Beaumont. New York: Dance Horizons Republications, 1970.

Ravaldi, Claudia, Alfredo Vannacci, Enrica Bolgnesi, Stefania Mancini, Carlo Faravelli, and Valdo Ricca. "Gender Role, Eating Disorder Symptoms, and Body Image Concern in Ballet Dancers." Journal of Psychosomatic Research 61 (2006): 529–35.

Regan, Kate. "This Ballerina Is No Fragile Swan." San Francisco Chronicle, November 10, 1985.

Rico, Laura. "Keeping Dancers on Their Toes: New Technique Allows MRIS of Ballet Dancers En Pointe, Aiding Injury Treatment and Prevention." University of California, Irvine. www.uci.edu/features/2010/08/feature_ballet_100830.php.

Ries, Frank W.D. "Nijinska, Bronislava." In International Dictionary of Ballet. Edited by Martha Bremser. London: St. James Press, 1993.

Robbin-Challan, Louise. "Social Conditions of Ballet Dancers of the Paris Opera in the Nineteenth Century." Choreography and Dance 2, no. 1 (1992): 17–28.

Romanovsky-Krassinsky, Marie (Princess). Dancing in Petersburg: The Memoirs of Kschessinska. London: Gollancz, 1960.

Rowes, Barbara. "Baryshnikov Picks a New Partner with Classic Grace, Cynthia Harvey." People, January 1981.

Russell, Jeffrey A. "Anatomy and Motion of the Ankle in Female Ballet Dancers." Phd diss., University of Wolverhampton, 2010.

Schorer, Suki, and Russell Lee. Suki Schorer on Balanchine Technique. New York: Alfred A. Knopf, 1999.

Schulman. Jennie. "National Ballet of Canada," Back Stage, October 30, 1998.

Sechelski, Denise S. "Garrick's Body and the Labor of Art in Eighteenth-Century Theater." Eighteenth Century Studies 29, no. 4 (Summer 1996): 369–89.

Siegel, Marcia B. "Growing Old in the Land of the Young." The Hudson Review 29, no. 2 (Summer 1976): 249–54.

Smith, Gary. "Rex Harrington a True Ballet Star." Hamilton Spectator, November 27, 1998.

Sobolevskaya, Olga. "Anastasia Volochkova: A Perfect Scandal," RIA Vesti, October 3, 2003. http://english.pravda.ru/society/stories/09-10-2003/3866-volochkova-0.

Solway, Diane. *Nureyev, His Life.* New York: William Morrow, 1998.

Sorell, Walter. *Dance in Its Time.* Garden City, NJ: Anchor Press/Doubleday, 1981.

———. "The Diaghilev Era." In *The Dance Anthology.* Edited by Cobbett Steinberg. New York: New American Library, 1980.

Souritz, Elizabeth. *Soviet Choreographers in the 1920s.* Durham: Duke University Press, 1990.

Springer, John. "I'm Not Fat, Says Ballerina Faulted for 'Too Many Sugarplums.'" December 13, 2010. www.today.com.

Statistical Insights on the Arts, vol. 3, no. 1. Hill Strategies Research Inc., September 2004. Report funded by the Canada Council for the Arts, the Department of Canadian Heritage, and the Ontario Arts Council.

Statistics Canada 2006 Census. Employment Income Statistics in Constant (2005) Dollars, Dancers. www12.statcan.ca/census-recensement/index-eng.cfm.

Summers, Anne. "On Begging to be a Bridesmaid in a Ballerina Dress: Some Meanings of British Fashion in the 1950s." *History Workshop Journal* 44 (Autumn 1997): 226–32.

Swift, Mary Grace. "Dancers in Flames." *Dance Chronicle* 5, no. 1 (1982): 1–10.

Taylor, Jeffrey. "The Dancer, the Tsar, and the Boy Who Believed He Was the Romonov's Lost Heir." *Express on Sunday*, July 30, 2006, 58–59.

Toepfer, Karl. "Orgy Salon: Aristocracy and Pornographic Theatre in Pre-Revolutionary Paris." *Performing Arts Journal* 12, no. 2/3 (1990): 110–36.

Tölgyes, T. and J. Nemessury. "Epidemiological Studies on Adverse Dieting Behaviours and Eating Disorders Among Young People in Hungary." *Social Psychiatry and Psychiatric Epidemiology* 39 (2004): 647–54.

Trachtman, Paul. "Degas and His Dancers," *Smithsonian* (April 2003): 89–95.

Turner, Bryan S., and Steven P. Wainwright. "Corps de Ballet: The Case of the Injured Ballet Dancer." *Sociology of Health & Illness* 25, no. 4 (2003): 271–72.

U.S. Census Bureau. 2000 Census. Earnings by Detailed Occupation: 1999: United States: Females. www.census.gov/hhes/www/income/data/earnings/call2usfemale.html.

Verghis, Sharon. "Best Foot Forward." *Sydney Morning Herald*, December 14, 2002.

Vigée-Le Brun, Louise-Elisabeth. *The Memoirs of Elisabeth Vigée-Le Brun, Member of the Royal Academy of Paris, Rouen, Saint-Luke of Rome, Parma, Bologna, Saint-Petersburg, Berlin, Geneva and Avignon.* London: Camden Press, 1989.

Volkov, Solomon. *Balanchine's Tchaikovsky.* Translated by Antonina W. Bouis. New York: Simon and Schuster, 1985.

Wainwright, Steven P., and Bryan S. Turner. "'Just Crumbling to Bits'? An Exploration of the Body, Ageing, Injury and Career in Classical Ballet Dancers." *Sociology* 40 (2006): 237–54.

Walker, Morley. "A Place in Her Hart: Former RWB Star Has Fond Memories of Winnipeg But Her Life Now Is in Toronto." *Winnipeg Free Press*, April 17, 2008.

Walker, Susan. "Ballet Shows Its Muscles." *Toronto Star*, November 22, 1997.

———. "Some Signs of Life After Dance; Their Bodies Pushed to the Brink, Dancers Seek Second Careers with Help of a Local Agency." *Toronto Star*, January 31, 2008.

"Weight of the Law Lifts Swan Lake Star Back to Starlight." *Adelaide Advertiser.* November 28, 2003.

Wente, Margaret. "The Glasco Fiasco (Act XVII) in which the National Ballet's Belligerent Ballerina Triumphs in Court, But Loses Friends." *Globe and Mail*, July 4, 2000.

Winter, Marian Hannah. *The Pre-Romantic Ballet.* London: Pitman, 1974.

Woodcock, Sarah C. "Archives of the Dance: Later Dance Holdings of the Theatre Museum." *Dance Research: Journal of the Society for Dance Research* 8, no. 1 (Spring 1990): 62–77.

———. "Margaret Rolfe's Memoirs of Marie Taglioni: Part I." *Dance Research: The Journal for the Society for Dance Research* 7, no. 1 (Dance History Issue, Spring 1989): 3–19.

Wyman, Max. *Evelyn Hart: An Intimate Portrait.* Toronto: McClelland and Stewart, 1991.

Yokel, Nathalie. "Légendaire Emma Livry." *Danser* 195 (January 2001): 22.

Young, Susan. "From Ballet to Boxing, The Evolution of a Female Athlete." In *My Life at the Gym.* Edited by Jo Malin. Albany: SUNY Press, 2010.

Zorina, Vera. *Zorina.* New York: Farrar, Straus and Giroux, 1986.

ACKNOWLEDGMENTS

THIS BOOK REPRESENTS my very own dance marathon: intensely and exhaustingly performed with the help of numerous partners who nudged me along, keeping the momentum going. To all of you, I offer my heartfelt thanks. But to name names: my children, Vladimir and Isadora Barac, who for months ate at the dining-room table surrounded by ballet books and never once complained. This book would never have been launched without the encouragement and enthusiasm of my publishers at Greystone Books, in particular Nancy Flight and Rob Sanders. My agent, Hilary McMahon of Westwood Creative Artists, continues to push me forward, so my gratitude also to her. At my workplace, the *Globe and Mail* newspaper, *Style* editor Danny Sinopoli cheered me on and helped nail down the subtitle. The *Globe*'s photo librarian, Paula Wilson, gave me a crash course in sourcing and buying my own images, and Harry Kokolakis in IT Support, patiently showed me, during his time off, how to collate them electronically. In New York City, Peter Rohowsky, executive manager of the Art

Archive at Art Resource, volunteered to track down far-flung historic images of obscure ballerinas and claimed that gazing at rare pictures of Pavlova was his just reward. Gotta love that. Phyllis Collazo of the *New York Times* also helped track down hard-to-get images and was super fast and friendly about it. Cameron Tolton, professor emeritus at Victoria University, the University of Toronto, helped with the French translations and listened to my ballerina gossip, goading me on, of course. I bow to him. On the topic of scholars, Cheryl Belkin Epstein, dance historian at Canada's National Ballet School, and Caroline O'Brien, a costume designer on faculty at Ryerson Theatre School, Ryerson University, read the manuscript in its later stages and generously gave astute suggestions, which definitely made the book better. Thank you also to Selma Odom, professor emerita, Department of Dance, York University, for her kind support of the project. At the Toronto Reference Library, performing arts librarian Lee Ramsay helped me source centuries-old documents and shared her own ideas. To her I owe the expression, "bonfire ballerina." Ballet company publicists who unstintingly fulfilled my requests for information, despite their already busy schedules, include Katharina Plumb, manager of media relations, New York City Ballet; Kelly Ryan, director of press and public relations, American Ballet Theatre; Caitlin Gillette, communications and special projects associate, New York City Ballet; and Eli Wallis, publicist, the Australian Ballet. My deepest appreciation.

Last but not least, given the subject matter, I want to thank the ballerinas, all of them—past, present, and future—for kindling in me a love of dance in the first place, a fire that won't soon burn out. In writing this book, I rediscovered so many ballerinas whose accomplishments have tended to be forgotten in the march of time. I am so happy to resurrect their names for a new generation of ballet lovers. There are so many ballerinas, and any omissions I have made can be chalked up to a lack of space, not a lack of interest. In particular, I thank the former ballerina Svea Eklof, who lent me her Balanchine books and shared with me stories of dancing in his company. She became my friend even though, by members of her particular sorority, dance critics are often regarded as the enemy. She could see that my heart was in the right place.

Finally, this book is dedicated to Victor Barac, my very own *danseur noble*, who held me up when I thought I might fall. I couldn't have done it without you.

INDEX

248